CW01262070

BENTLEY
Since 1965

Many of the innovations introduced with the Brooklands coupé spilled over onto the Azure T. This picture shows the wing vents, body-colour grille surround and mirror bodies, and the two-piece 20in wheels.

BENTLEY
Since 1965

JAMES TAYLOR

The Crowood Press

First published in 2012 by
The Crowood Press Ltd
Ramsbury, Marlborough
Wiltshire SN8 2HR

www.crowood.com

© James Taylor 2012

All rights reserved. No part of this publication may be reproduced or transmitted in any form or by any means, electronic or mechanical, including photocopy, recording, or any information storage and retrieval system, without permission in writing from the publishers.

British Library Cataloguing-in-Publication Data
A catalogue record for this book is available from the British Library.

ISBN 978 1 84797 371 9

Typeset by Jean Cussons Typesetting, Diss, Norfolk

Printed and bound in Malaysia by Times Offset (M) Sdn Bhd

CONTENTS

	Introduction and Acknowledgements	6
CHAPTER 1	STANDING IN THE SHADOW	7
CHAPTER 2	TWO-DOOR EXCLUSIVITY	23
CHAPTER 3	THE GREAT REVIVAL	39
CHAPTER 4	CONTINENTAL RENAISSANCE	64
CHAPTER 5	ARNAGE	85
CHAPTER 6	VOLKSWAGEN AND LE MANS	104
CHAPTER 7	A GT FOR THE TWENTY-FIRST CENTURY	117
CHAPTER 8	FLYING SPUR	140
CHAPTER 9	AZURE AND BROOKLANDS	149
CHAPTER 10	A NEW GRAND BENTLEY	161
CHAPTER 11	VERY SPECIAL BENTLEYS	174
	Appendix – Bentley Identification Numbers Since 1965	185
	Index	189

INTRODUCTION AND ACKNOWLEDGEMENTS

It's an extraordinary but fascinating story, how the Bentley marque was sadly neglected in the 1960s and 1970s; of how it was revived by a single new model in the 1980s; and of how it gradually rose to out-sell its Rolls-Royce stable-mate in the first half of the 1990s. Then, separated from Rolls-Royce at the end of that decade, it went on to even greater things – including a win at the world-renowned Le Mans 24-hour race – under new ownership.

Above all, though, this book tells the story of the products that have carried the Bentley name since 1965, a year that in many ways represented a low point for the Bentley marque. With the arrival of monocoque construction, and its associated inflexibility, there was no room for a real standalone Bentley, and the marque simply became a badge-engineered Rolls-Royce with its own inverted-snob appeal. It has come a long way since then.

Since the early 1990s, Bentley marketing has been characterized by the creation of a variety of niche and special-edition models, all of them capable of being individualized further through the bespoke Personal Commission and later Bentley Mulliner programmes. One result of this has been a huge and very confusing variety of different Bentleys, characterized by a profusion of limited editions, some specific to individual countries and others available globally. So, one of the missions of this book is to provide a path through the modern-Bentley maze.

However, the modern-Bentley story is really only just beginning, and in years to come there will certainly be much more of the story to tell. Details will become clear of abandoned projects, as well as of new cars not even planned when this book went to press. So for the moment, this book pretends to do no more than to tell as much of the story as it is possible to tell.

It is important to understand how dates are used in this book. Calendar-year dates are straightforward, and '1996' means exactly that. However, a '1996 model-year' or '1996 season' car does not necessarily mean that a car was built in the 1996 calendar-year. The Bentley model-year usually began in September (or thereabouts) of the previous year; so, a 1996 model-year car could have been built any time between September 1995 and the end of 1996 model-year production in summer 1996.

Special thanks to Keith Jones and to Malcolm Bobbitt for the loan of a number of pictures used in this book. For many of the pictures, I am grateful also to the Public Relations Department of Bentley Motors and to Newspress Ltd.

WHO MADE BENTLEYS?

The Bentley brand has retained a strong identity through several changes of ownership since its foundation in 1919.

1919–31	Bentley Motors Ltd, an independent motor manufacturer, based at Cricklewood in London.
1931–39	Bentley Motors (1931) Ltd, a subsidiary of Rolls-Royce Motor Cars Ltd, based at Derby.
1946–71	Bentley Motors Ltd, a subsidiary of Rolls-Royce Motor Cars Ltd, based at Crewe.
1971–80	Bentley Motors Ltd, a subsidiary of Rolls-Royce Motors Ltd, based at Crewe.
1980–98	Bentley Motors Ltd, a subsidiary of Rolls-Royce Motors Ltd, based at Crewe. Both marques were owned by Vickers plc.
1998 onwards	Bentley Motors Ltd, based at Crewe and owned by the Volkswagen Group in Germany.

CHAPTER ONE

STANDING IN THE SHADOW

When Rolls-Royce began to contemplate resuming production of cars at the end of the Second World War, the plan for what became known as the 'rationalized range' was already in place. It had originally been drawn up in the late 1930s by Alec Harvey-Bailey, Chief Engineer of the Car Division, who reasoned that the company could achieve greater profitability by sharing major components between one range and the next. The interruption of the war, of course, delayed the execution of the plan.

Yet despite the implications of the 'rationalized range' philosophy, it was clear that the company wanted to maintain a clear distinction between the Rolls-Royce and Bentley ranges. The first post-war car from Crewe was, in fact, a Bentley and not a Rolls-Royce. The 1947 Bentley Mk VI, with its 'standard steel' body by Pressed Steel, was presented as an owner-driver sports saloon, and the Rolls-Royce Silver Wraith model, which followed it in 1948, was a much larger, grander car intended for bespoke coachwork and the chauffeur-drive market.

When the Rolls-Royce Silver Dawn arrived in 1951 to give the marque a presence in the owner-driver saloon market, it may have shared the Bentley Mk VI chassis and body, but it was by no means a clone of that car. The distinction was still very clear: the Silver Dawn had a single-carburettor version of the 6-cylinder engine, which made it rather more sedate than the twin-carburettor type standard in the Bentley.

The distinction was to be reinforced further. When the new Bentley Continental was announced in 1952, it came with a high-performance derivative of the 6-cylinder engine and taller gearing to give higher top speeds. It was also intended for lightweight coachwork, in order to maintain that performance – although as time went on, the cars became increasingly heavier and lost some of their performance edge.

So it was that Bentley and Rolls-Royce remained quite distinctive marques in the early 1950s. Rolls-Royce offered a sedate owner-driver saloon (the Silver Dawn) and a larger chassis (the Silver Wraith) intended for chauffeur-driven duties and for bespoke coachwork. Bentley offered a quick sports saloon (the Mk VI, upgraded in 1952 as the R-type) and an ultra-fast long-distance touring car (the Continental). There was no doubt about the distinction.

A CHANGE OF EMPHASIS

Things continued in much the same vein when the second generation of post-war cars from Crewe arrived in 1954. When the new owner-driver Rolls-Royce Silver Cloud was announced, the Silver Wraith continued in production to cater for the chauffeur-drive market. On the Bentley side, the new S-type saloon was admittedly closer in specification to the Silver Cloud than the Mk VI and R-type had been to the Silver Dawn – in fact it was identical mechanically, except for the availability on very early models of a manual gearbox that could not be had on the Rolls-Royce derivative. But, from 1955, the sporting character of the Bentley marque was again thrust to the fore with a new S-type Continental chassis that featured a higher-compression engine, taller gearing, a lower radiator shell and, once again, that option of a more sporting, manual gearbox.

So the Bentley buyer of the late 1950s was still able to buy a car that was distinctively different from the Rolls-Royce with which it shared much of its engineering and appearance. However, from 1957, the manual-gearbox option for Bentley saloons and Continentals was discontinued. The Bentley S-type saloon thus became a Rolls-Royce Silver Cloud with a Bentley grille and different badging. That same year, Crewe permitted four-door bodywork to be mounted on the Continental chassis for the first time, the mould-breaking design being H. J. Mulliner's Flying Spur. Suddenly, the distinctiveness of the Continental model was also under attack.

The distinction between the two marques became even more blurred from 1959, when the new V8 engine was put into the Clouds and S-types to create the Silver Cloud II

■ STANDING IN THE SHADOW

and Bentley S2. Raised gearing in the saloons reduced the distinction between standard saloon and Continental chassis, and by the time of the Silver Cloud III and Bentley S3 in 1963, the only real difference lay in the height of the radiator grille. Two-door bodies, originally designed for the Continental chassis, were by this time being ordered for fitment to the Rolls-Royce chassis, and the Bentley as a distinctive sporting marque had effectively ceased to exist.

All this visible change was paralleled by developments at Crewe, out of the public eye. As early as February 1954, it had been clear that the third generation of post-war cars would have to move with the times and abandon the traditional separate-chassis construction in favour of monocoque structures. No serious work was done on this third generation until 1958, but at that point the intention to give the Bentley marque its own clear identity was still very much in evidence.

Initial plans were for a range of three cars. The Rolls-Royce saloon, codenamed Tibet, would have a 123in wheelbase and the new 6.2-litre V8 engine that was to enter production in 1959. The Bentley saloon, codenamed Burma, would use the same basic body structure but with a shorter front end; its wheelbase would be 119.5in and it would be powered by the new 4-litre F-60 6-cylinder engine. Then the platform of the Bentley would be shortened by another 6in, and on this 113.5in wheelbase would be built a two-door sporting successor to the Continentals. This car had the codename of Korea and would have the 6.2-litre V8 engine to deliver maximum performance.

So, in the late 1950s, the plan was to retain the sporting character of the Bentley marque in a Continental-type model. In the saloon market, there was a subtle change of emphasis, and the Bentley would play second fiddle to the Rolls-Royce by being a smaller – and presumably noticeably cheaper – car. But, one way or another, a Bentley would be a Bentley and a Rolls-Royce would be a Rolls-Royce.

Inevitably, there was some cross-fertilization of ideas. As the 1960s got under way, there were plans on the drawing-board for a Bentley version of the Tibet car (codenamed

Scale models from the styling studio: on the left is the Rolls-Royce Tibet, and on the right is the Bentley Burma. Plans for separate models were abandoned and Burma eventually developed into the new saloon, badged as both Bentley and Rolls-Royce.

STANDING IN THE SHADOW

There was only ever one Bentley Korea prototype, built in 1961 with a body by Park Ward. It linked the idea of the Bentley name with a high-performance car.

Borneo) and a Rolls-Royce version of the Burma (codenamed Tonga). Only the Korea project for a new Bentley Continental remained untainted.

Exactly what was behind this cross-fertilization of formerly separate projects has never been officially revealed, but it was almost certainly a drive to reduce manufacturing costs. Despite the planned overlaps between projects, the cost of tooling up for three different monocoques with two different engines was going to be enormous. With its tiny sales volumes, Crewe was not going to be able to justify the outlay.

A FUNDAMENTAL SHIFT

The first casualty of this new line of thinking was the Continental, which was cancelled in September 1961. But before the end of the year, an alternative plan had presented itself. This was an alliance with the British Motor Corporation. The basic idea seems to have been that the new Bentley saloon could be built far more cheaply if it were to share its bodyshell with the ADO 53 Austin Princess, BMC's top-of-the-range 3-litre model. With a little careful detail work, that mass-produced monocoque could be modified to take on a family resemblance to the Tibet and Burma cars that Crewe was working on. With the new Rolls-Royce F-60 6-cylinder engine, and an appropriately high standard of interior finish, it would make a very passable Bentley. The new project took on the codename of Java, and occupied a good deal of time during 1962.

There was a second project along the same lines. This one was called Bengal and aimed to develop a new Bentley from the bodyshell of the Austin-Morris 1800 saloon. This required rather more re-engineering, as the BMC car had been designed for front-wheel drive and transverse engines, whereas the Bentley would have rear-wheel drive and its F-60 engine mounted conventionally north–south.

Both these projects demonstrated quite clearly that there had been a fundamental shift in Crewe's perception of the Bentley marque. Shorn of its sporting Continental replacement, it was now seen as the name for a smaller and cheaper car positioned below the Rolls-Royce. The rot had set in with the Burma project, and had now become more advanced with Java and Bengal.

But something dissuaded Crewe from going ahead with this plan. Perhaps it was the fear that an alliance with BMC – the maker of cars for Everyman – would damage the image of the Bentley marque. One way or another, both Java and Bengal had been cancelled as Bentley projects by the end of 1962.

Both, however, had a new lease of life under BMC. The modified Princess bodyshell, drawn up for Java, entered production in 1964 as the Vanden Plas 4-litre R, complete with the 4-litre Rolls-Royce F-60 engine (now known as the FB-60) that had been planned for Java and a very Bentley-like grille. The modified 1800 bodyshell, with its extended bonnet and

■ STANDING IN THE SHADOW

boot sections, was further developed and became the Austin 3-litre in 1968 with BMC's own 6-cylinder engine. Neither car was very successful, so perhaps Crewe's instincts had been right.

COMING TOGETHER

The cancellation of Korea and then of the Java and Bengal projects left only Burma on the stocks as a new Bentley. Originally planned as a 119.5in wheelbase car with the 4-litre F-60 engine, it now came to the fore as the basis of a new saloon for both the Rolls-Royce and Bentley marques.

In practice, both Burma and the larger (Tibet) Rolls-Royce project were cancelled, and the new Rolls-Bentley saloon was put together from the most successful elements of the two projects. It brought together the 6.2-litre V8 planned for Tibet with the overall size planned for Burma and was known within the Crewe works as the SY model. In addition, plans were made for an alternative two-door body style to be built by Mulliner-Park Ward (which had become a wholly-owned Rolls-Royce subsidiary in 1959) on the same platform. This could also form the basis of a drophead coupé.

Significantly, however, the opportunity to give the Bentley marque its own identity, by making the two-door a Bentley-only model, was not taken up. Both two-door and four-door variants of the third-generation post-war cars from Crewe were to be badged according to customer choice as Rolls-Royce or Bentley derivatives and would have the same mechanical specification. The move to monocoque construction had, in effect, destroyed the distinction between the Rolls-Royce and Bentley marques.

ON SALE

None of that prevented a Bentley version of the new saloon from going on sale in October 1965, alongside the mainstream Rolls-Royce model. There were two Bentleys on their own stand at that month's Earls Court Motor Show in London, and three examples of the new Rolls-Royce on that marque's stand. The Rolls-Royce took the name of Silver Shadow; the Bentley was, more prosaically, a T series. It differed from the Rolls-Royce in only insignificant details, such as the radiator grille with its winged B mascot and appropriately reshaped bonnet panel pressing, the wheel trims and the winged B in place of the Rolls-Royce logo at various places around the car. The engine cam covers, too, carried the Bentley name, where the Rolls-Royce cam covers were cast with the double-barrelled name.

ALD 47B was a hand-built prototype of the SY car, and was pictured here on test in late 1964. It was clearly close to the production configuration.

STANDING IN THE SHADOW

The original Bentley T series, latterly known as the T1, was an extremely advanced car on its announcement in 1965. The car was essentially a Rolls-Royce Silver Shadow with Bentley trimmings and a special bonnet to suit the more rounded Bentley grille.

So the big question was: what was the Bentley for? It was for those who had traditionally bought a Bentley in preference to a Rolls-Royce – or indeed any other make – and who did not want to change their allegiance. In the later years of the T series cars, it was also said that the Bentley was for the owner who wanted a car that was less ostentatious than the Rolls-Royce but who did not want to compromise on the quality of the car itself. There was probably a lot of truth in this, and more so after Britain's long-serving Conservative governments finally gave way to left-wing Labour administrations in the later 1960s.

It was not long before Crewe recognized its mistake in not developing a distinctive Bentley model. Bentley sales dropped from 40 per cent of Crewe's output to around 8 per cent during the lifetime of the first-series SY cars from 1965 to 1976. The Bentley marque was perceived as so insignificant that Britain's best-selling weekly motoring magazine, *Autocar*, did not bother to test a Bentley derivative of the SY range until 1979 – thirteen years after it had been introduced.

Arguably, the day could have been saved if the two-door SY derivatives introduced in 1966 had been marketed as Bentleys, so giving the marque a distinctive visual identity, even if the mechanical specification had remained the same as that of the Rolls-Royce saloons. But those cars had been conceived in the first half of the 1960s when the Bentley name was not viewed as important – and besides, customer demand for Rolls-Royce versions of what had previously been sold as Bentley Continental models towards the end of 1965 strongly suggested that producing the cars only as Bentleys might have been a mistake. So they were built as both Rolls-Royce and Bentley variants, and again the Bentley found far fewer takers than the Rolls-Royce.

THE T-SERIES DESIGN

Whether badged as a Bentley or a Rolls-Royce, the new SY range was a considerable engineering achievement. Its monocoque bodyshell was manufactured for Crewe by Pressed Steel at Cowley, and was among the largest car monocoques of its day. It boasted carefully conservative styling by John Blatchley, rather slab-sided by comparison with the curvaceous Silver Cloud range but very much in tune with the trends of the mid-1960s. Bonnet, boot-lid and doors were all made of aluminium alloy to save weight, and the shell was zinc-dipped to resist the corrosion that was already bringing about the early demise of many early monocoque cars from other manufacturers.

Harry Grylls' engineers at Crewe were also well aware of the road-noise problems that could affect monocoque structures, and as a result they chose to mount the bodyshell on heavy steel sub-frames that were insulated from the shell

■ STANDING IN THE SHADOW

TOP LEFT: **The Bentley grille was always the most obvious distinguishing feature of the marque in the 1960s and 1970s, and for most markets it came with a three-dimensional winged B mascot.**

TOP RIGHT: **If the styling of the T series was a little square for some tastes, there were exquisite detail touches. Typical were the door handles.**

MIDDLE LEFT: **Even the handle on the bootlid combined sturdy construction with elegance. The winged B logo was the only indication of the car's identity visible from the rear.**

BELOW LEFT AND RIGHT: **The Bentley T saloon was a clone of the Rolls-Royce Silver Shadow, and it is hard to be certain that the cars seen under construction here are indeed Bentleys – although the curved shoulders of the bonnet panels do suggest the slightly softer profile used on the T series.**

by specially developed mountings. These mountings, made by Delaney Gallay under the trade name of Vibrashock, certainly played their part in preventing the transmission of road noise into the bodyshell. On the negative side, however, they also tended to make the driver feel rather eerily isolated from the road under the car. Compliant front mountings on the front sub-frame made things worse, causing the steering to feel rather vague. These factors, and the deliberately light feel of the steering, provoked a number of negative comments from customers and road-testers alike in the early days.

For the first time on a car from Crewe, the suspension was all-independent. There was really no alternative: beam axles imposed limitations on both handling and ride comfort, and manufacturers further down the market, such as Jaguar, Triumph and Rover, were already showing the way ahead with all-round independent suspension. Mercedes-Benz in Germany were also clearly wedded to it, and their new 600 saloon, introduced in 1963, made clear that they were aiming for a slice of the traditional Rolls-Royce market.

However, steel coil-springs all round, with double wishbones on the front wheels and semi-trailing arms on the rears, only told part of the SY story. Inside each coil spring was a traditional telescopic damper, and the top of that damper was connected not to the bodyshell, but to a hydraulically controlled height-control ram mounted on the shell. These rams were operated from a high-pressure hydraulic system that was pressurized by a pump driven by the engine, and their purpose was to ensure that the ride height, and therefore the trim of the car, remained constant in spite of variations in the load.

Unlike more modern systems, the height-control rams were not designed to reduce roll in cornering, and it was excessive roll from the soft suspension that occasioned more negative comment in the SY range's early days. The cross-ply tyres fitted as standard were also a source of complaint because they did not give the levels of grip available from modern radial designs, but the Crewe engineers were unwilling to approve radials at that stage because they believed they made the cars more noisy.

High-pressure hydraulics also played their part in the braking system, which, in the interests of safety, was immensely complex. At the wheels, things looked relatively conventional, with twin diametrically-opposed callipers on each front disc and a single four-piston calliper on each rear disc. However, the complication lay in the brake-actuating system.

There were in fact three separate braking systems – four, if the cable-operated handbrake is added into the equation.

By later standards, the cross-ply tyres on the original Bentley T look positively skinny. They certainly offered nothing like the standards of grip that would be associated with later models from Bentley.

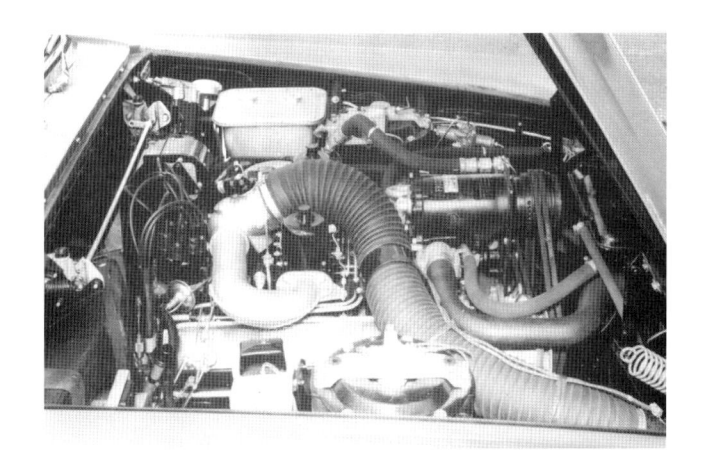

Crewe generally revealed little about its engines, and even publicity pictures were few and far between. The two SU carburettors are clear here, and beyond them the reservoir for the hydraulic systems. To the right is the air-conditioning pump.

STANDING IN THE SHADOW

LEFT: **Even though the Silver Shadow and T series were built on the same assembly lines, the fictional separation between the two marques was carefully preserved. The board in front of this early T series claims that the coachwork was by Bentley Motors (1931) Ltd. On the left, Crewe's Sales Director, Dr Llewellyn Smith, shows some of the underbonnet features to his wife.**

MIDDLE: **Two-tone colour schemes were popular on the T series, and this early car shows a typical configuration, with the colour boundary running along the bright belt-line that passed through the door handles.**

BELOW: **This is the interior of a mid-1970s car. Early cars did not have the centre console faired into the dashboard. Note the discreet B logos on the instruments and pedal rubbers. The ICE head units in this example are considerably more modern than the car itself.**

A second hydraulic pump on the engine fed an accumulator with brake fluid, which remained under pressure until the driver operated the brake pedal. This then released fluid under pressure to the braking system to operate the brakes. The primary high-pressure system accounted for 47 per cent of the total braking, operating one pair of front callipers to give 31 per cent of the total braking and delivering a further 16 per cent of braking power at the rear. A secondary high-pressure system operated on the other pair of front callipers, again delivering 31 per cent of the total braking. The final 22 per cent of braking came from the third hydraulic circuit and acted on the rear wheels only by way of a conventionally pressured hydraulics. Crewe claimed that this added 'feel' to the system, which would otherwise have amounted to little

SPECIFICATIONS FOR BENTLEY T-SERIES MODELS

Years of manufacture   1965–76

Build quantity
1,712 (all standard saloons)

Engine
1965–70
6230cc (104.14mm × 91.44mm) ohv V8
Twin SU carburettors   9:1 compression ratio (8:1 optional)
195bhp at 4,000rpm (estimated)
290lb ft at 2,500rpm (estimated)

1970–76
6750cc (104.14mm × 99.1mm) ohv V8
Twin SU carburettors   9:1 compression ratio (8:1 optional)
198bhp at 4,000rpm (estimated); less for US models
330lb ft at 2,500rpm (estimated)

Transmission
RHD cars to 1968
Four-speed GM Hydramatic automatic gearbox built by Rolls-Royce, with fluid coupling and electric selection.
RHD cars from 1968 and all LHD cars
Three-speed GM400 Turbo-Hydramatic automatic gearbox with torque converter.

Suspension
Independent front suspension with coil springs, twin wishbones, anti-roll bar, hydraulic telescopic dampers and high-pressure hydraulic self-levelling system. (High-pressure self-levelling system deleted in late 1969; top wishbones with single transverse arms from summer 1972.)
Independent rear suspension with coil springs, semi-trailing arms, hydraulic telescopic dampers and high-pressure hydraulic self-levelling system.

Steering
Power-assisted recirculating-ball steering by GM Saginaw.

Brakes
Disc brakes on all four wheels, with 11in diameter. Three separate hydraulic circuits (two from 1975), with high-pressure hydraulic system.

Wheels and tyres
15in steel disc wheels with 6in rims
1965 to summer 1972   8.45 × 15 cross-ply tyres
Summer 1972 to spring 1974   205VR15 radial tyres
Spring 1974 on   235/70-15 or HR70HR15 radial tyres

Vehicle dimensions
Wheelbase
1965–74   119.5in (3,035mm)
1974–76   120in (3,050mm)
Overall length   203.5in (5,169mm)
Overall width   71in (1,803mm) to spring 1974
71.7in (1,821mm) from spring 1974
Overall height   59.75in (1,518mm)
Weight   4,659lb (2,113kg) unladen, with half-full fuel tank

Performance
Max. speed   115mph (108km/h)
0–60 mph   10.9sec
Fuel consumption   15mpg (18.87ltr/100km)

■ STANDING IN THE SHADOW

more than a progressive on–off switch as far as the driver was concerned.

The engine, of course, was the 6.25-litre V8 that had been introduced in 1961 on the Silver Cloud range. With around 200bhp – Crewe never quoted exact figures – this comfortably made the new SY saloons into 120mph (193km/h) cars. In the Silver Cloud, there had been some design compromises because the new engine had to be fitted into an engine bay designed many years earlier for an in-line 6-cylinder. For the SY range, the cylinder heads were redesigned to make the spark plugs more readily accessible for servicing, and the exhaust manifolds were made less restrictive. In addition, the auxiliary drive at the front of the engine was redesigned to drive the high-pressure hydraulic pumps for brakes and suspension.

It went without saying that the gearbox on all models would be automatic. There was already a four-speed automatic transmission in production at Crewe, a licence-built and modified version of the General Motors Hydramatic that had been designed in the USA. However, there had been considerable advances in transmission design since this had been introduced, and it was important for the SY range to remain ahead of the pack.

In practice, two updates went into production. Exactly why is unclear (it may have had something to do with production volumes), but right-hand-drive cars were introduced with an updated version of the existing transmission, while left-hand-drive cars had a new three-speed type. The updated four-speed had lighter aluminium castings than the earlier cast-iron gearbox, it had a freewheel between first and second speeds to smooth out downchanges, and range selection was made by an electrically-operated servo instead of by the rod linkage used before.

The new three-speed gearbox was another General Motors design, this time the one introduced on Cadillac and Buick models in 1963 and known as the Turbo-Hydramatic, or GM400. Unlike the earlier transmission it featured a torque converter, and unlike the earlier transmission it was not built under licence at Crewe but was imported from the USA. Three years further on, this more modern transmission was standardized on right-hand-drive cars as well.

The SY range was originally planned to remain in production for at least ten years, but actually lasted fifteen years before it was replaced. There were several reasons why. The bankruptcy of the Rolls-Royce Group in 1971 (caused by excessive costs in the aero-engine division) was a key factor, and the constant changes in safety and emissions regulations in the company's largest market of the USA also consumed precious engineering resources, which Crewe might have preferred to devote to preparing new models. A series of industrial disputes in the late 1970s can also not have helped what was by then known as Rolls-Royce Motors.

FIRST-SERIES SALOONS

Delays in obtaining bodyshells from Pressed Steel meant that the first production models of the new T series were not delivered until the spring of 1966, by which time Crewe had also announced the companion-model two-door cars, which are described in Chapter 2.

Reaction to initial criticisms of the cars also seemed to be rather delayed, although the truth was that in any small-volume operation, such as the one at Crewe, it actually takes a long time for changes to be perfected and then introduced on production. So, it was 1968 before much changed.

The development of the first-series SY cars built between 1965 and 1976 represented a gradual process of improvement, but there was no doubt that the last cars were much better in many areas than their forebears. Most of the changes were quite subtle, and one of them – the introduction of long-wheelbase variants in May 1969 – did not impact on the Bentley marque at all. However, there were two key factors that drove the major changes to the first-series cars. These were the demand for better handling dynamics and the changing safety and exhaust emissions requirements of the US market.

Handling disappointed many drivers from the very start. Crewe's engineers had focused on delivering a soft and compliant ride, assuming that owners were not going to throw their cars about in an unseemly manner. Unfortunately, buyers of the middle 1960s expected better dynamics, even from a car in this class – and it would be nice to think that Bentley buyers, with their more sporting expectations, were the ones who complained most loudly.

One way or another, changes were introduced in 1968, when the addition of a rear anti-roll bar and a stiffer front anti-roll bar went some way to reducing cornering roll. The steering ratio was also raised to add a little more 'feel' for the driver, but the dynamics were a long way from perfect yet. The next stage came early in 1970, when a smaller steering wheel with a 16in diameter made a further improvement to the feel of the steering, and then in August 1971 a changed steering ratio helped a little more. Realistically, though, these changes were just tinkering with the problem, and something more radical was in preparation at Crewe.

The more radical change arrived in mid-1972, later than new engineering director John Hollings would have liked, thanks to delays brought about by the need to devote engineering resources to meeting US regulations. It was known as the compliant suspension, and finally allowed Crewe to fit radial tyres in the knowledge that they would not increase noise levels or harm the ride. It consisted of stiffer sub-frame mountings, wider front tracks and a different top link for the front suspension, while the Panhard rod between sub-frame and bodyshell at the rear was also eliminated.

That, however, was not the final dynamic change for the first-series cars. From spring 1974, longer, re-shaped rear trailing arms widened the track and also increased the wheelbase by half an inch to the full 120 inches. A similar increase in track was made at the front, and fatter 235/75 × 15 radial tyres both put more rubber on the road and demanded subtly flared wheelarches to provide adequate clearance. Compared with the very first SY cars, the handling was now very much improved – but towards the end of the 1980s, an aftermarket kit of stiffer coil springs and anti-roll bars developed by Harvey Bailey Engineering made clear how much more could have been done to sharpen the handling without detriment to the ride.

The ever-changing US Federal requirements were a nightmare for many manufacturers in the late 1960s and early 1970s. Broadly speaking, they demanded higher levels of passive safety and lower levels of exhaust emissions. The result of the first was usually to increase weight, while the result of the second was usually to decrease engine power and torque. For a small-volume manufacturer such as Rolls-Royce Motors, the most cost-effective solution was to standardize the Federal specification for all cars, as far as possible, and from May 1969 that was exactly what they did.

From that month, Bentley T series and Rolls-Royce Silver Shadow models all took on a redesigned facia, with additional crash padding, re-arranged switches and instruments, warning lamps instead of the ammeter and oil pressure gauge, and a new centre console that linked the facia with the transmission tunnel and housed the radio and a variety of switches. In addition, recessed door latches and recessed grab handles were fitted, to reduce the risk of injury in an accident.

Those changes took care of the safety requirement. New carburettors in spring 1969 were a first nod to the emissions regulations, but it was clear that more far-reaching changes would be needed. So from summer 1970, all models had a longer-stroke edition of the V8 engine, now with a swept volume of 6.75 litres. It did not make much difference to the car's performance, but it did offset the effect of the exhaust emissions controls demanded in the USA (and, increasingly, in other countries as well), and it did offset the gradually increasing weight of the cars.

Rationalization prompted the standardization on all derivatives of the GM400 three-speed automatic transmission in autumn 1968. It was at least partly responsible also for the arrival of the ventilated front brake discs in June 1973, a few months after their introduction on the Corniche models. However, changes in other areas were mainly driven by the search for greater refinement and greater reliability. Typical of the refinement changes were the addition of a viscous fan to the engine in autumn 1968 to reduce noise and the introduction of central locking and a new ICE system with four door-mounted speakers in summer 1970. Reliability was enhanced by the change from dynamo to alternator in late 1969, and the change to a stainless steel exhaust system at about the same time took one formerly consumable item off the maintenance schedule.

There were deletions, too, which reflected experience of the cars in use. So the swivelling front quarter-lights were replaced by fixed windows during 1968 because owners simply did not use them, and the end of 1969 saw the front ride-levelling system deleted because it had proved unnecessary. Near the end of first-series production, in autumn 1975, the braking system was also altered and the conventional hydraulic system to the rear wheels was deleted. Brake 'feel' was restored artificially by the use of a rubber block, which provided resistance to the brake pedal.

THE SECOND-SERIES CARS

It was Crewe's practice to introduce substantially revised versions of its cars about three years before they were due to be replaced. They had done this in 1952 with the big-bore engine that turned the Bentley Mk VI into an R-type, and again with the twin-headlamp nose and other revisions that created the Bentley S3 out of the earlier S2 in 1962. Now it was the turn of the SY range, and in early 1977 a whole series of changes was announced. As far as the Bentley derivatives were concerned, the cars were now known as T2 types. They and their Rolls-Royce counterparts would remain in production until October 1980.

■ STANDING IN THE SHADOW

SPECIFICATIONS FOR BENTLEY T2 MODELS

Years of manufacture   1977–80

Build quantity
558 (standard saloons)
10 (long-wheelbase models)

Engine
6750cc (104.14mm × 99.1mm) ohv V8
Twin SU carburettors; Bosch K-Jetronic fuel injection for 1980 Californian cars
9:1 compression ratio to autumn 1975
8:1 compression optional
8:1 standard in Europe and 7.3:1 standard for Australia, Japan and USA
240bhp at 4,000rpm (estimated); approx. 200bhp from autumn 1975
Torque figure not available

Transmission
Three-speed GM400 Turbo-Hydramatic automatic gearbox with torque converter
Ratios   3.08:1, 4.558:1, 7.638:1, reverse 6.406:1
Final drive ratio   3.08:1

Suspension
Independent front suspension with coil springs, twin wishbones, anti-roll bar and hydraulic telescopic dampers.
Independent rear suspension with coil springs, semi-trailing arms, hydraulic telescopic dampers and high-pressure hydraulic self-levelling system.

Steering
Power-assisted rack-and-pinion steering.

Brakes
Disc brakes on all four wheels, with 11in diameter. Two separate hydraulic circuits, with high-pressure hydraulic system.

Vehicle dimensions
Wheelbase   120in (3,050mm) for standard saloons
                                    124in (3,150mm) for long-wheelbase models
Overall length   204.5in (5,194mm) for standard saloons
                                    208.5in (5,296mm) for long-wheelbase models
Overall width   71.7in (1,821mm)
Overall height   59.75in (1,518mm)
Track   60in (1,524mm), front
                                    59.6in (1,514mm), rear
Weight   4,930lb (2,237kg) unladen, for standard saloons
                                    5,020lb (2,277kg) unladen, for long-wheelbase models without division
                                    5,260lb (2,386kg) unladen, for long-wheelbase models with division

Performance
Max. speed   119mph (191.51km/h)
0–60mph   10.1sec
Fuel consumption   14.5mpg (19.52ltr/100km)

STANDING IN THE SHADOW

The T2 looked very much like the earlier T series cars, but noticeable even to the casual observer was the change from chromed bumpers to large black 'impact bumpers' on all models. These met a Federal requirement that bumpers should protect the bodywork – particularly safety-critical fittings like the lights – from damage in a low-speed impact. In the beginning, the requirement covered speeds up to 5mph, and on US models of the car there were damper struts behind the bumpers, which controlled the force with which they would be pushed in towards the body. The struts were omitted from cars for other markets, but the large black bumpers remained. From 1978 there was then a minor change when a headlamp wash-wipe was made standard. It had actually been on cars delivered to Scandinavian countries for some years.

Under the skin, there had been further dynamic improvements for the T2 models. Steering was much sharper thanks to a new power-assisted rack-and-pinion system in place of the old re-circulating ball-type; revised front-suspension geometry and a smaller diameter rear anti-roll bar made their own contribution, and a 15.25in diameter steering wheel gave just the right amount of 'feel'.

There had, of course, been further changes to meet the latest exhaust emissions regulations, and the engines were now fitted with tamper-proof HIF7 carburettors, which reduced the top-end power somewhat. However, the addition of the less restrictive twin-pipe exhaust system from the Corniche was enough to ensure that performance was not noticeably affected. It was not the final solution, however. Californian emissions regulations had for some time been tighter than those in the rest of the USA, and the only way to meet them from 1980 was by changing to the more finely controlled fuel metering available from a Bosch K-Jetronic fuel-injection system. Other markets continued to receive carburettor types until production ended.

There were interior changes when the T2s came on-stream, too. The cars were fitted with the split-level air-conditioning system that had been introduced earlier on the Corniche models, and with this came a new facia. It incorporated a distinctive panel of warning lights alongside the traditional twin-dial instruments, thumbwheel controls for the new air-conditioning system, and a short centre section that was no longer linked to the oddments tray on the transmission tunnel. In fact, it anticipated the facia that would be used on the SZ models scheduled to replace the SY range in 1980 and, though the change was not visible, was differently constructed from earlier facias. The latest US safety regulations had prompted a change from solid wood (which could splinter under impact and cause injury) to an alloy armature to which wood-veneer was glued.

Perhaps most interesting for the Bentley marque in these final years of SY production was that a total of ten long-wheelbase Bentley derivatives were built. Like the Rolls-

Subtly fatter wheelarches over wide radial tyres helped give the T2 of the mid-1970s a more substantial look. Longer front bumper wraparounds helped, too. The lenses on the wings were for US-specification marker lights, not used in the UK.

■ STANDING IN THE SHADOW

Royce versions introduced in 1969, they had an extra four inches in the wheelbase, which all went into providing more legroom for rear-seat passengers. They had the same Everflex vinyl roof and smaller rear window, and they were available either with or without a division.

It appears that the long-wheelbase cars were built to special order and because of persistent customer demand. This quite clearly revealed the existence of a Bentley lobby within Crewe's customer-base, and perhaps the company's decision to accept these orders was an early reflection of a change of attitude towards the Bentley marque. This change of attitude would certainly become apparent in the early years of the next generation of saloons from Crewe.

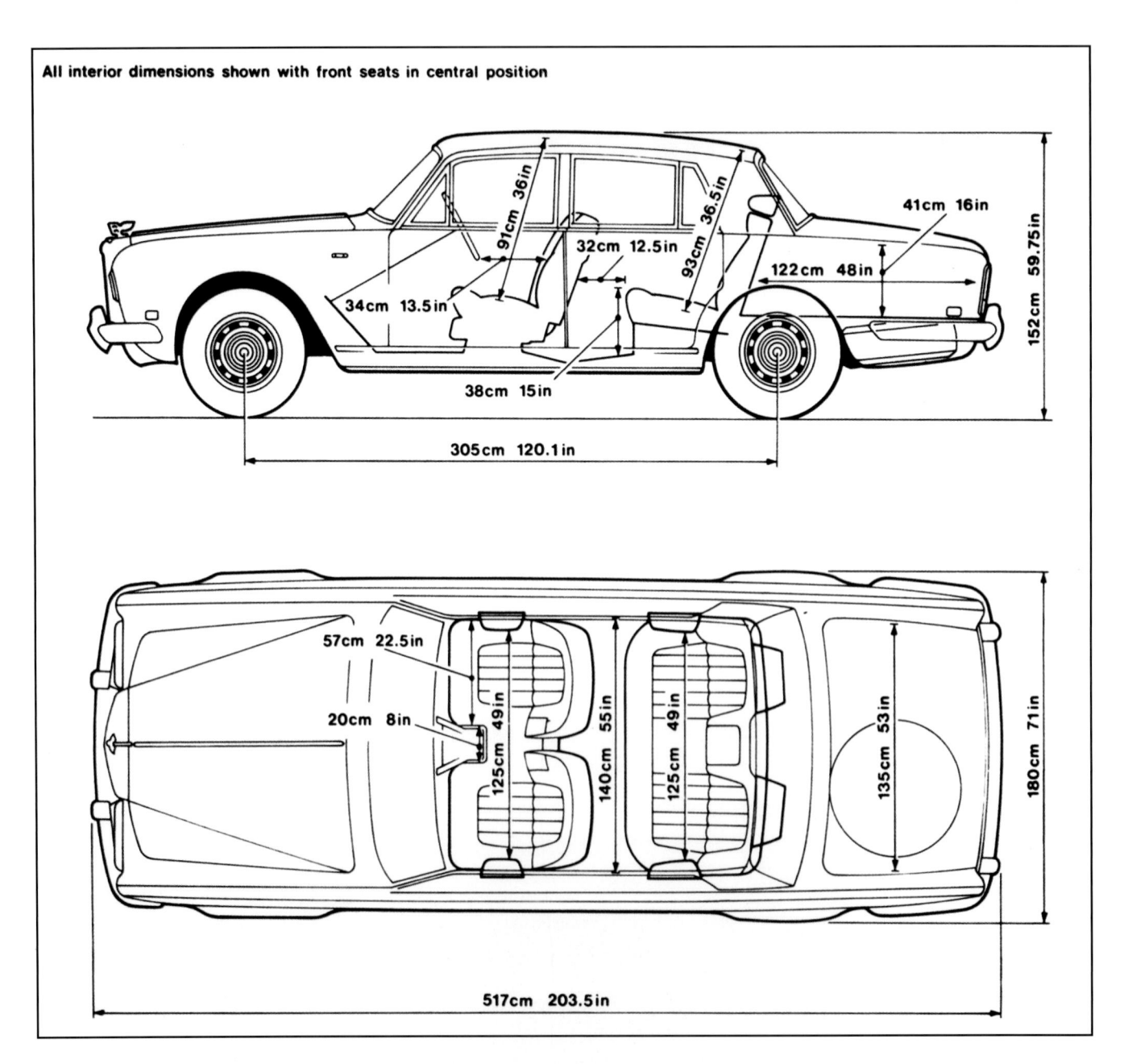

The generous interior dimensions of a 1976 T series are clear from this drawing prepared for sales brochures. The boot, too, was vast by contemporary standards, measuring a full 4 feet from front to back.

STANDING IN THE SHADOW ■

ABOVE: **Wearing the 1900 TU number plate, which was one that the company transferred from car to car, this is a 1978 Bentley T2. The rubber bumpers and front air-dam are apparent, as are the big door mirrors. This car has the alternative style of two-tone colour split, with the second colour covering only the roof panel.**

RIGHT: **With the impact bumpers, made of neoprene rubber, came a shorter version of the Bentley grille. Clear on this T2 are the headlamp wipers.**

21

■ STANDING IN THE SHADOW

TOP AND BELOW: **Two-tone colour schemes always suited the T series, even though they were no longer fashionable by the time this car was built in 1977. The air dam was omitted from US-specification cars.**

22

CHAPTER TWO

TWO-DOOR EXCLUSIVITY

The switch from separate-chassis construction to monocoque had enormous repercussions, both for Crewe and for some of the companies that had traditionally depended on its products for their own existence. It had been a fairly straightforward business to build a bespoke body style on a rigid chassis frame, but this was no longer possible with a monocoque. New bodies had to be engineered, as well as designed, so that they would cope with the stresses that a monocoque was designed to withstand, and the coachbuilders who had traditionally worked with Rolls-Royce and Bentley products were simply not equipped to deal with that.

Nevertheless, Crewe was rightly convinced that the market for expensive, typically two-door, alternatives to its standard four-door saloons would not disappear. So it came up with a strategy that would meet the market demand, but with an in-house design: there would be two-door saloon and convertible variants of a standard style that would be built by the company's Mulliner, Park Ward coachbuilding division in London. These would be available with both Bentley and Rolls-Royce badges to maximize the variety of options on offer.

This decision really sounded the death knell for the few remaining coachbuilders that had been working on Bentley and Rolls-Royce chassis. Their numbers had in any case dwindled in recent years, but a key independent that remained in business was James Young, who were owned by the Jack Barclay dealership chain and were based in Bromley, Kent. Young's drew up a plan to deliver a two-door variant of the Silver Shadow, and secured Crewe's agreement to introduce it before the in-house two-door model reached the market, but the car was very much a last-ditch effort. By the time the last of just fifteen Bentley models and thirty-five Rolls-Royce examples had been completed in 1967, Young's activities were

There was no scope for traditional coachbuilders with the new monocoque Bentley and Rolls-Royce models, but James Young gamely created a two-door car by modifying the standard shell. Its lines were too rigid to be a great success.

23

TWO-DOOR EXCLUSIVITY

in terminal decline and the company closed its doors later the same year.

The James Young T-types and Shadows were simply conversions of the standard four-door, with a single long door on each side in place of the two doors of the standard saloon. There were modifications inside, such as tipping front seats to afford access to the rear, but otherwise the cars were unchanged. They had limited appeal (although there was no doubt about their exclusivity) and were, in all honesty, not particularly attractive either to look at or from a practical point of view.

Crewe's own solution to the two-door problem was altogether superior, and the car that was introduced as a two-door saloon ('coupé' in the USA) in March 1966 was an elegant and timeless design that reflected the best of the company's abilities. It was perhaps interesting that a Bentley variant showed the new style to the world at the Geneva Motor Show that month, but the event had no longer-term significance. The convertible models followed in autumn 1967, partly because they needed extra development but also because resources simply did not allow the introduction of both new bodies at the same time.

The two-door models, rather unimaginatively known simply as that and lacking a proper name of their own at this stage, had been designed by Rolls-Royce styling chief, John Blatchley, in conjunction with the team at Mulliner, Park Ward. The MPW involvement was critical to the project because the plan was always for these cars to be built at the coachbuilding division's premises in Willesden, North London – a strategy that led to some complicated and costly movements of part-completed cars between London and Crewe.

Characteristic of the two-door body was a gentle kick-up in the lines just ahead of the rear wheels, a feature that gave the body so much more character than the nearly straight lines of the four-door T series and Shadow. More rounded contours everywhere, and particularly at the rear, gave these cars a sleekness and an elegance that still marks them out more than forty years after they were designed. For most of their long production life (the saloons were available for only fourteen years but the convertibles for a remarkable twenty-eight years) they had no direct rivals in their field.

Both two-door saloon and convertible bodies had light-alloy bonnets, boot lids and doors as a way of saving weight, but there was no disguising their overall weight. The convertibles were even heavier than the closed cars, thanks largely to extensive reinforcement of the underframe and sills to compensate for the loss of a fixed roof. The hood and hood mechanism were also heavy in themselves, the hood being beautifully constructed with a sound-damping layer between the inner wool headlining and the outer cloth covering. It was, of course, power-operated, and a switch on the centre console brought into operation electrically-driven hydraulics that raised or lowered it in a smooth and pleasing sequence. As was normal at the time, the rear window was made of transparent plastic to allow it to fold with the hood, and a leather hood bag could be fitted over the folded hood behind the seats to tidy the profile when the car was open to the elements.

The lines created for the two-door derivatives of the Shadow/T series range by Mulliner Park Ward had a beautiful flowing elegance. The rather severe and formal lines of the roof carried some family resemblance to the parent saloons, but these models were the spiritual ancestors of later two-door Bentleys such as the Continental R and the Brooklands coupé.

TWO-DOOR EXCLUSIVITY

Two-tone paintwork was generally less common on the two-door models, and this early T series is something of a rarity.

Constructing these cars was a very lengthy and complicated process. Every stage was, of course, almost entirely dependent on hand-building, and each car took around twenty weeks to complete – plus an extra week or so if it was a convertible. This compared with a mere twelve weeks for a standard four-door saloon.

Once the T series or Shadow underframes had been delivered to Willesden from Pressed Steel at Cowley, it took three weeks to build the basic superstructure of the two-door body. The part-completed shells were then shipped to Crewe, two at a time, where they were rust-proofed and painted with undercoat up to the 'guide coat' stage. Still at Crewe, five more weeks were spent on fitting all the running-gear. They then returned to Willesden for finishing.

'Finishing' took several more weeks. An extra week at the beginning of this stage went into the construction and fitting of the convertible hood on those cars that were to have one. Two more weeks were devoted to the final paint process, and a further three weeks were needed to fit the upholstery, the wood, the glazing and the brightwork. The apparently completed cars then spent two weeks going through an exhaustive series of checks and tests before they were ready to be released to the dealers who would supply them to waiting customers. It was no surprise that they were so expensive: a two-door saloon cost some 50 per cent more than a standard four-door, and a convertible even more.

There was just one disappointing aspect of the new two-door models, and that was their dynamic qualities. They had exactly the same powertrain and suspension as the four-door saloons, and although the 6230cc V8 would whisk them swiftly and silently up to 120mph (193km/h), the whole car was set up as a long-distance cruiser, and was no happier than the four-door saloon at being hustled through a series of bends. The cross-ply tyres would squeal if the car was cornered too quickly, and the steering was finger-tip light and so well-damped that it conveyed very little information to the driver about what the front wheels were doing. Nevertheless, many customers were perfectly happy with the cars' combination of qualities: at that time, cars of this size were simply not expected to handle like a sports car at speed.

With hindsight, Crewe's failure to give the cars handling and performance that better fitted their visual promise looks like a missed opportunity, but the fact was that the Mulliner Park Ward division was kept fully occupied meeting orders. Most were for Rolls-Royce examples: in the five years during which the cars were built in their earliest form, there were just ninety-eight Bentley saloons and a mere forty-one Bentley convertibles against 571 Rolls-Royce saloons and 504

■ TWO-DOOR EXCLUSIVITY

Rolls-Royce convertibles. It was, admittedly, Crewe's policy to introduce new features on these flagship cars some months ahead of their introduction on the four-door saloons. So, for example, air conditioning became standard equipment in spring 1969 on the two-doors, while it was not standardized on the four-door cars until the end of the year. However, the extra build-time of the two-door cars absorbed some of the advantages of early introduction, and, in any case, major changes to items such as the engine and transmission were made at the same time right across the range.

The two-door cars had no real sporting pretensions and, as this example shows, not even a rev counter among the instruments.

The two-door saloons ('coupés' in the USA) were accompanied by drophead versions of the same bodyshell. The tread-plate on the door sill bears the name of the coachbuilder – H. J. Mulliner, Park Ward.

26

SPECIFICATIONS FOR BENTLEY TWO-DOOR, CORNICHE AND CONTINENTAL MODELS

Years of manufacture
1966–71 (two-door MPW saloons and convertibles)
1971–84 (Corniche)
1984–94 (Continental)

Build quantity
(See separate sidebar)

Engine
1965–1970
6230cc (104.14mm × 91.44mm) OHV V8
Twin SU HD8 carburettors
9:1 compression ratio (8:1 optional)
195bhp at 4,000rpm (estimated)
290lb ft at 2,500rpm (estimated)
1970–1980
6750cc (104.14mm × 99.1mm) OHV V8
Twin SU HD8 carburettors (1970–1977); twin SU HIF7 carburettors (1977–1986); single four-barrel Solex carburettor for some export territories; Bosch K-Jetronic fuel injection for 1980 Californian cars; Bosch K-Jetronic fuel injection for USA and Japan from 1985MY, for Australia from 1986MY, and standardized from 1987MY; Bosch MK-Motronic engine management system from 1989MY
9:1 compression ratio to autumn 1975, 8:1 compression optional; thereafter 8:1 standard in Europe and 7.3:1 standard for Australia, Japan and USA
198bhp at 4,000rpm (estimated) to 1986; less for US models; 225bhp (approx) with Solex carburettor; 240bhp from 1987
330lb ft at 2,500rpm (estimated); torque figure for Solex carburettor and fuel injected engines not available

Transmission
RHD cars to 1968
Four-speed GM Hydramatic automatic gearbox built by Rolls-Royce, with fluid coupling and electric selection.
RHD cars from 1968–92 and all LHD cars to 1992
Three-speed GM400 Turbo-Hydramatic automatic gearbox with torque converter.
All cars, 1992–94
Four-speed GL480-E GM automatic gearbox.

Suspension
Independent front suspension with coil springs, twin wishbones, anti-roll bar and hydraulic telescopic dampers.
Independent rear suspension with coil springs, semi-trailing arms, hydraulic telescopic dampers and high-pressure hydraulic self-levelling system.

Steering
Power-assisted recirculating-ball steering by GM Saginaw (1966–76); power-assisted rack-and-pinion steering (1977–94).

Brakes
Disc brakes on all four wheels, with 11in diameter. Three separate hydraulic circuits (two from 1975), with high-pressure hydraulic system.

Wheels and tyres
15in steel disc wheels with 6in rims
1966 to summer 1972	8.45 × 15 cross-ply tyres
Summer 1972 to spring 1974	205VR15 radial tyres
Spring 1974 on	235/70-15 or HR70HR15 radial tyres

Vehicle dimensions
Wheelbase	119.5in (3,035mm)
Overall length	191.5in (5,169mm) with metal bumpers
	192.5in (5,194mm) with neoprene bumpers
Overall width	72in (1,829mm)
Overall height	58.75in (1,492mm) for saloons
	59.75in (1,518mm) for convertible
Track	57.5in (1,460mm), front and rear
Weight	4,978lb (2,258kg) unladen, for Corniche saloon
	5,124lb (2,322kg) unladen, for Corniche convertible

Performance
(Figures for mid-1970s Bentley Corniche)
Max. speed	120mph (193km/h)
0–60 mph	9.6sec
Fuel consumption	13mpg (22ltr/100km)

■ TWO-DOOR EXCLUSIVITY

1971 – THE CORNICHE

As ever, the issue of resources prevented Crewe from forging ahead with changes that would make the two-door cars more different from the four-doors. However, the company did take note of customer preferences and comments, and by the end of 1970 was ready with a package of improvements, known internally as Gamma, which would give the Mulliner Park Ward models some of the special qualities that they needed. One improvement, perhaps long overdue, was to give them a distinctive name, and the one chosen was Corniche. It conjured up all the right images of sunny, coastal roads (called the Corniches) between the glamorous Mediterranean resorts of Nice and Monte Carlo – and there was no doubt that many of the cars had found owners among the inhabitants of those wealthy and fashionable places.

The press launch was planned as a ride-and-drive event based at Nice, when journalists would have the opportunity to drive the cars on those breathtaking coastal roads that hugged the cliffs and looked over the sea. But a month before it was due to take place, Rolls-Royce called in the receivers in a move that surprised and shocked observers everywhere. The company's problem had not been in the car division, but rather in the aero-engine division, where development of the new RB211 jet engine had run massively over-budget. Fortunately, the decision was taken to go ahead with the launch in March 1971, while feverish activity went on behind the scenes to ensure the survival of the two arms of the company. In the end, the car division and the aero-engine division were separated – and the Rolls-Royce and Bentley marques lived to fight another day.

Central to the Corniche specification was the new 6750cc version of the V8 engine, which would reach the four-door models only later in the year. However, the Corniche version of the engine was special, and boasted some 20 per cent more power thanks to revised cam timing, a less restrictive air cleaner and a larger diameter exhaust system. Of course, Crewe did not disclose the actual engine power outputs, but maximum power was probably around 198bhp. For the USA, however, emissions requirements meant that Corniche models had the same engine as the standard T series and Silver Shadow. It was simply too expensive to homologate two different versions of the engine for the USA at this stage.

The Corniche models also had some distinctive exterior features, of which one was a neat and discreet plate badge on the boot lid that simply read 'Corniche'. It set a style that Crewe has followed ever since. Much more obvious to onlookers, however, were the new wheel trims, which were

In 1971, the two-doors became the first cars to receive the new 6.75-litre engine, received some styling changes, and were re-named Corniche models. Here, a 1976 Corniche drophead stands next to a T series saloon from which it was derived.

TWO-DOOR EXCLUSIVITY

The Corniche models had different wheel trims from the standard saloons, wearing either the B for Bentley or the double-R logo.

BELOW: **Despite the space eaten up by the convertible hood and its mechanism, the Corniche drophead still offered ample space for four passengers and ample luggage room in the boot as well.**

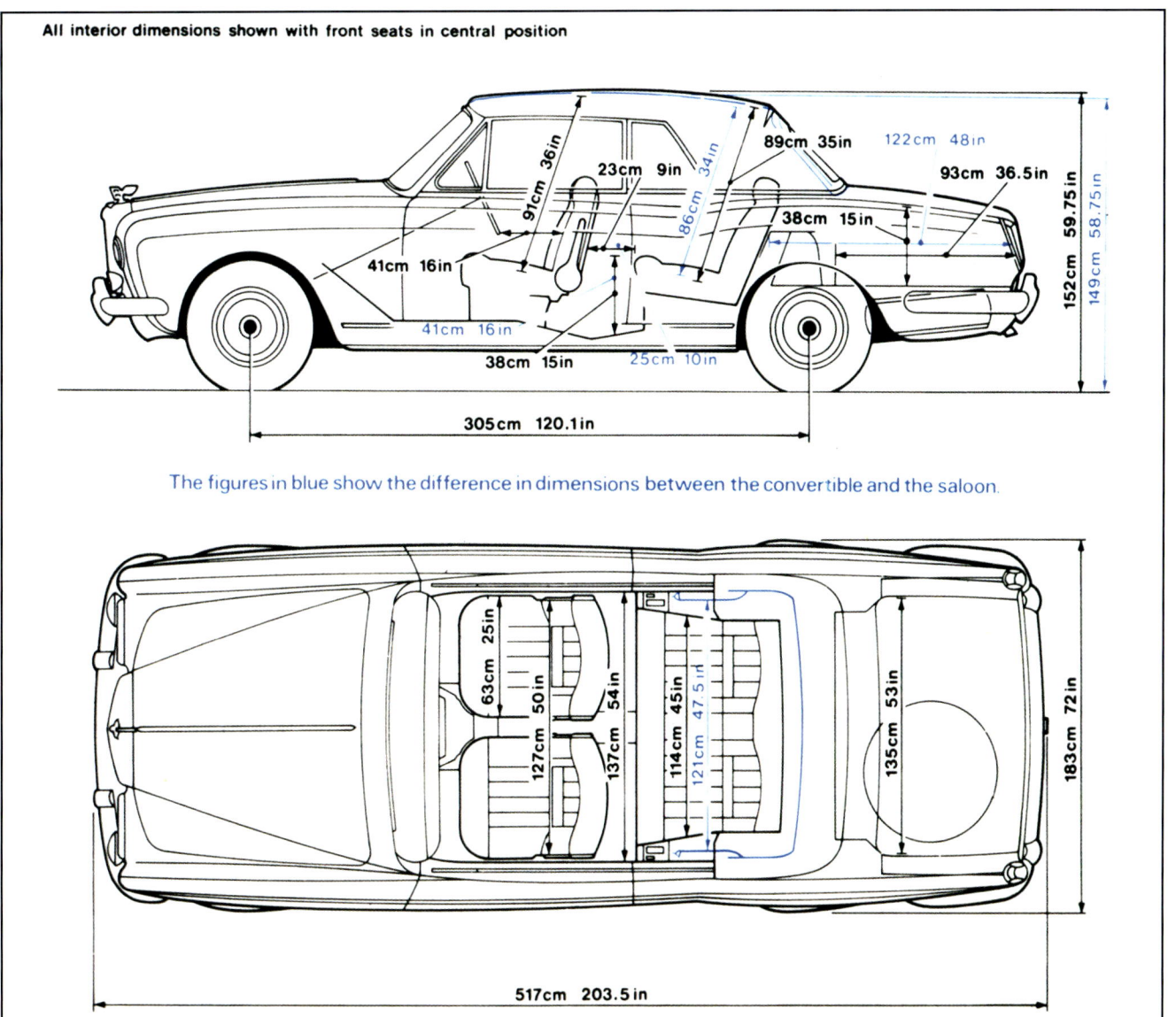

All interior dimensions shown with front seats in central position

The figures in blue show the difference in dimensions between the convertible and the saloon.

29

TWO-DOOR EXCLUSIVITY

simpler than the earlier type that had been shared with the saloons – and also, supposedly, improved the flow of cooling air to the brakes. The radiator grilles were deeper front-to-rear than before (although this was not obvious unless early and late cars were seen side-by-side), and there were other minor differences, such as rectangular reversing lights instead of the round ones on the earlier cars. The saloon versions also had an Everflex roof covering as standard, usually in a contrasting colour that set off the car's lines very well. In later years, however, the Everflex roof tended to date the Corniche's appearance because vinyl roof coverings went out of fashion and remained permanently associated with the 1970s.

The interior had also come in for attention, and the dashboard was noticeably different, even though it followed the same basic style as before. New for the Corniche models, and unique to them, was a rev counter, where older models had a combined instruments dial; the displaced instruments were accommodated in four smaller dials inboard of the speedometer. The centre console had also been redesigned, and a new three-spoke steering wheel with a wooden rim gave a slightly more sporting ambience to the driving position. Being slightly smaller than the earlier type, with a 15in (381mm) diameter, it also helped to make the steering feel slightly heavier and more sporty; sadly, though, there had been no changes to the suspension to support this. Ventilated front disc brakes were also part of the Corniche upgrades, although they were not actually introduced until later in 1971, and the very first cars were delivered with the solid discs introduced in 1966.

The new engine did make a difference, as Geoffrey Howard commented in *Motor* magazine after trying the new cars at the press launch in southern France. 'It really feels now as if the engine is large enough for the huge size and weight of the body, and its step off the mark from rest is now most impressive.' There were improvements elsewhere, too. 'No claims are made for suspension improvements, but there has been a progressive programme of development in this department and the latest car is much better than previous ones. Most of our criticisms of poor directional stability and slow steering have been answered and the new small wheel helps a lot in giving the driver more feel of what is going on. There is still very strong understeer, largely disguised by the power steering, and excellent straight line running.'

Prices once again reflected the fact that the two-door cars were the flagships of the Crewe range (unless, of course, the big Rolls-Royce Phantom limousines were included in the equation). A four-door Bentley T series saloon cost £9,925, and a Corniche saloon cost £12,758. There was, of course, a price differential to make clear that the Bentley was only second-best: the Rolls-Royce Corniche saloon cost an extra £71.

The two Corniche models continued with the same basic specification right through until March 1981, when the saloons went out of production. The convertible, however, remained available as a Corniche until May 1984 – an astonishingly long run of just under thirteen years. Nor was it finished yet: renamed the Continental, it carried on for another ten years until 1994. In the meantime, though, there had been many changes of detail – and some of real significance.

CORNICHE – THE FIRST 10 YEARS

Broadly speaking, changes to the Corniche range followed those made to the T series and Silver Shadows – or, more accurately, led them, because it was still policy at Crewe to introduce changes on the two-door cars first. For most of the first ten years of the Corniche's life, it remained the flagship of the range, but there was a period between 1975 and 1977 when it was temporarily replaced in that role by the new Rolls-Royce Camargue. The Camargue, however, was never offered as a Bentley (although one car was specially built with Bentley features), and therefore has no real place in the present story. As far as the Bentley marque was concerned, its flagship in the 1970s was always the Corniche range. Sales, though, continued to favour the Rolls-Royce variants heavily.

The most important changes over the first decade of the Corniche's life began with the arrival of compliant front suspension in early 1972 and the reversion, not long afterwards, to a 16in (406.4mm) thin-rimmed steering wheel. Then 1974 brought the large, black bumpers and a modified front end with a shorter radiator grille that gave the bumpers room to move backwards (on US models only, which had damper struts) and with plain panels where the air intakes had once been under the headlamps. The cars lost some of their attractiveness at this point, but the overall shape of the body remained unchanged. Flared arches over wider, low-profile tyres followed, and then in mid-1975, for markets where exhaust emissions were not a sensitive issue, engine power was increased by means of the four-barrel Solex 4A1 carburettor that had recently been introduced for the Rolls-Royce Camargue. US models, however, and cars for many other markets, retained the earlier engine specification with its twin SU carburettors.

THE UNIQUE BENTLEY CAMARGUE

In the early 1970s, Rolls-Royce identified a market for a new flagship coupé that would embody the very latest technology and would appeal to a small but determined number of customers who were determined to have not only the best but also a car that was very distinctive.

The car, codenamed Delta during its development phase, was based on the underframe and running-gear of the SY (Silver Shadow and T series) family. A distinctive appearance was achieved by subcontracting the body design to the Italian styling house of Pininfarina, who had already built a one-off two-door Bentley fastback coupé on the SY underframe for industrialist Sir James Hanson in 1968. The plan was to market this new flagship only as a Rolls-Royce, not least because it was intended as the most expensive model in the owner-driver range and could not therefore be marketed with the less prestigious Bentley badges.

Such was Crewe's thinking in the early 1970s, although it is interesting that the Delta prototypes all wore Bentley-style grilles when they were out on test because this supposedly made them less conspicuous. It is also undeniable that the Bentley grille suited the proportions of the Pininfarina body very well; the Rolls-Royce grille had to be stretched rather uncomfortably to fit for the production cars.

The car was marketed as the Rolls-Royce Camargue, and 530 were built between 1975 and 1985, when production came to an end. A plan to fit it with the turbocharged V8 was abandoned in favour of using that engine in the Bentley Mulsanne. However, a single Bentley version was built in 1985 to meet the request of a very special customer – the Sultan of Brunei, a fanatical and wealthy collector of special cars for whom Crewe would go on to undertake a number of individual commissions (see Chapter 11).

Since then, and as prices of the Camargue have tumbled, several owners have had their cars fitted with Bentley grilles and other markings to make them more distinctive. There is also little doubt that these fake Bentley Camargues look more attractive than the real thing, whose appearance has always divided opinions quite sharply.

The epitome of elegance: an early chrome-bumper Bentley Corniche drophead shows how stunning the cars could look.

■ TWO-DOOR EXCLUSIVITY

ABOVE: **The Corniche drophead was subject to the same safety requirements as any other car. Here, a bodyshell undergoes a side-impact test associated with US safety regulations.**

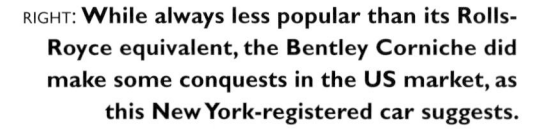

RIGHT: **While always less popular than its Rolls-Royce equivalent, the Bentley Corniche did make some conquests in the US market, as this New York-registered car suggests.**

Two-tone treatments were still being specified during the rubber-bumper era of the Corniche. This coupé was destined for the USA, and has no bonnet mascot or front air-dam; the square number plate is also to US standards.

TWO-DOOR EXCLUSIVITY

Next came the deletion of the conventional hydraulic circuit from the braking system, exactly as on the four-door saloons. Then February 1977 brought a whole range of changes, which matched those on the T2 versions of the Bentley. Corniche models took on a front air-dam below the bumper (although this was omitted from US cars), modified front suspension geometry and Burman rack-and-pinion steering. There was also a new facia.

However, the biggest and most important change to the Corniche models in this period was one which did not affect their four-door saloon contemporaries. From March 1979, all Corniches took on the modified rear suspension that had been designed for the forthcoming Bentley Mulsanne and Rolls-Royce Silver Spirit saloons (see Chapter 3). This tightened up the chassis dynamics a little – enough at least to make the latest Corniche with its rack-and-pinion steering, wide tyres and uprated rear end a very different proposition on the road from the original two-door cars of the mid-1960s.

The new rear suspension was fitted to a modified subframe. It brought Girling gas struts in place of conventional dampers, and these were relocated behind the line of the halfshafts, having earlier been mounted concentrically with the coil springs. The springs themselves were shorter and had a softer rating, and there was a minor increase in the rear track as a result of all these changes. At the same time, mineral oil replaced brake fluid in the car's high-pressure braking and self-levelling systems.

During 1980, cars destined for California took on a fuel-injected version of the 6750cc engine. The Bosch K-Jetronic injection system was extended to cars for other US states later in the year, but 1980 had another and larger significance in the Corniche story because the final saloon bodyshells were assembled during the autumn. Although production did not officially end until March 1981, the gap of a few months was actually used for assembly of the final cars to meet orders. From then on, the Corniche was available only as a convertible.

These changes also coincided with some quite major changes at the Mulliner Park Ward body plant in Willesden. In 1979, production was transferred from the old Park Ward factory in High Road to new buildings that had been erected opposite the Rolls-Royce Service Station in Hythe Road. Work began on a new Service Station in School Road, Acton, and the old Service Station was extensively modernized to take the Mulliner Park Ward operation. Three years later, in 1982, the whole move was complete and Corniche convertibles began to emerge from Hythe Road.

1984 – THE CONTINENTAL

It is interesting that Crewe had at one stage given some serious consideration to a two-door convertible derivative of the SZ (Mulsanne and Silver Shadow) body design, which would, presumably, have replaced the Corniche if it had gone into production. The design progressed to a full-size model (badged as a Rolls-Royce), but there was no doubt that the more prosaic front end lacked the sensuous lines of the Corniche.

From June 1984, the Corniche name stayed with Rolls-Royce, while the Bentley dropheads became Continentals. Note the headlamp wipers on this example, and the wheelarch trims associated with the Continental.

33

■ TWO-DOOR EXCLUSIVITY

The Continental was undeniably a car to be seen in, though not all were as eye-catching as this 1985 model, finished in Tudor Red for the singer Elton John. The Parchment leather trim had contrasting red piping, and the car had the very latest alloy wheels. The body-colour grille slats were a standard Continental feature.

TWO-DOOR EXCLUSIVITY

Research also showed that Corniche buyers also tended to be conservative, which argued against changing the older body design. The mechanical and suspension elements were, after all, so closely related to those of the SZ saloon range that it would be an easy job to keep the Corniche up-to-date mechanically as the SZ was developed during production.

Instead, the Corniche convertible was updated for the 1985 season in June 1984 and, although the Corniche name was retained for Rolls-Royce derivatives, Bentley models were given a clearer identity of their own through the use of a new and evocative name. From now on, Bentley versions of the car would be called the Continental. It was a name that sat well with the car's image, and that reached back into Bentley's glamorous past.

OPPOSITE & THIS PAGE: **The Continental formula barely changed from the mid-1980s to the end of production a decade later. From the start of the 1986 model-year, the front number-plate was relocated on the bumper, and there were always different lighting arrangements for US-market cars: two of those pictured here have the side marker lights required by US Federal regulations.**

35

■ TWO-DOOR EXCLUSIVITY

With the Bentley Continental name came grille slats that were painted in the body colour, and body colour was used for the bumpers and mirror bodies as well. The new combination worked very well visually, making the massive bumpers less intrusive on the overall shape of the car and making it look more modern without harming its timeless appeal. Slim chrome strips were also added to the wheelarch edges. There were further revisions to the seats and dashboard. Sales began to increase, fuelled partly by the new focus on the Bentley marque as qualitatively different from Rolls-Royce, which had been initiated with the launch of the Bentley Mulsanne Turbo in 1982.

It is interesting that, in 1986, Crewe looked seriously at making a removable hardtop for the Continental, creating the solid roof out of GRP to reduce weight. However, the project – which would have created a car known internally as CZS – did not come to fruition. The next specification changes did not, in practice, occur until March 1987, when all variants of the Continental took on the new Bosch fuel-injected engine that went into the latest versions of the Mulsanne saloon, together with the latest ABS braking system. However, relatively few Continentals were built before there were more changes that November for the 1988 season.

The 1988-season changes brought memory-set buttons for the electric front-seat adjusters. These buttons were located on a longer centre console, and there were also additional door handles that allowed rear-seat passengers to open the doors themselves, plus changes to the locks. Rolls-Royce versions of the car took on the new name of Corniche II, but the Bentley remained a plain Continental.

More major changes had to wait until 1992, when the Continental took on some of the new elements that had been drawn up for the new Continental R coupé. In the meantime, though, there were annual upgrades. The 1989 models, introduced in November 1988, had a new sports steering wheel, revised seat trim with the horizontal seams seen on the Turbo R, a stowage box in the rear-centre armrest, a slightly modified facia with an outside temperature gauge and an analogue clock, and a modified dim-dip system for the headlights. For 1990, November 1989 brought a redesigned facia, which, like that introduced on the Mulsanne saloons at the same time, had a new warning module. Rolls-Royce variants took on the Corniche III name; Bentleys remained simply Continentals. Notable was that the Continental did not gain the new automatic ride-control system that was introduced for the Mulsannes and the Continental R; that would come later. Then for 1991, the August 1990 changes made a catalytic converter available as a no-cost option in the UK, and added a higher-specification radio-cassette system with ten speakers and a CD changer.

1992–95 – THE FINAL YEARS

Engineering changes associated with the new Continental R coupé inevitably had their impact on the Continental convertible in its final years. For Rolls-Royce, the February 1992 upgrades to the convertible resulted in a model called the Corniche IV, but the Bentley remained a simple Continental.

Still elegant after all those years… this late Continental has a UK specification without side markers but with indicator repeater lamps set high on the front wings.

TWO-DOOR EXCLUSIVITY

The single Pininfarina-bodied car was no great beauty, with a very heavy appearance from some angles. The car has since been modified with T2-style rubber bumpers and Corniche wheel trims.

37

■ TWO-DOOR EXCLUSIVITY

Production figures: Bentley SY two-door models, 1965–95

Model	Years	Saloon	Convertible
James Young	1965–67	15	
MPW T-series	1966–71	98	41
Corniche	1971–80	63	
Corniche	1971–84		77
Continental	1984–94		421
Continental Turbo	1992–95		8 (*)
Overall totals		**176**	**547**

(*) Total disputed; see main text.

The most far-reaching changes were in the powertrain department, where the engine now took on a Bosch MK-Motronic management system and the old three-speed GM 400 automatic gearbox gave way to a new four-speed, again manufactured by General Motors in the USA. The 4L80-E transmission featured not only an overdriven top gear, but also a torque converter that locked up above a certain road speed in order to reduce power losses. It came with electronic controls that allowed a winter setting (in other words, reduced the risk of wheelspin under acceleration) and, eighteen months later, in September 1993, was further upgraded with what Crewe called Shift Energy Management. This reduced engine torque briefly during upshifts in the gearbox, to ensure that the changes were as smooth and unobtrusive as possible.

Other, more minor, changes in February 1992 brought motorized central locking in place of the earlier solenoid-operated type, and also a change to 235/70 × 15 tyres on alloy wheels. But Crewe had not yet finished with the Continental, and 1993 brought further changes, in two groups. First, January saw a redesigned convertible top that now disappeared completely into the bodywork when lowered and incorporated a glass rear window – as many other high-quality convertible models were now doing. An automatic dimming rear-view mirror was added, together with a single-unit Alpine radio-cassette head unit with a remote control for the rear passengers. The Bentley badge changed to feature a green background.

Then changes in September 1993 brought more power from the latest redesign of the V8 engine, Shift Energy Man-

agement for the automatic transmission (as already noted), and – at long last – the Adaptive Ride Control that was already used on the Bentley saloons and the Continental R coupé. The Continental drophead also gained a passenger's side airbag as standard, and the seats were redesigned to reflect the latest style of Bentley upholstery with swooping curves for pleats.

Those changes were the last made to the Continental, which went out of production in 1994 to make way for the new Azure convertible derived from the Continental R coupé. There was, however, one final twist in the tale of the big convertible. Beginning in 1992, Crewe had responded to the wishes of a small number of customers who wanted their Continentals to have the blistering performance that had now become available through the turbocharged engines used in other Bentley models. So a very few Continental Turbo models were built, the last one being delivered in 1995. Some sources claim that there were eight cars in all, but others believe there were no more than three, and that all of these were built for the Sultan of Brunei (see Chapter 11). The Brunei cars – and presumably the others, if they existed – had reinforced sills, body modifications to accommodate the intercooler and its ducting, a Turbo R exhaust system and 16in wheels from the Continental R with 255/60ZR16 tyres.

THE PININFARINA BENTLEY

One T series four-door underframe (CBH 4033) was supplied to the Italian coachbuilder Pininfarina in late 1967 or early 1968 to form the basis of a show special. Pininfarina designed for it a two-door coupé body, number PF 917, with sloping rear roofline and finished it in dark Velvet Green.

The car had right-hand drive and was displayed at the 1968 Turin Motor Show as a 'Coupé Speciale'. It was bought by the industrialist James Hanson (later Lord Hanson) and registered as BGC 225G. It was sold on through HR Owen in London during 1980 and was later fitted with black bumpers as used on the later T2 models and with Corniche-style wheel trims. Some commentators have suggested that this car inspired Pininfarina's design for the Rolls-Royce Camargue.

CHAPTER THREE

THE GREAT REVIVAL

The 1980s were the critical period in the revival of the Bentley marque. Even though David Plastow had set Rolls-Royce Motors on course as early as 1974 to re-establish Bentley as separate and different from Rolls-Royce, lead times were inevitably long in such a small company. The changes had to be made in line with resources, and those resources were uncomfortably finite. There was also the issue that Bentley customers at that time still tended to be rather conservative, and it could have been a marketing mistake to rush through a number of radical changes all at once.

As far as the public was concerned, the rebirth of Bentley coincided with the introduction of the replacement model for the Silver Shadow range of cars. The company did not have the resources to develop an entirely separate model-range to carry the Bentley badge, and so the new SZ saloon that was introduced in 1980 would have to do duty for both the Rolls-Royce and Bentley marques. At that time, it would have taken considerable prescience to determine the way things would go over the decade ahead, because the only indication of what was to come lay in the name given to the Bentley version of the new car. Instead of being reduced to a mere letter, as it had been with the R-type (Silver Dawn), S-type (Silver Cloud) and T-type (Silver Shadow), the Bentley equivalent of the new Rolls-Royce Silver Spirit had a name of its own. It was called the Mulsanne, and it was the choice of that name that gave a clue to what might happen next. Mulsanne was the name of the famous straight section of the Le Mans racing circuit – and in that, it harked back to the glorious racing days of Bentley at Le Mans in the 1920s.

To be fair, the 1980 Mulsanne was a clone of the Rolls-Royce Silver Spirit. It was not until 1982 that things became more interesting. That year saw the introduction of the Bentley Mulsanne Turbo, a high-performance derivative featuring a turbocharged engine that was not available in Rolls-Royce versions of the car. It was a step in the right direction, but it was not yet enough: the car shared its luxury-limousine dynamics with the Silver Spirit and was criticized for its lack of sporting characteristics beyond the massively impressive straight-line performance that came with the turbocharged engine.

Two years later, the next stage became clear. July 1984 brought the Bentley Eight, an entry-level variant of the SZ saloon, which was deliberately intended to bring the Bentley marque within the range of a new set of customers – typically, younger and slightly less wealthy ones who might otherwise have been tempted by rival luxury saloons from Mercedes-Benz or BMW. Among its key features was sharper handling.

David Plastow was Chairman of the Rolls-Royce car division from 1972–80, and the initial impetus to distinguish the Bentley marque more effectively from Rolls-Royce came from him.

■ THE GREAT REVIVAL

The Mulsanne was the Bentley version of the SZ range. As introduced in October 1980, it was indistinguishable from the companion Rolls-Royce Silver Spirit, except by badging and the Bentley grille. However, plans were already afoot to make more of the Bentley marque.

The rear seat of a Mulsanne was a magnificent place to be for long-distance travel, but passengers would have been hard-pressed to tell whether they were in a Silver Spirit or a Mulsanne.

That handling package, further improved in a number of ways, reached the turbocharged car in March 1985 to create the Bentley Turbo R (the Mulsanne name was dropped for this variant), which became a legend in its own lifetime thanks to its astonishing combination of high performance with sporty handling.

It was the Turbo R that was pivotal in making the distinction between the Bentley and Rolls-Royce marques clear to the buying public. It also allowed Crewe to re-introduce Bentley as a separate marque to the USA, where previously it had been available only to special order through Rolls-Royce dealerships. Between November 1987 and November 1988, the three Bentley models (Eight, Mulsanne S – the latest version of the Mulsanne – and Turbo R) were launched in the USA, where the marque swiftly gained a valuable foothold.

Further important changes followed. From 1988, the Bentley front end was further distinguished by four round headlamps instead of the original rectangular lamps shared with the Rolls-Royce. And by 1991, as Chapter 4 shows, the

THE GREAT REVIVAL

marque was generating enough revenue for Crewe to launch a real Bentley-only model in the shape of the stunning Continental R. (Also worth noting is that some of the development effort that had gone into the Bentley did eventually feed back into the Rolls-Royce variants of the SZ saloon: the long-wheelbase Silver Spur was made available in late 1994 with the turbocharged engine and the name of Flying Spur.)

Even so, Bentley's upward progress was not entirely uninterrupted. In fact, the marque suffered some severe problems in the early 1990s, which were a period of recession in the Western world when sales of all luxury cars suffered. Bentley kept its head above the water by regularly offering new features on its cars, so keeping them fresh and attractive. Their specification moved on at a pace that their mass-market rivals, from companies such as Mercedes-Benz and BMW, could not emulate. These incremental changes also enabled the marque to distance itself from the Rolls-Royce models that still looked very similar at a pace that the factory's resources could comfortably accommodate. There were

Though it looked very similar indeed to a standard Mulsanne, 1982's Mulsanne Turbo was a huge step forward for the Bentley marque. At first, the only special exterior features were the body-colour grille surround and discreet 'Turbo' badges on the wings and bootlid.

This was what made the Mulsanne Turbo so special – a turbocharged version of the 6.75-litre Rolls-Royce V8 engine. Sadly, the handling lagged somewhat behind the car's new-found performance.

■ THE GREAT REVIVAL

ABOVE: **The Bentley Eight** was another element in the rebirth of the marque, priced lower to attract customers who had previously considered a Bentley beyond their reach. It re-introduced the mesh grille and used discreet wing badges like the Mulsanne Turbo – but they simply read 'Bentley'.

LEFT: **There were few obvious** cost-cutting measures in the Eight, but comparing this with the picture of an early Mulsanne's rear cabin, the absence of mirrors in the rear quarters and the net instead of a map pocket on the seat back are obvious.

THE GREAT REVIVAL

More cost was saved (but how much in reality?) by using straight-grain wood-veneer instead of figured wood in the cabin.

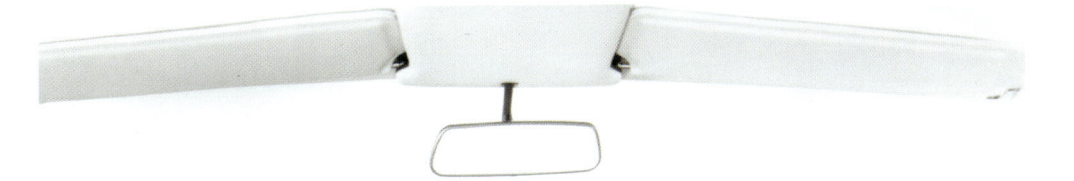

With reworked suspension, the turbocharged car became the Turbo R – no longer a Mulsanne. Suddenly, sporty alloy wheels and bright red paint no longer looked out of place on a Bentley.

■ THE GREAT REVIVAL

There were no very special changes at the rear of the Turbo R – and even the badge plates on the bootlid still read simply 'Bentley' and 'Turbo'.

On the Turbo R, the centre console now flowed into the main dashboard to give a more sporty 'cockpit' feel, and the instruments included a rev counter alongside the speedometer.

For 1989, paired round headlamps on a black background made the cars more distinctive from their Rolls-Royce cousins. The alloy wheels had different centre caps, too. The number-plate had moved to the bumper in 1985, when headlamp washers had replaced the original wipers.

44

THE GREAT REVIVAL

special editions, too, which helped to keep sales alive because they offered an additional degree of exclusivity within what was already an exclusive market. It was a very far cry from the 1960s and 1970s, when changes had occurred very slowly indeed; it was also, and continues to be, very confusing for observers and chroniclers of the Bentley marque.

IN THE BEGINNING

All this development of the Bentley marque had been completely unforeseen when work began on the successor to the Silver Shadow and T-series saloons in 1969. At that stage, the perennial issue of resources was again paramount. The Shadow range had been extremely costly to put into production, mainly because it was the first monocoque design from Crewe, and the company could not contemplate delivering another all-new car to replace it. Instead, large elements of the Shadow itself would have to be carried over to the new saloon. In practice, that meant the underframe, suspension and powertrain would be basically unchanged, even though they would benefit from evolutionary upgrades.

The new car would, however, have to look very different. Styling was entrusted to Fritz Feller, who had succeeded John Blatchley at Crewe, and the early 1970s saw a series of five quarter-scale models (known as Styles A to E) created. All were broadly similar, the main differences lying in the headlamp treatment, and all carried Rolls-Royce grilles. Bentley variants, at this stage, were very much of secondary importance. These quarter-scales all showed that the aim was to make the new model look lower and more rounded than the Shadow range.

There was no Style F; instead, a full-size model known as FS1 was created, and this led quickly on to a second one called FS2, which differed mainly in having a narrower roof that made the car look rather less bulky. Meanwhile, two full-size running prototypes had been built on the basis of the Style C proposal, and the first of these began testing in April 1975. These were known at Crewe as Z-1 and Z-2. Six more prototypes, numbered Z-3 to Z-10, were built to the production style between then and 1978. The first two prototypes were used to test components because they were unrepresentative of the production design. The later six included LHD, long-wheelbase and US-specification cars, and the final one was used to train production staff, being dismantled and rebuilt several times in the process. Most of these prototypes were fitted with dummy Bentley grilles that had their surrounds painted in the body colour so that they were less conspicuous. Ironically, the Bentley grille with painted surround would be chosen for the mould-breaking Mulsanne Turbo models in 1982.

One particular problem in this period was the threat of changing US regulations. Crash safety regulations were one problem; exhaust-emissions regulations were quite another. There was also the problem that US manufacturers had been 'downsizing' since the first oil crisis in 1973, with the result that the Rolls-Royce 6.75-litre V8 engine was beginning to look large and out of step with the times in a country where large engines had once been the norm. So the later 1970s saw Crewe working on no fewer than three different engines for US market versions of the SZ.

Of these, one was an emissions-optimized version of the existing 6750cc V8, known as the L410E type. (The 410 represented the 4.10in bore of the standard engine; the E appears to have stood for emissions-controlled.) The second was known as the L380, and was a 5352cc engine with a 3.80in bore; it was being tried with a GM 200 automatic transmission. The third was the L725, which appears to have been a bigger capacity engine with a swept volume of 7.25 litres. The L725 appears to have been the first casualty, probably during the mid-1970s, and the L380 was cancelled some time around late 1981. The L410E project of course led to the production US-specification engine.

Two pre-production US-specification cars were built in 1979–80, along with ten cars to the rest-of-the-world specification. Of these, one was damaged in an accident, and its major components were re-used in another experimental car known as LGB-2. LGB stood for Light Gauge Body: right from the start, Crewe had been concerned about the weight of the SZ, and a special body with some thin-gauge panels had been built and baptized LGB-1. Also an issue during the development of SZ was the use of lead filler, which not only added weight but was also a potential hazard for those building the cars. So the SZ body had been designed to minimize the number of panel joints and to improve the quality of seal landing faces so that less filler was needed. Plastic filler was also tried experimentally, but was not satisfactory.

1980 – THE FIRST CARS

As introduced in October 1980, the Bentley Mulsanne was hard to distinguish from its Rolls-Royce Silver Spirit stablemate. The wheel trims looked the same from a distance,

THE GREAT REVIVAL

SPECIFICATIONS FOR BENTLEY SZ MODELS

Years of manufacture 1980–98

Build quantity
10,078 (standard wheelbase)
1,832 (LWB)
(For a more detailed breakdown, see sidebar)

Engine
Non-turbo types	6750cc (104.14mm × 99.1mm) ohv V8
1980–86	Two SU HIF7 carburettors with 9.1 compression ratio for most markets; Bosch K-Jetronic fuel injection with 8:1 compression for Australia, Japan and North America. 198bhp at 4,000rpm; torque figures not disclosed
1987–95	Bosch K-Jetronic fuel injection with 9.1 compression ratio for all markets. 238bhp at 4,000rpm; torque figures not disclosed
1996	Zytek electronic engine-management system with 8.7.1 compression ratio for all markets. 238bhp at 4,000rpm; torque figures not disclosed
Turbocharged types	6750cc (104.14mm × 99.1mm) ohv V8
1982–85	Single Solex 4A1 carburettor, with Garrett T04B turbocharger; 8.1 compression ratio. 298bhp at 3,800rpm and 450lb ft at 2,450rpm
1986–88	Bosch KE3-Jetronic fuel injection, with Garrett T04B turbocharger; 8.1 compression ratio. 328bhp at 4,000rpm; torque figures not disclosed
1988–93	Bosch MK-Motronic engine-management system, with Garrett T04B turbocharger and intercooler; 8.1 compression ratio. 328bhp at 4,000rpm; torque figures not disclosed
1994–96	Bosch MK-Motronic engine-management system, with Garrett T04B turbocharger and intercooler; 8.1 compression ratio. 355bhp at 4,000rpm and 420lb ft of torque
1995 (Turbo S)	Zytek electronic engine-management system, with Garrett T04B turbocharger and liquid-cooled intercooler; 8.1 compression ratio. 430bhp at 4,000rpm
1996–98 (Turbo R)	Zytek electronic engine-management system, with Garrett T04B turbocharger and liquid-cooled intercooler; 8.1 compression ratio. 385bhp at 4,000rpm
1997–98 (Brooklands)	Zytek electronic engine-management system for all markets, with Garrett T04B turbocharger with Transient Boost system; liquid-cooled intercooler; 8.1 compression ratio. 400bhp at 4,000rpm
1998 (Turbo RT)	Zytek electronic engine-management system for all markets, with Garrett T04B turbocharger with Transient Boost system; liquid-cooled intercooler; 8.1 compression ratio. 420bhp at 4,000rpm and 650lb ft at 2,100rpm

Transmission
1980–91	Three-speed GM400 Turbo-Hydramatic automatic gearbox with torque converter
1991–98	Four-speed General Motors 4L80-E automatic gearbox with torque converter

(Note: The changeover to the four-speed transmission took place gradually over 1991–92; see main text.)

Suspension
Independent front suspension with coil springs, lower wishbones, transverse top links with brake reaction arms, anti-roll bar and hydraulic telescopic dampers.
Independent rear suspension with coil springs, semi-trailing arms, anti-roll bar, hydraulic telescopic dampers and high-pressure hydraulic self-levelling system.

THE GREAT REVIVAL

Steering
Power-assisted rack-and-pinion

Brakes
Disc brakes on all four wheels, with 11in diameter; ventilated discs at front, solid discs at rear. Two separate hydraulic circuits, with high-pressure hydraulic system. Bosch ABS from 1986.

Wheels and tyres
Mulsanne, Mulsanne Turbo, Mulsanne S and Brooklands to 1995: 15in steel disc wheels with 6in rims and 235/70HR15 tyres.
Brooklands, 1996–97: 16in alloy wheels with 7in rims and 255/60ZR 16 tyres.
Brooklands, 1998: 17in alloy wheels with 7.5in rims and 255/55WR17 tyres.
Turbo R, 1986–93: 15in alloy wheels with 275/55VR15 tyres; 255/65VR15 tyres optional.
Turbo R, 1993: 16in alloy wheels with 7in rims and 255/60ZR 16 tyres.
Turbo R, 1994 on: 17in alloy wheels with 7.5in rims and 255/55WR17 tyres.

Vehicle dimensions

Wheelbase	120.5in (3,061mm) for standard saloons
	124.5in (3,162mm) for long-wheelbase models
Overall length	209in (5,309mm) for standard saloons
	213.17in (5,414mm) for North American specification standard saloons
	213in (5,411mm) for long-wheelbase models
Overall width	74.3in (1,887mm) over body
	79in (2,008mm) over door mirrors
Overall height	58.75in (1,492mm)
Weight	4,950lb (2,245kg) unladen, for standard saloons
	4,960lb (2,250kg) unladen, for Australian specification standard saloons
	4,866lb (2,208kg) unladen, for Japanese specification standard saloons
	4,980lb (2,259kg) unladen, for North American specification standard saloons
	5,120lb (2,320kg) unladen, 1990 model-year Eight and Mulsanne S
	5,050lb (2,290kg) unladen, 1990 model-year Eight and Mulsanne S for North America
	5,270lb (2,390kg) unladen, 1990 model-year Turbo R
	5,360lb (2,430kg) unladen, Brooklands
	5,400lb (2,450kg) unladen, Turbo R
	5,440lb (2,470kg) unladen, for long-wheelbase Turbo R
	5,011lb (2,273kg) unladen, for long-wheelbase models

Performance

Max. speed	115mph/185km/h (early Mulsanne)
	135mph/217km/h (Mulsanne Turbo)
	140mph/225km/h (Turbo R from 1986)
	147mph/237km/h (Turbo R from 1993)
	150mph/242km/h (Turbo RT)
	155mph/250km/h (Turbo S)
0–60mph	10.3sec (early Mulsanne)
	7sec (Mulsanne Turbo)
	6.9sec (Turbo R from 1986)
	6.3sec (Turbo R from 1993)
	5.8sec (Turbo S and Turbo RT)
Fuel consumption	12–16mpg (18–24ltr/100km)

THE GREAT REVIVAL

although of course the Bentley version had a winged B motif in their centres, and both cars had the same rectangular headlamps. Paired rectangular lamps were specified for the USA, but the Bentley Mulsanne was not marketed there and so this specification was found on only a tiny number of cars built to special order. The key difference on the outside lay in the grille, which on the Bentley was an all-chrome item to the expected style. The front bumper, straight on the Silver Spirit, was slightly curved on the Bentley to protect this grille effectively. Inside, the differences were only in the motifs, with winged Bs in the Bentley, where the Rolls-Royce had the paired Rs. Both variants of the car had a facia that was almost identical to the one used in the final Silver Shadow II and Bentley T2 cars – again evidence that Crewe had to take care with spending money on development.

The new car had the same 6750cc V8 engine as the one it replaced, still with twin SU carburettors, except for the USA where fuel injection was fitted to ensure compliance with emissions regulations. As before there was a three-speed GM Turbo-Hydramatic 400 gearbox. Differences in the rear suspension made the wheelbase half an inch longer than in the earlier cars. There were still semi-trailing arms with coil springs and self-levelling, but the angle of the semi-trailing arms' pivots had been increased from 16 degrees to 21 degrees 38 minutes. The springs were also shorter and softer than before, while the sub-frame that carried the rear suspension had been completely redesigned to increase rigidity and to help insulate the cabin from road noise.

The interior equalled Crewe's traditional best, with a relaxing and expensive ambience created by the juxtaposition of top-quality leather, burr walnut wood trim and Wilton carpets with lambswool over-rugs. The front seats were, of course, power-adjustable, and the switchgear was designed as much for its appearance and feel as for its actual function. Perhaps it did not come up to the latest best practice in terms of ergonomics, but few potential buyers would have been put off by that. Most probably did not even comment on the adoption of an American-style foot-operated parking brake in place of the traditional twist-grip handbrake. Leather was standard, but cloth seat-facings were available to order, and would certainly have been preferable to leather in many hot-climate territories, even though the peerless split-level air-conditioning system carried over from the Shadow range was a standard feature.

Few changes were made in the first two years of production. Early cars suffered from wind noise around the front windows at high speeds, and so stronger window frames were introduced to reduce the tendency of the originals to be sucked outwards. However, this modification alleviated the problem rather than cured it. Long-wheelbase cars became available in June 1981, with an extra 4 inches in the wheelbase. All of that went into the rear passenger area and was matched by longer rear doors. There was a smaller rear window, too. Interesting was that the long-wheelbase bodyshells were built as such by Pressed Steel, who of course were also building the standard shells at their Cowley works; on the Shadow range, the shells had actually been 'stretched' by the Mulliner Park Ward division in London.

The year 1981 also saw a refinement package introduced on all the SZ models. The main effect of this was to reduce noise levels inside the car, a result that was achieved mainly by better isolation of the engine and front suspension from the bodyshell, using softer rubber mountings.

1982 – THE MULSANNE TURBO

'It is a marvellous treat,' said *Autocar* magazine in its issue dated 23 October 1982, 'to feel such a large car surge forward as the Bentley Turbo does'. That was a classic of understatement, almost as typically British as the car they were writing about. Nearly two years later, *Autosport* (dated 28 June 1984) was just as taken with the car, although its reservations were also quite clear: it described the Bentley Mulsanne Turbo as 'a superb carriage for those who put comfort before cornering and who want a very high speed cruising ability as well'.

In many ways, the decision to make the first distinctive Bentley a turbocharged car had been inevitable. As is so often clear in this period of the Bentley story, a lack of resources prevented anything more ambitious. The 7.25-litre engine that was under development experimentally might have delivered the extra performance that the marque needed, but it was cancelled early on. Turbocharging the existing V8 engine was an obvious solution: turbocharging was becoming popular as a way of getting more performance out of an engine without automatically incurring a major fuel-consumption penalty, and it was a solution that demanded re-development of an existing engine, rather than the much more expensive solution of starting from scratch.

The SZ saloon had been signed-off for production in 1974, and only details changed between then and 1976. At that point, the launch specification was frozen, and the work that

THE GREAT REVIVAL

The Mulsanne S combined some of the sporting features of the turbocharged cars with the naturally-aspirated engine. The UK price list (*below*) from the 1989 model-year shows that there were several items of optional equipment.

followed was devoted to future upgrades. The first turbocharged prototype was built in 1977, and the Mulsanne Turbo joined the Bentley range in April 1982, after an announcement at the Geneva Show in March. As already noted, of key importance was that it had no Rolls-Royce equivalent: this was a

BENTLEY MULSANNE S

Recommended Basic Price	£60,658.00
Car Tax	£5,054.83
VAT	£9,856.92
Recommended Retail Price	**£75,569.75**

BENTLEY MULSANNE S OPTIONAL EQUIPMENT

	Recommended Basic Price £	Car Tax £	VAT £	Recommended Retail Price £
Fire extinguisher	34.00	2.83	5.52	42.35
Whitewall tyres	98.00	8.17	15.93	122.10
Facia top roll in hide	198.00	16.50	32.18	246.68
Rear parcel shelf in hide	50.00	4.17	8.13	62.30
Cloth headlining	198.00	16.50	32.18	246.68
Hide headlining	594.00	49.50	96.53	740.03
Non-standard hide upholstery	198.00	16.50	32.18	246.68
Non-standard paint	718.00	59.83	116.67	894.50
Special Paint Formulations	1,128.00	94.00	183.30	1,405.30
Two tone paint schemes	326.00	27.17	52.98	406.15
Birds eye maple veneer	155.00	12.92	25.19	193.11
Burr walnut veneer	155.00	12.92	25.19	193.11
Black lacquered woodwork				
Bench rear seat		No extra charge if requested on order
Picnic tables to rear of front seats	615.00	51.25	99.94	766.19
Everflex roof covering	594.00	49.50	96.53	740.03
Rear seat arm rest compartment with opening lid	164.00	13.67	26.65	204.32
Badge bar	34.00	2.83	5.52	42.35
Refrigerator to boot	440.00	36.67	71.50	548.17
Cocktail cabinet to centre console	396.00	33.00	64.35	493.35
Lambswool rug to boot	176.00		26.40	202.40
Leather covered steering wheel	52.00	4.33	8.45	64.78
4 black rubber mats	58.00		8.70	66.70
Bentley seats	686.00	57.17	111.48	854.65

Bentley Turbo RT production

	Standard series	Mulliner
Long-wheelbase	194	49
Short-wheelbase	2	7
Total:	**196**	**56**

Production totals, by type

Mulsanne (1980–87)	482 standard wheelbase
	49 long-wheelbase
Mulsanne Turbo (1982–85)	495 standard wheelbase
	24 long-wheelbase
Eight (1984–92)	1734
Turbo R (1985–98)	4,657 standard wheelbase
	1,508 long-wheelbase
Mulsanne S (1987–92)	905 standard wheelbase
	61 long-wheelbase
Brooklands (1992–98)	1,429 standard wheelbase
	190 long-wheelbase
Turbo S (1994–96)	60
Brooklands R (1997–98)	100
Turbo RT (1997–98)	252
Grand total	11,910

■ THE GREAT REVIVAL

Bentley-only model, which made the marque distinctive at long last. It was also a revelation in terms of the accelerative performance that could be achieved from such a large luxury car with a weight in excess of 2 tons.

Early work on turbocharging the 6.75-litre V8 was sub-contracted to Broadspeed at Southam, and Crewe lent the company a late Silver Shadow I as a mobile test-bed. This responded very well to the turbo treatment, delivering around 50 per cent more torque and 10 per cent more power than standard. It also astonished everyone involved with the project by achieving 140mph (225km/h) on test – although Broadspeed did recommend suspension and tyre changes! Broadspeed were also involved with the turbocharger installation on a second car in 1976, and this time the host vehicle was the very first Rolls-Royce Camargue prototype. The same car was fitted in 1977 with a turbocharged version of the experimental 7.25-litre V8 engine, but these experiments went no further.

Once the basic principle of turbocharging the V8 had been proved, development reverted to Crewe. There was a great deal of work to be done, especially on refinement and in dealing with the considerable extra under-bonnet heat that the turbocharged engine generated. A small team of engineers working under Jack Read developed the production installation, settling on a single-turbocharger installation because there was not enough room for the more obvious solution of twin turbochargers, with a single one fed from each exhaust manifold. Space was very much at a premium, and some ancillaries, among them the PAS pump, had to be relocated to accommodate all the new under-bonnet hardware.

The single turbo was a Garrett AiResearch T04B type, mounted at the front of the right-hand exhaust manifold and fed from that and, through a cross-over pipe, from the left-hand manifold as well. Maximum boost was 7.5psi, delivered at 3,000rpm, and a wastegate or dump valve opened to reduce pressure if it reached 8psi. The exhaust manifolds themselves were made of a special high-temperature nickel-iron alloy.

The engine was still carburettor-fed but, in place of the twin SUs of the standard V8, it had a single four-barrel Solex carburettor similar to that used on the Rolls-Royce Camargue variant of the engine. This had been chosen mainly because it allowed enough throughput of air for the turbocharger to deliver its best, whereas the two SUs were more restrictive. The idea of combining the turbocharger with the Bosch injection system already used on emissions-controlled engines was also given brief consideration, but was rejected because of the likely development costs. One regrettable result of the need to use that Solex carburettor was that the turbocharged car would not meet emissions regulations in its original production form, and could therefore not be sold in Australia, Japan or North America.

The single carburettor was contained in a pressurized airbox on top of the engine to maintain even pressures in the float chamber and at the mouth of the carburettor. A valve in the airbox opened when the throttles were closed after running open, and the unwanted pressure from the turbocharger was then recirculated through a pipe and back to the intake side of the turbocharger. Fuel-pump pressure was maintained at 4psi higher than the pressure inside the airbox, to prevent fuel being forced back through the system.

With the lower 8.0:1 compression ratio already used for US versions of the engine, the turbocharged V8 did not suffer from poor off-boost performance and was not subject to the detonation that afflicted high-compression turbocharged engines. Nevertheless, there was also a knock sensor, which could retard the ignition by as much as 8 degrees to avoid engine damage. The pistons, too, were special, being made of aluminium with steel reinforcing struts to compensate for the different expansion rates of the pistons and the cast-iron cylinder liners.

All this delivered around 50 per cent more power and torque than the standard engine, and although Crewe never officially revealed the figures at this stage, homologation papers for the West German market revealed that the early Mulsanne Turbo had 298bhp at 3,800rpm and 450lb ft at 2,450rpm. These were in a completely different league from those for the standard 6.75-litre V8, and they demanded changes elsewhere. There was a larger capacity exhaust system with twin outlets, a strengthened torque converter for the three-speed gearbox and a taller final drive of 2.69:1, together with strengthened rear-axle components. Even with that taller gearing, the Mulsanne Turbo would still readily spin its rear wheels under acceleration. The specially-designed Avon Turbospeed 235/70 × 15 tyres could safely handle the car's huge weight at its 135mph (217km/h) governed maximum, but their grip was sometimes less than enthusiastic drivers might have wanted.

And there lay the problem with the Mulsanne Turbo. Nobody could fail to admire its straight-line performance, with a 0–60mph time of 7sec and a 0–100mph time of 18sec, but there was little doubt that its dynamics were disappointing. Spring and damper rates were unchanged from the standard Mulsanne, unless a buyer ordered the optional stiffer front dampers, with the result that the car would float over bumps taken at speed and would roll alarmingly in corners. It did have remarkable reserves of grip, but its behaviour did not inspire confidence in the driver. So, for the moment, Crewe had to be content with making waves in the automotive world purely on the basis of that straight-line performance. It was enough: the Mulsanne Turbo was an extraordinarily accurate opening salvo in the battle to put the Bentley marque back at the forefront of high-performance luxury motoring.

It was typical of the times that the Mulsanne Turbo was barely distinguishable from a standard Mulsanne at first sight: perhaps Crewe could not get away from the idea that its cars needed to be discreet, even though public tastes were already beginning to change. There were just two external features that told an onlooker what the car was. These were a body-coloured surround to the radiator grille and a discreet plate on the boot lid that read 'Turbo'.

Things went quiet at Crewe for a time after the Mulsanne Turbo's launch, which, appropriately enough, took place at Le Mans in France. September 1982 brought a new ICE system (the Bosch Toronto radio-cassette) and November 1983 saw improved door locks. But the next stage in Bentley's rebirth did not occur until July 1984.

1984 – THE BENTLEY EIGHT

Crewe knew very well that the Mulsanne Turbo needed some suspension upgrades to fulfil its performance potential. The problem was once again one of resources, and it had simply not been possible to re-engineer the V8 and re-engineer the suspension at the same time. So the engine was introduced first because it gathered maximum publicity; the suspension followed just over two years later in July 1984.

However, this was only a partial revision of the suspension; the full re-work was still nearly a year away. It brought stiffer spring rates and firmer damping to give tauter handling to the SZ, and it was at this stage available only on a new entry-level model called the Bentley Eight.

The term 'entry-level' was of course relative, because the Bentley Eight was carefully priced just under £50,000 at £49,497. That sort of money would very nearly buy two of Mercedes-Benz's superb 500SEL saloons, but in Crewe's terms it represented the bargain basement because the standard Mulsanne then cost £59,937 and the Mulsanne Turbo £61,743.50. It was also some £13,500 cheaper than the cheapest version of the Rolls-Royce Silver Spirit. It was, though, still a massively expensive luxury car.

However, the tauter suspension was part of a carefully designed package, which made the car more appealing to a new type of customer. Crewe thought that the typical new customer might have been some ten years younger than their traditional customers (so, aged between 35 and 45), and might otherwise have been tempted by a top-specification BMW 7 Series or Mercedes S Class. The Eight was distinguished externally by a mesh grille in place of the standard slatted type, a styling caprice supposed to remind onlookers of the mesh grilles used on the later Le Mans racing Bentleys of the 1920s. It also had a plate badge on the boot-lid that read 'Eight'.

To the casual onlooker, it was hard to work out where Crewe had saved the money that allowed such a massive reduction in the showroom price. In fact, the difference in manufacturing costs alone would probably not have allowed Crewe to cut so much off the price. The fact was that the Eight was a loss-leader, designed to attract more sales and to justify a lower profit margin in that way. There were deletions from the standard specification, of course, but it was arguable that they hardly mattered. So the standard interior trim was cloth, and when leather was specified at extra cost there was less of it in some of the less-visible areas. Instead of the carefully matched burr walnut wood trim, there was straight-grain walnut with a less glossy finish. Rear passengers had to manage without lambswool over-rugs and the traditional 'companion sets' of mirrors and lights in the rear quarter-panels; they also had to stow oddments in nets rather than pockets on the backs of the front seats. The dashboard was simpler, too, dispensing with the digital computer console of the standard Mulsanne. But that was all: this was a Bentley that cossetted its users just as much as the more expensive variants, went just as well as the standard Mulsanne and actually handled rather better.

Despite this collection of advantages, Crewe proceeded with its usual caution. The Eight was available only in its home market for the first nine months, and was not made available for export until March 1985.

Soon after the Eight was introduced, some more minor changes were announced. The 1985-model cars, available from September 1984, had their radio aerial relocated to the left-hand rear wing, while the front fog lights were deleted and a headlamp power wash replaced the original wash-wipe system. Less visibly, the central locking was revised, the heated rear window now had an isolator and the door mirrors now contained heating elements. There were minor changes inside, too, with a modified centre console, additional lighting and an upgraded ICE system. The dipswitch was now relocated on

■ THE GREAT REVIVAL

the steering column and the intermittent wipe control gained three extra functions.

1985 – THE TURBO R

Crewe's package of improvements for the turbocharged car was finally ready for introduction at the Geneva Show in March 1985, and at that point the Bentley Mulsanne Turbo gave way to the Bentley Turbo R – although, in practice, Mulsanne Turbos continued to come off the assembly lines until September 1985 in order to meet existing orders. The significance of that letter R was never officially confirmed, although Sales and Marketing Director Peter Ward did suggest at the Crewe launch that it stood for Roadholding and Refinement, which certainly got the message across.

The Turbo R addressed almost all the shortcomings of the original turbocharged model at once, and immediately secured a huge amount of positive publicity for the marque. Key among those shortcomings had been handling and grip, and a comprehensive package of improvements had been developed to deal with them by a team working under Phil Harding as Chief Engineer, Vehicles. There were no changes to the springs or to the suspension geometry, but there were new anti-roll bars, the front one 100 per cent stiffer than before and the rear one 60 per cent stiffer. Damping, too, had been stiffened up, primarily in rebound rather than in bump. At the rear of the car, the roll stiffness had been increased by adding hydraulic damping between the tops of the self-levelling struts, while further lateral stiffness came from a Panhard rod inserted between the rear sub-frame and the bodyshell.

Of course, none of that was visible. What onlookers could see, however, was the new alloy wheels with fatter tyres, which made their own important contribution to the car's behaviour. The new alloys – the first on a Bentley – had wider 7.5in rims and were manufactured by Ronal in Germany; the tyres were now 275/55VR15s, made by Pirelli to their P Zero specification with Kevlar reinforcement. They were, as it turned out, only a temporary measure because Crewe was working with Avon to produce a special tyre for the Turbo R, and when the special tyre became available in early 1986 as the Turbospeed CR27, the Pirellis were relegated to an extra-cost option.

The new wheels were the key visual change for the Turbo R, which of course also had its own plate badges on the boot as well. A closer look would reveal that the car also had a deeper front air-dam than other members of the SZ family. This had been developed to improve high-speed stability and reduced front-end lift by 15 per cent, while also reducing drag by a useful 7 per cent.

These changes made a decisive difference to the way the Turbo R drove. A reduction of 50 per cent in the steering's power assistance greatly improved feel (although some commentators still thought the steering was too light), and shortly after production began, leather trim added to the steering wheel made the rim thicker and made its own small contribution. There was some body shudder over poor surfaces, but it was a fair trade-off for the improvements in the car's handling. 'Turn-in is sharp and secure with no hint of scrubby understeer at brisk cornering speeds,' said *Motor*, comparing a Turbo R with a Mercedes 500SEL in its issue of 3 August 1985. 'Only when hammering along indifferent rural secondaries does the Bentley begin to lose its composure and accurate directional control, partly as a result of tyre deflection by cambers and ridges.'

At £68,420 without extras, the Turbo R was now the most expensive Bentley variant of the short-wheelbase SZ. Even more expensive was the long-wheelbase Turbo R, a model that sold steadily alongside the more glamorous short-wheelbase car but remained little known outside its own customer base. There were extras to be had for extra cost on both versions of the car. The Everflex roof covering, standard on the long-wheelbase cars, could be ordered for the short-wheelbase versions (although it seems to have remained rare). Also optional were Fiamm air horns with a 'quiet' setting for town use and to meet regulations in some European countries; walnut picnic tables for the rears of the front seats; a lidded compartment in the rear armrest; a cocktail cabinet in the centre console; a small fridge in the boot and lambswool covering for the boot, as well.

The Turbo R would have its own enormous impact on the renaissance of the Bentley marque, and by late 1985, a healthy 22 per cent of cars built at Crewe were wearing Bentley badges. Just three years earlier, the total had been a miserable 5 per cent. The changes wrought in just three years since the introduction of the Mulsanne Turbo were having exactly the desired effect.

The momentum created by the launch of the Turbo R was more than enough to keep the Bentley marque in the limelight for the next couple of years until the next major upgrade for the SZ range was ready. But minor changes were made to keep the three-model range of Eight, Mulsanne and Turbo R fresh. There was of course, also the Continental convertible in the Bentley range, as Chapter 2 makes clear.

THE GREAT REVIVAL

From October 1985, it became clear that the work that had gone into creating the Turbo R had not been purely for the benefit of that model; the R had simply introduced the changes because it was the flagship model and would gain more attention. The suspension changes developed for it became standard on the Eight and Mulsanne as well, so helping to distinguish the Bentley-badged cars yet further from their Rolls-Royce counterparts, which remained wedded to the softer suspension. However, the Mulsanne and, optionally, the Eight had narrower 6.5in alloy wheels to the same pattern as the Turbo R's, and they retained their 235/70 tyres rather than taking on the 275/55 tyres of the turbocharged car. It was clearly important for the flagship model to retain its handling edge.

Two further small changes affected all the 1986-model cars, and both were visible from the front. The number plate, originally underneath the bumper, was now repositioned more neatly in the centre of the bumper itself, and the original headlamp wiper system was replaced by simpler washer jets.

1987 – FUEL INJECTION AND ABS

The next round of upgrades was still some way off, but Crewe managed to give the impression of continuing momentum by announcing what was really the 1988-season specification, as early as September 1986. The revised cars were not in practice available for the best part of a year, although enough had been built in the first months of 1987 for a press ride-and-drive exercise to be held at the Hungaroring, Hungary's new Grand Prix racing circuit, in May that year. To keep the momentum going, an injected car was taken to the Millbrook circuit in September 1987 for an assault on the national one-hour distance record, where it travelled a distance only a few yards short of 141 miles, taking the record from a Lamborghini Countach.

The most important changes affected all models in the Bentley range, and they were the standardization of fuel injection and anti-lock brakes. The ABS was a Bosch system and was, in all honesty, somewhat overdue on cars in the luxury class – especially one with the performance of the Turbo R. The fuel injection was again by Bosch and was an important step for the marque: although fuel injection had been standard on Crewe's cars for the USA for some years, that had been of little value to Bentley because the cars had not been marketed there. North America was already the largest market in the world for Rolls-Royce cars, and Bentley's absence from the market had been something of a handicap. With the standardization across the range of fuel injection, which allowed their cars to be tuned to meet local emissions regulations, Bentley could now become a standalone marque across the Atlantic.

However, fuel injection was not the only change to the engine. The 6750cc V8 had in fact been extensively re-worked in other areas as well. The crankcase had been redesigned and was now lighter, while there were thicker walled cast-iron cylinder liners, new lower friction pistons and upgraded main bearings. The ports in the cylinder heads had also been re-shaped to improve gas flow, the exhaust manifolds had been modified, and a new flywheel reduced the already small incidence of vibration.

Crewe had subcontracted some of the development work on the new injection systems to Ricardo at Shoreham. For the Eight and Mulsanne models, the engine had a Bosch K-Jetronic injection system, but a more sophisticated KE-Jetronic with additional electronic control was used on the Turbo R engine. With the KE-Jetronic came twin distributors, one for each bank of cylinders, and one very beneficial effect was that the car would now start instantly; carburettor-fed versions of the turbocharged engine had often needed a little churning on the starter before they would fire up. In terms of figures, the Eight and Mulsanne now boasted 20 per cent more power than before, with 238bhp; the Turbo R had 10 per cent more power, with 328bhp. That delivered performance of 0–60mph in just under 7sec, and with the speed limiter now removed, the car would power on to over 140mph (225km/h).

Changes elsewhere were more subtle, but no less valuable. The new-found engine power allowed Bentley to fit taller axle ratios, so improving fuel consumption – although it was still a struggle to better 14–15mpg (19–20ltr/100km) in any of the models. All models also took on an engine-oil cooler and a larger radiator as safeguards against the additional stresses from their extra power. The Mulsanne also took on the wider wheels and tyres of the Turbo R, making it even more different than before from its Rolls-Royce Silver Spirit sibling.

On the outside, there was a choice of six new paint colours, and a new one-piece chin spoiler was added, together with a pair of small but effective foglights. Inside, the major change was to the seats, which were now somewhat thinner than before but were better shaped to improve lateral support. Their power adjustment system had also been improved, with a shaped switch (similar to the one used by Mercedes-Benz)

53

■ THE GREAT REVIVAL

instead of the rather confusing toggle switch, and a four-position memory. New safety belts with low-friction inertia-reels were added, and the cooling capacity of the air-conditioning system was increased. The Turbo R took on a rev counter next to the speedometer – again a feature it should really have had before – and there were other minor dashboard and console changes involving the warning lights and switches. The Mulsanne took on a three-spoke steering wheel.

As soon as these revised models came on-stream, the assault on the US market began. The first model to be introduced there was the Eight, which went on sale in November 1986. That was followed eleven months later in October 1987 by the Mulsanne S (the latest version of the Mulsanne; see below), and then in November 1988 the Turbo R completed the range. During 1988, US models were briefly fitted with motorized seatbelts, although these were dropped when twin airbags became standard a year later to meet the Federal requirement for passive restraints. There had, in the meantime, been yet more changes and one result was that the first year's production of US-specification Bentley Eights was the only one to have the twinned rectangular headlamp units.

1988–91 – TWIN HEADLIGHTS, THE MULSANNE S AND AUTOMATIC RIDE CONTROL

For the 1988 season that began in August 1987, there were yet more upgrades for the range. The Eight was now sold with leather upholstery and companion sets in the rear quarter-panels as standard, and a number of changes turned the Mulsanne into a Mulsanne S, complete with boot-lid badge to confirm its identity. Those changes were body-coloured door mirror housings, the rev counter and 170mph speedometer from the Turbo R (but with a straight-grain walnut dash as in the Eight unless to special order), and a new centre console, which reached from dashboard to floor in an unbroken sweep.

The 1989 changes, introduced in June 1988, gave the Bentley range even more individual identity by replacing the SZ's rectangular headlamps with twin 7in round units that met requirements in the USA, as well as in other world markets. On these first cars, the paired lamps were set against a black background. A power-wash system was standard, and in the UK a modified dim-dip system was fitted. All models took on bright cantrail trim unless fitted with an Everflex roof covering, and the Eight gained alloy wheels (which were already standard in the USA), body-colour mirror housings and a boot-lid badge with the winged B against a black background. The Turbo R took on a winged B with a red background, together with a shallow, rear skirt panel that contained a hinged flap; its front air-dam, sill extensions and the new rear apron were all painted in the body colour.

However, the 1989 Turbo R also brought with it an important engine upgrade. Neither the original Mulsanne Turbo nor the subsequent Turbo R had been equipped with an intercooler – a device for cooling the air forced into the induction

By the end of the 1980s, the Turbo R was recognized as a formidable performance car even though, as this picture makes clear, it was still a big and heavy four-door luxury saloon.

THE GREAT REVIVAL

system, so increasing its density and consequently its combustive power. For 1989, an air-to-air intercooler was fitted, and the maximum power of the revised engine went up by just over 10 per cent to 328bhp. There were important torque gains, too. All this was overseen by another new engine-management system, this time a Bosch MK-Motronic type.

September 1989 brought the 1990-season modifications, which were paralleled on Rolls-Royce versions of the SZ range by a name-change to Silver Spirit II and Silver Spur II. All models took on a new dashboard with a warning module containing a gearchange indicator; a new ten-speaker ICE system and a remote anti-theft alarm arrived, along with powered lumbar adjustment for the front seats. The Mulsanne S and Turbo R gained an automatic ride control system, which allowed three different damper settings ranging from sport to comfort, and this also reached the Eight in April 1990. Then from July, catalytic converters in the exhaust system became a no-cost option for the UK market; they were already standard wear on US models and would progressively become standard for the rest of the world.

For the USA, where Bentley had now become well established, the 1989 cars all had twin airbags – a feature they would not have in most markets until the 1994 model-year. North American Bentleys also had the convenience of one-touch front window switches and heated seats with adjustable lumbar support. A leather-trimmed steering wheel was standard on all models, and the seat belts were no longer motorized.

1991 – FOUR-SPEED AUTOMATICS

From 1991, the Eight, Mulsanne S and Turbo R were joined by a fourth Bentley model. The new Continental R was closely related to the four-door saloons mechanically, but its role was to differentiate the Bentley marque from Rolls-Royce even more clearly than before. The developments that would enable this process to take place would have their impact on the saloons as well in the coming years.

The Continental R, as Chapter 4 explains, was the first Bentley to have a new four-speed gearbox. Again manufactured by GM in the USA, this was known as the Hydramatic 4L80-E, and to three lower gear ratios closely similar to those of the older three-speed transmission it added an overdrive fourth. The overdrive fourth lowered engine revs at higher speeds, bringing the twin advantages of reduced noise and reduced fuel consumption. It must be said, though, that the reduction in engine noise was detectable only by a machine, while the reduction in fuel consumption was usually negated by driver enthusiasm! An additional feature was that this electronically controlled gearbox had three settings, for Sport, Economy and Winter.

The four-door saloons did not all get this new gearbox at once. Along with two other new features – motorized central-locking in place of the solenoid type, and a high-mounted third brake-light – it was rolled out progressively over a period of some fourteen months. The top models had all these

The Eight had done its job of attracting new buyers, and was replaced for 1993 by the Brooklands model, which also replaced the Mulsanne S. Comparing this 1994 model with the original Mulsanne makes clear how far Bentley had come in just under a decade and a half.

55

■ THE GREAT REVIVAL

By this stage, the naturally-aspirated models looked very much like the turbocharged cars, but there were differences: note the difference between the wheels on this 1994-model Turbo R and those on the Brooklands of the same time.

features first, and they worked their way down the range. So the changes began with the Turbo R in June 1991, moved on to the Mulsanne S from January 1992 and finally reached the Eight in August 1992. For the Mulsanne S, however, the changes were to be short-lived because the model was discontinued in April 1992.

1992 – THE BROOKLANDS

Not many Eights had the new features, either, because that model also went out of production, in this case during January 1993. Both Mulsanne S and Eight were replaced by a new model called the Brooklands, which entered production in October 1992 as a 1993 model.

The Eight had proved that few buyers really wanted the entry-level trim specification with such things as cloth upholstery, but it had done its intended job of bringing the Bentley marque to the attention of a new group of customers. So the Brooklands specification was closely similar to that of the old Mulsanne S. For its first year in production, but no longer, it was distinguished by special green-enamelled badges.

The Brooklands brought other new features to the range. It previewed a new front air-dam and it dispensed with the chrome strip along the centre of the bonnet, so giving a cleaner and more sporting look. On the inside, the pleated leather door trim was new and, perhaps most important, there was now a console-mounted gear selector in place of the steering-column type that had been used for so long. This change had been previewed on the Continental R (see Chapter 4) and gave the interior a far more sporting ambience than before.

As for the Turbo R, the 1993 models introduced in September 1992 had new 16in wheels with 255/60VR16 tyres, and had the same green enamel on their boot and wing badges as the Brooklands. They, too, had the console-mounted gear selector. There was also a self-dimming electro-chromatic rear view mirror, and yet another new ICE unit. This time, it was an Alpine head unit with a remote control for rear seat passengers, and it came with a six-CD changer.

1994–95 – AIRBAGS, ELECTRONICS AND THE TURBO S

The 1994-model four-door saloons were announced in August 1993, and again there were two basic models. The Brooklands had the naturally-aspirated engine and the Turbo R the turbocharged type; both could be had in either standard or long-wheelbase form.

THE GREAT REVIVAL

For the 1994 model-year, the turbocharged engine took on Transient Boost Control. Though it was still essentially the same engine as before, cosmetic cover panels both made it look different and tidied up the underbonnet view.

From the outside, there were few distinguishing features. The Brooklands, however, now had black enamel badges and the Turbo R once again had red enamel. On the Brooklands, the wheel centre caps were redesigned with a black enamelled centre badge in place of the cast-in B on earlier wheels. The Turbo R meanwhile had new 16in alloy wheels with wider rims. Both cars now had the plain bonnet without a chrome strip.

There were more significant changes inside, where a passenger's side airbag was now standardized and the front seat-belt installations were modified. The steering-column shroud was now swathed in black leather and there was a new lockable stowage compartment below it. The seats, too, had been redesigned, now offering better lumbar support from redesigned cushions and squabs together with better lateral support from longitudinal pleating. Electric adjustment was already standard, of course, but now came with a four-position memory. In line with latest industry practice, the air-conditioning system was now filled with R134 gas, which was not harmful to the ozone layer.

Electronics lay behind some valuable changes to the turbocharged engine. A new management system incorporated what Bentley called Transient Boost Control, which gave a brief burst of additional power for overtaking if the accelerator was floored. Arguably, the principle dated back to the 'blower' Mercedes of the 1920s and 1930s, when full engine power from the supercharger was to be used only for brief periods because it put the engine under a strain it could not withstand for long. The Bentley system certainly took the engine closer to its design limits than ever before, giving about 20 per cent more power when in use. However, there was no risk of engine damage because the electronics governed a gradual transition back to 'normal' mode long before there was any real risk of putting strain on the engine. Cars with the new system did boast better performance than

The 1995-model Turbo S introduced the idea of limited editions to the Bentley range, and previewed some of the changes planned for the 1996 models. Note the seven-spoke alloy wheels, borrowed from the Continental R coupé, the shallower grille and the new air-dam. The S also boasted red Bentley badges on the rear pillars, and a painted coachline.

57

■ THE GREAT REVIVAL

ever, though, with a 147mph (237km/h) maximum, a 0–60mph time of 6.3sec and simply stunning mid-range acceleration. Perhaps to ensure that using the additional urge did not raise noise levels unduly, the engine was now encapsulated in plastic shrouds as well.

On top of this, electronics in the gearbox-control system now provided what was called Adaptive Shift Control. Once again, this was a new development in the automotive industry, and it was important for the Bentley image to be in the forefront of technological changes. ASC software allowed the gearbox to 'learn' the driver's style and to modify the gearchange shift points to suit it. So, if the car was being driven gently, the gearchange points would be lower down the rev range; if it was being driven hard, gearchanges would be delayed until higher revs to give maximum acceleration. Either way, the changes themselves were nearly undetectable to those inside the car.

At the end of the 1994 calendar-year, Bentley Motors made available a limited edition model on the standard wheelbase under the name of Turbo S. The plan was to build no more than 100 of these, and in fact just sixty were eventually made, with the final examples being delivered in 1996. The car was sold only in Europe (including the UK), Asia and the Middle East, and was an ultra-high performance derivative that previewed some of the changes planned for the 1996 models.

Central to the Turbo S was its engine, offered in the small-volume Continental S at the same time, as Chapter 4 explains. It featured a new management system developed by motor racing specialists Zytek in Britain. Zytek had been chosen for the job partly because of their acknowledged expertise but also because, as a small company, they could respond to modification requests more rapidly than could a large company like Bosch. This flexibility enabled Bentley to offer regular upgrades to the venerable V8 engine over the next few years, and suited their 1990s policy of continuous range refreshment. Bentley also added exclusivity to the Turbo S by making the underbonnet layout different from that of any previous Turbo model – and also different from that of the later Turbo Rs that would have a similar engine.

However, the Zytek management system was not the only new feature. Out went the air-to-air intercooler and in its place came a water-to-air intercooler. The new headline figures were 386bhp and 553lb ft of torque, and the maximum speed of the new car was governed to 155mph (250km/h) – the highest yet on an SZ derivative. A viscous limited-slip differential was standard, along with 17in seven-spoke wheels wearing 255/55WR17 tyres.

1996 – THE 'NEW' TURBO R AND THE TURBO R SPORT

For the first half of the 1990s, development of the Turbo R had proceeded by small increments. However, Bentley Motors

Bentley held something back for the 1996 models, of course. Even a quick glance at this Turbo R will reveal the re-shaped door mirrors and the absence of front quarter-lights.

58

THE GREAT REVIVAL

ABOVE: **For 1996, the Brooklands models had new wheels, similar to earlier types but with fewer intermediate spokes.**

RIGHT: **This is the dashboard of a 1996-model Brooklands. While the traditional figured wood-veneer does not disappoint, the gear lever is now on the console rather than the steering column. The steering wheel of course contains an airbag.**

■ THE GREAT REVIVAL

saw the changes for the 1996 model-year cars introduced in autumn 1995 as being more far-reaching – and in fact referred to the 1996-model Turbo R as the 'new' Turbo R.

The Brooklands model was still available, of course, and it shared a major cosmetic makeover with the Turbo R. This began at the front end, where the four-door Bentleys shared with their Rolls-Royce sisters a redesigned bumper and air-dam assembly and a radiator grille shortened by 2in at the bottom. The new air dam incorporated large mesh grilles that matched the radiator grille. At the rear, the spare wheel had moved from its underfloor position to inside the boot, as on the Continental R, and this allowed a new rear bumper and valance assembly to be installed. The new bumpers and the side sills were all finished in body colour.

There were further exterior novelties, as well as a new range of paint colours. Most obvious was that the quarter-lights had been deleted from the front doors, and that there were new and more aerodynamic door mirrors. The seven-spoke wheel design from the Continental R that had been previewed on the 1995-model Turbo S limited edition now became standard wear, with a 16in size for the Brooklands and a 17in size for the Turbo R.

There were several interior changes, too. The steering wheel now came with electric tilt adjustment, and moved automatically to its highest position to facilitate entry and exit. Favoured positions could, of course, be stored in the seat memory, too. There were new interior colours, and the front seats had been modified in detail to give an extra inch of headroom. Their armrests now included stowage boxes, while on the dashboard the ICE head unit could be discreetly concealed by a hinged flap to deter thieves. A new centre console layout incorporated a different ashtray and cigarette lighter unit, and rear-seat passengers now had their own individually controllable cold-air vents.

On the mechanical side, the viscous-coupled differential previewed on the Turbo S was now standard equipment, and, of course, both versions of the engine now had the Zytek EMS3 management system. The Brooklands models had some 6 per cent more torque than before, which allowed them to cope with the taller 2.69:1 final drive from the turbocharged cars. The combination was claimed to deliver an 11 per cent improvement in fuel economy. At the same time, lower-profile tyres improved the handling and roadholding. As for the Turbo R, its additional torque was claimed to improve both acceleration and fuel economy, which was supposedly 6 per cent better than before.

There was still room for limited editions, however, and for 1996 a special limited-production Turbo R Sport was made available on the standard wheelbase for European markets only. This was available in two new colours, Black Garnet and Black Emerald, and the mesh of the grille was painted in body colour as well. Special features of the interior were a new dashboard with a dark carbon-check Kevlar finish and contrasting bright instrument bezels, and a panel integrating a satellite navigation screen, GSM telephone and the ICE system. There were also larger disc brakes, which were claimed to give a stopping time of just 4.96sec from 100mph (161km/h). Like the other 1996 models, it was limited to a top speed of 150mph (241km/h), at least partly to protect the 155mph (250km/h) exclusivity of the limited-edition Turbo S.

1997 – TURBOCHARGERS BECOME UNIVERSAL

The four-door Bentley range was trimmed a little for the 1997 model-year, in anticipation of the new Arnage models to be released in 1998. The standard-wheelbase models of the Turbo R went out of production, leaving only long-wheelbase models available, while the Brooklands received a major performance upgrade by taking on a turbocharged engine.

There were few exterior revisions, though. A wider range of paint options was welcome, but altogether more distinctive were the bright-finish alloy wheels that became standard. Inside the cars, occupants were treated to seat-belt pre-tensioners, redesigned head restraints and extended front-seat cushions, while less immediately apparent were the new self-arming anti-theft system and automatic dimming for the headlamps.

Mechanical improvements were also few. The Turbo R now had an electronic traction control system (called ETAS – Electronic Traction Assistance System) and large-diameter micro-alloy front brake discs, while both of these items became options for the Brooklands models. The biggest change was perhaps that made to the Brooklands itself, which now came with a turbocharged engine. This was known as the Light Pressure Turbo engine, and developed 300bhp – much the same as the Turbo R engine of ten years earlier. It was, of course, a quite different engine, having benefited from the upgrades developed in those ten years, and its arrival delivered a welcome performance boost for the Brooklands, which was beginning to look quite slow against rivals from other makers. The turbocharged Brooklands could now hit

THE GREAT REVIVAL

60mph (97km/h) from rest in just 7.9sec, which was a very respectable time indeed for such a large and heavy car.

1998 – THE END OF THE LINE

A great deal happened to Bentley during the 1998 model-year. For a start, as Chapter 6 shows, the marque was separated from its Rolls-Royce sibling and was sold to a new owner. It was also destined to be the last season of production for the SZ series, which was due to be replaced in spring 1998 by the new Rolls-Royce Silver Seraph and Bentley Arnage models, which are covered in Chapter 5.

So for 1998 the Bentley derivatives of the SZ range were characterized by two new models, each with a limited-edition derivative. These limited editions were characterized by the Mulliner name; with the anticipated split between the two marques, the Mulliner Park Ward name, which had for so long been associated with special coachbuilt models from Crewe, was itself divided, the Park Ward name remaining with Rolls-Royce.

The least expensive of the 1998-season cars was the Brooklands R, which took on the stiffer suspension and 17in wheels associated with the Turbo R, together with the high-performance braking system from the Continental T. There were subtle exterior recognition points: a mesh grille instead of the slatted type, body-colour headlamp surrounds, and new bumpers with a black lower lip and black mesh inserts in the front air-dam. A thicker steering wheel rim added a little more meatiness to the steering.

The top-model regular-production four-door for 1998 was the Turbo RT, which went out in fine style with the 400bhp Continental T powertrain that brought 0–60mph in 5.8sec and a maximum speed of 150mph (242km/h). It had distinctive five-spoke 17in alloy wheels, broadly similar to an earlier design but without the paired smaller spokes between the main spokes, together with the same front-end revisions as the Brooklands R. In theory, every Turbo RT was a long-wheelbase model, but at this stage of the game Bentley Motors was happy to entertain requests for variations from standard, and it appears that some Turbo RTs were built with the standard wheelbase.

Then, of course, there were the two limited-edition Mulliner special series. There was plenty of scope for personalizing these from the array of options that Bentley offered publicly, but once again, several highly bespoke cars were delivered.

For 1998, the Brooklands R Mulliner brought dark wood-veneer trim with chrome instrument surrounds.

■ THE GREAT REVIVAL

Right at the end of SZ production came the Brooklands RT, offered only in long-wheelbase form (unless the customer insisted). The five-spoke alloy wheels were an easily recognizable feature.

BELOW: **For the very fortunate few, there was an RT Mulliner limited edition, with this distinctive mesh panel in the rear apron.**

There were 100 numbered examples of the Brooklands R Mulliner, which came as standard with dark wood-veneers and contrasting chrome instrument surrounds. The Turbo RT Mulliner, however, was something else again.

There were just fifty numbered examples of this model, which was made very special indeed by being fitted with the 420bhp turbocharged engine from the latest Continental coupé. Acceleration of the long-wheelbase model was now equal to the fastest of the short-wheelbase Turbo Rs, with a 5.8sec 0–60mph time, and top speed was limited to 155mph (250km/h). The car was made to look the part, too, with very noticeably bigger wheelarch flares covering wider tracks, 18in five-spoke alloy wheels on 255/55WR18 tyres, new bumpers, aprons and sills, and a mesh insert in the rear apron.

The sporting theme was hammered home inside, with a push-button starter (which was quickly imitated by several other makers), drilled metal pedals, and black lacquer facia and centre console with chromed instrument bezels. Instead of wood, the door tops were trimmed in black leather, and the headrests all carried an embroidered winged B. Slightly less sporting, but no doubt much appreciated by buyers, were power-adjustable rear seats.

Further individualization was available from the options list. The bonnet and front wings could be fitted with vents, a matrix grille and those who insisted could even have a large white racing number roundel on the front doors. Chrome sports wheels and chromed door mirrors were on the cards, as were chromed headlamp surround panels. Those who did not take to the standard (and very attractive) black-lacquer finish on the dash and console could order other wood finishes or machine-turned aluminium. Lastly, to keep rear-seat passengers aware of exactly how fast the car was travelling, it was possible to have the ultimate caprice of a second speedometer fitted to the rear of the centre console. And some owners insisted on adding their own personal touches even to that list…

DEALER SPECIAL EDITIONS

Once Bentley had started the ball rolling with its factory-built special editions in the 1990s, demand for their perceived exclusivity skyrocketed around the world. As production of the SZ models drew to a close, a number of dealers gained factory permission to create their own limited editions, to some extent as a way of clearing old-stock cars before the arrival of the new Arnage.

Details of these limited editions are necessarily sketchy but, for example, the Turbo RT Olympian was produced in 1998 by London Bentley dealer Jack Barclay. Four cars are thought to have been built, all with the 18in five-spoke alloy wheels from the RT Mulliner and with 'Olympian' boot-lid badges.

The known (or, at least, claimed) dealer special editions are listed below.

Brooklands derivatives

- Indonesian Brooklands
- Trophy Edition Brooklands

Turbo R derivatives

- HR Owen Bentley Turbo R
- Indonesian Turbo R
- Newport Beach Turbo R
- Turbo RT Olympian
- Weybridge and Mead Turbo R

CHAPTER FOUR

CONTINENTAL RENAISSANCE

If the 1982 Mulsanne Turbo was the model that gave the Bentley marque its first distinctive product since the 1960s, it was the 1991 Continental R that made clear Crewe was serious about re-establishing the Bentley brand. This car, based on the platform and running-gear of the Turbo R, added a distinctive two-door coupé body to the already heady mix of mechanical elements to create a hugely desirable machine with much, if not all, of the appeal and magic of the legendary R-type Continental of 1952.

In fact, the Continental R was a long time in the making. Back in the early 1980s, Rolls-Royce Managing Director David Plastow had been behind the original plan to create a two-door Bentley in the mould of the R-type Continental, but it was a plan that had to be realized gradually.

Once again, we have to remember that Rolls-Royce Motor Cars was a small company with limited resources. Much as it might have liked to develop an all-new model to re-establish the Bentley marque, it simply could not. That was why the new Continental had to be created on the basis of existing hardware – and the platform of the Turbo R provided both the highest performance Crewe could offer at that stage and an existing and readily identifiable link to the Bentley name. Only if the concept was successful in the market-place could more money be found to develop it further and to make it more distinctively different from the Turbo R on which it was based. For the moment, the striking new body design was the critical feature that made the Continental R what it was.

That body design had seen its first incarnation in 1985, when Rolls-Royce had exhibited what it called Project 90 at the Geneva Motor Show during March. The name itself indicated that there was not much chance of this car seeing production before 1990, if it saw production at all, and the

The 1985 Project 90 concept sketched the lines of a new Bentley coupé very effectively, but the design was used only as a springboard…

had a long wait in store. The first two years' worth of production had already been sold before the car was even formally announced.

Underneath its stylish new body, the car was essentially a modified Turbo R. It had the familiar turbocharged version of the 6.75-litre V8 engine with 333bhp, this time driving through a new four-speed GM Hydramatic transmission (which would also reach the Turbo R itself soon afterwards).

This transmission had a 0.75:1 overdrive top gear for better fuel economy, together with a lock-up feature on the torque converter. It also had the dual-mode arrangement that was increasingly becoming expected at the top end of the market: a switch mounted in the top of the selector knob selected Sport mode, altering the electronic control program to deliver upshifts at higher speeds and to make the kickdown more sensitive.

Transmission
Four-speed GM 4L80-E automatic gearbox with torque converter; switchable Sports mode and converter lock-up on top gear.

Suspension
Independent front suspension with coil springs, lower wishbones, automatically variable ride control and anti-roll bar.
Independent rear suspension with coil springs, semi-trailing arms, dampers with automatically variable ride height control, and anti-roll bar.

Steering
Power-assisted rack and pinion.

Brakes
Disc brakes on all four wheels, ventilated at the front.
From mid-1996: 13.4in (340mm) Micro-alloy ventilated front discs.

Wheels and tyres
Continental R: 16in alloy wheels with 7.5in rims and 255/60 ZR16 tyres; later 17in alloy wheels with 7.5in rims and 255/55WR17 tyres.
Continental T and SC: 18in alloy wheels with 8in rims and 285/45ZR18 tyres.

Vehicle dimensions
Wheelbase	120.5in (3,060mm) (Continental R and S, and Azure)
	116.5in (2,959mm) (Continental T and SC)
Overall length	210.5in (5,346mm) (Continental R and S)
	206.3in (5,241mm) (Continental T and SC)
	210.3in (5,342mm) (Azure)
Overall width	81in (2,058mm) over mirrors
Overall height	57.6in (1,463mm) (Continental R)
	56.9in (1,447mm) (Continental T)
	58in (1,475mm) (Azure)
Weight	5,564lb (2,524kg) unladen (Continental T)
	5,295lb (2,402kg) kerb weight (Continental R)
	5,754lb (2,610kg) kerb weight (Continental SC and Azure)

Performance
Max. speed	145mph/233km/h (Continental R, 1991)
	150mph/242km/h (Azure, 1995; electronically limited)
	151mph/243km/h (Continental R, 1995)
	170mph/270km/h (Continental T, 1998)
	155mph/250km/h (Continental SC, 1999; electronically limited)
0–60 mph	6.6sec (Continental R, 1991)
	6.1sec (Continental R and Azure, 1995)
	5.5sec (Continental T, 1998)
Fuel consumption	14mpg (20ltr/100km) (Continental R, 1991)
	13mpg (22ltr/100km) (Continental R, 1995)
	15mpg (19ltr/100km) (Azure, 1995)
	15.1mpg (19ltr/100km) (Continental T, 1998)

That Sport control was also linked to a second new feature, which was an electronic damper control. Selecting Sport mode automatically brought in the most sporty (and hardest) setting for the dampers; there were also Comfort and Standard settings, which were selected by a separate switch. In fact, the whole suspension system had been revised as compared to the Turbo R, with stiffer springs and damper settings to give a more sporty feel to the handling at all times. The basic suspension layout was otherwise the same as on the Turbo R, and the new 16in five-spoke alloy wheels (with three inset spokes between each of the main spokes) ran on 255/60 ZR 16 tyres.

In all fairness, the revised suspension was something of a compromise. It certainly did give the car a more sporting feel than the Turbo R, but it also thumped and crashed quite noticeably at low speeds over rough surfaces. The tyres also failed to provide enough grip for enthusiastic use of the accelerator on wet surfaces or tight corners, and more than one commentator, when the Continental R was new, mentioned an urgent need for a traction control system. There was in fact one in the pipeline, but it had simply not been ready in time for the car's launch. The steering, a power-assisted rack-and-pinion set-up, also came in for criticism because it gave insufficient feedback to a driver who was pressing on.

At £175,000 ($261,800 in the USA), the Continental R was the most expensive car then available from Crewe. It was also a classic example of the old adage that 'less equals more': despite the elevated price tag, it offered much less room inside than a Turbo R saloon, plus a smaller boot. To give enough room for elegant entry and exit, the two doors had to impinge on the low roof panel. But what the car did offer was presence and prestige. The gentle coke-bottle kick-up in the waistline hinted at the lines of the older Corniche coupé based on the T-series cars, although the overall shape was much squarer, in the contemporary idiom. The two-door configuration of course brought with it the desirable image of a personal car rather than a family saloon. Sitting on the same 120½in (3,060mm) wheelbase as the Turbo R, the Continental R was 3in (75mm) longer overall, 1½in (38mm) wider and stood only ½in (12mm) lower than the saloon.

The slatted Bentley grille had a body-colour surround, and the front featured paired 7in round headlamps which were so much more stylish than the rectangular headlamps of the saloon. The rear had no badge on the first cars, and no doubt the thinking was that the winged B motif that swung away to reveal the bootlid release was enough to explain to the curious and envious that this was the new Bentley. The boot lid also boasted an integral rear spoiler, pressed into its shape, which hinted at the high speeds of which the car was capable.

The interior was exquisitely finished in leather and wood in the finest Crewe tradition, with a thin-rimmed but leather-bound steering wheel that contained an airbag as standard. (In fact, the first few pre-production models, which became demonstrators, had a three-spoke wheel with no airbag.) A striking change of direction for Crewe was the location of the gear selector lever on the centre console above the transmission tunnel; previous practice had been to have it on the steering column, but Crewe believed the central position gave the interior a more sporting ambience.

On the negative side, the effects of the coupé body style were very noticeable to rear-seat passengers, and tall passengers were likely to find long-distance travel rather uncomfortable. The seats were set rather high for tall drivers, who were likely to find their heads uncomfortably close to the leather headlining. The cushions of all four seats were criticized as rather short when the car was new, and in fact the considerable body roll that set in if the Continental was driven energetically made clear that the seats offered too little sideways support as well. Probably some of its buyers complained, too, because revised seats appeared on later versions of the car.

Nobody, however, complained about the straight-line performance, which was even better than that of the much-admired Turbo R saloon. The car was good for 145mph (233km/h), could reach 60mph from rest in 6.6sec (according to its makers), and would hit 100mph (161km/h) in just 16sec. And despite the shortcomings in the handling department, it delivered a quite extraordinary driving experience. In Britain, *Autocar* magazine summed it up best in a road test in its issue dated 23 August 1995: 'Like the QE2 winning a power boat race or a Boeing 747 looping the loop,' they said, 'it does things its size and shape suggest should not be possible'. Of course it could be criticized in detail, but the Continental R was nonetheless a remarkable achievement, and all the more so in view of its manufacturer's limited resources.

THE CONTINENTAL S

Demand for the car had satisfied all of Crewe's business requirements, and so further development went ahead; it was, of course, cautious at first. Although nothing seemed to be happening for the first few years of the Continental's existence, there were things going on behind the scenes. Not the least of these was a liaison with the Italian coachbuilders Pininfarina to produce a convertible derivative of the car that would replace the existing and now elderly Corniche and would be called the Azure. First, though, would come a small-volume derivative that would test the market for more performance from the two-door Bentley.

This car was introduced in 1994 with the name of Continental S. It was available for just one season – the 1995 model-year, which began in mid-1994 – and its key special feature was a more powerful engine that featured an air-to-water intercooler for the turbocharger. Just thirty-seven examples were built, but this was enough for the experiment to be counted a success. For the 1996 model-year, the more powerful engine became standard on the further upgraded Continental R.

THE 1996-MODEL CONTINENTAL R

Despite the increased power and performance, the 1996-model Continental R still had no traction control system. Crewe had made an attempt to improve grip by fitting lower profile Avon 255/55 tyres, but the car was still criticized for a lack of steering feel and for inadequate grip when pushed hard. The low-speed ride was now, to some minds, even lumpier than before.

However, the new and more powerful engine was a clear demonstration of Crewe's determination to keep the Bentley marque ahead. Now boasting 385bhp and 553lb ft of torque, it was mated to a taller final drive and the combined effect, according to its manufacturers, was to make the latest Continental R more economical than earlier versions. The cylinder heads had been modified by Cosworth Engineering (which was, of course, part of the Vickers Group to which Rolls-Royce and Bentley belonged), the induction system had been changed, and the original Bosch engine-management system had been replaced by a new one from Zytek, better known for their race-car engineering. Interestingly, it was with the 1996-model cars that Crewe abandoned its long-standing and legendary practice of describing engine output as 'adequate', and instead quoted power and torque figures. At least it avoided inaccurate speculation, and with the latest models, the figures were certainly something to shout about.

When *Autocar* magazine tested an example of the 1996 Continental R in August 1995, they reported a maximum speed of 151mph (243km/h) with 0–60mph acceleration in just 6.1sec. Fuel economy of 13mpg (22ltr/100km) was not in the socially acceptable league, but few buyers who could afford the £187,354 price of the car (it cost $322,895 in the USA) were likely to complain.

There had been minor interior changes, too. Most notable was that the steering column was now adjustable for rake, although it still had no reach adjustment. The steering wheel also moved upwards out of the way whenever the driver's door was opened, so making access easier, and moved back into place as the door was closed.

Fatter wheelarches and the shorter wheelbase gave the 1997-model Continental T a more aggressive appearance. This early car has red badges; later Ts switched to black.

■ CONTINENTAL RENAISSANCE

THE CONTINENTAL T

Improving the engine was one way of getting more performance out of the Continental, and was fairly predictable. What almost nobody expected was Bentley's next move, which was to produce a lighter companion model on a shorter wheelbase that went even faster and offered an even more sporty driving experience. They announced it at a ride-and-drive press event based around Lugano in Switzerland in June 1996 as a 1997 model, and called it the Continental T.

Reducing the wheelbase by 4in (100mm) did take out some weight, although not an enormous amount. However, tweaking the engine's management system a little further did make a big difference to the performance. The 6.75-litre turbocharged V8 in the Continental T now delivered an astounding 400bhp with 590lb ft of torque – and after the car had been on sale for about a year, the engine was further uprated to deliver 650lb ft of torque. This, as Crewe was wont to point out, was more than any other production car engine in the world.

That original figure of 590lb ft of torque was produced all the way from 2,000rpm up to 3,450rpm, and it gave the Continental T simply stupendous mid-range acceleration. The 0–60mph sprint time was improved, too, and was now claimed to be 5.8sec (although road testers writing for magazines usually recorded about 6.5sec, admittedly with fairly new cars that had probably not loosened up enough to deliver their full potential). Top speed was now electronically limited to the 155mph (250km/h) that had been adopted by consent among German manufacturers.

The new model was of course formidably expensive, at £220,000 in the UK and $350,645 in the USA (inclusive, of course, of $26,145 luxury tax, which would have bought a quite respectable small car at the time). By March 1997, the price had dropped very slightly to $347,740, but the matter was academic because all that year's US allocation had already been sold. The 'official' EPA (Environmental Protection Agency) figure for city driving in the USA was 11 miles per US gallon; *Car & Driver* magazine managed 10mpg (28ltr/100km) in their March 1997 road test, although *Road & Track* quoted 14.5mpg (19.5ltr/100km) overall – which was good going from the smaller US gallon. It appears, incidentally, that US cars achieved their peak engine figures at slightly higher revs than those for other markets. This was no doubt because of slightly different engine-management settings to meet Federal emissions requirements.

The interior of the Continental T dispensed with the traditional wood trim, replacing it with engine-turned aluminium and introducing additional brightwork. It deliberately suggested the great racing Bentleys of the 1920s.

CONTINENTAL RENAISSANCE

The changes for 1998 brought a mesh grille and smaller matching grilles under the headlamps. The existing mesh in the apron's vents was now bright rather than blacked-out.

Once again, Crewe had focused very carefully on the driving experience, and on delivering an appropriately sporty interior ambience to go with it. In fact, the interior of the original Continental T was not to everybody's taste. Instead of the expected wood trim, it featured an engine-turned aluminium dashboard, with instruments set in chrome bezels instead of the black bezels on the Continental. The machine-turned aluminium even extended in a strip along the door trims, and the only wood was on the centre console. The idea behind this was to evoke the style of racing Bentleys from the 1920s, and it certainly appealed to many customers.

Of course, the driving dynamics of the Continental T had also benefitted from yet more development. The 16in tyres of the Continental R had gone in favour of big 18in five-spoke alloys shod with Goodyear Eagle 285/45 tyres. Greater stopping power came from new 13.4in ventilated front disc-brakes, which were now made of Micro-alloy, a material with a higher carbon content than that used for earlier discs. The shorter wheelbase, too, made its contribution to the way the car could be hustled around corners, although the introduction (at long last) of electronic traction control that operated through the ABS sensors to prevent the car getting out of shape during over-enthusiastic use probably made the biggest difference.

The car was still not perfect, complained the motoring press. Rear headroom was quite severely limited thanks to interior adjustments associated with shortening the wheelbase, the ride could be quite hard and the body was prone to shudder over ridges. The steering still gave insufficient feedback to encourage a driver to explore the car's upper limits. But the Continental T certainly attracted the customers, and that was what mattered at Crewe.

SMALL CHANGES FOR 1998

The two-model range of Continental R and short-wheelbase Continental T remained unchanged for 1998, but there were incremental changes for both models. Most obvious were a honeycomb mesh radiator grille in place of the earlier slatted

71

CONTINENTAL RENAISSANCE

type, and matching mesh grilles under the headlamps. Both cars had interior changes, the straight pleats of the upholstery giving way to a very attractive style with gently curving pleats. The front seats were also re-shaped to give more support. The Continental T now had a chrome-plated gear selector lever and lever surround, but the engine-turned panels disappeared from the door trims, to be replaced by a more conventional treatment. Also new were sporty-looking drilled aluminium pedals.

The Continental T had yet another increase in engine power, taking power to 420bhp and torque to 650lb ft. Maximum speed was now de-restricted and was a claimed 170mph (274km/h), with 0–60mph coming up in 5.5sec, according to Crewe's own figures. The 285/45 tyres were now Pirelli P Zero types, which gave slightly better grip but at some cost to the ride and also noise level.

There was, of course, still more to come.

1999 – THE CONTINENTAL SC

The new model for 1999 was yet another surprise. Based on the short wheelbase of the Continental T, the Continental SC was what other manufacturers would have called a targa-top model, with removable roof panels above the front seats. The Bentley approach, however, was different. As far as Crewe was concerned, the new model was reviving the sedanca-coupé style that had been popular on Bentleys of the 1930s, and that was where the SC tag came from.

Crewe also insisted that the Continental SC had been designed in response to customer demand, although it must be said that the demand must soon have been satisfied because the SC remained in production for no more than a year and a half. When the last one was built, Crewe explained that the factory space was needed to enable increased production of Bentley Azure and Rolls-Royce Corniche convertible models. That may well have been true, but there is evidence to suggest that the car was not the success its makers had expected. When it was announced, the company estimated production at about eighty cars a year. When production ended, just seventy-nine examples had been built, of which only twenty-three had right-hand drive.

The body had been developed as a joint project between Pininfarina in Italy and Bentley at Crewe. There was a fixed roof section over the rear seat area, with a smoked glass panel overhead that both let in light and reflected the sun's heat to shield the occupants. Over the front seats were two separate smoked-glass panels, which could be lifted out and stowed under the boot floor, leaving the front-seat passengers exposed to the elements behind the windscreen. And that, really, was the point of the Continental SC. Where a sedanca coupé in the 1930s had been designed for the owner to

The short-lived Continental SC was developed jointly with Pininfarina, and just seventy-nine examples were built. It was based on the Continental T.

sit in the back, discreetly screened from public view, the new Bentley was designed so that onlookers would focus their attention on the front seats and on who was in them. The car was really designed for celebrities and others who wanted to be seen driving their expensive motor cars.

The SC Continental was indeed expensive: at £245,000 ($319,000 in the USA), it was the most expensive production Bentley yet. It was not, however, designed as the fastest. Although it had the short wheelbase of the ultra-quick Continental T, it did not have that car's special engine but rather the 400bhp, 590lb ft variant of the 6.75-litre V8 from the Continental R. Extra weight – about 350lb (160kg) of body reinforcement to compensate for the absence of a fixed front roof section – would in any case have made it slower than a Continental T. Governed to 155mph (250km/h), it was claimed to reach 60mph from rest in 6.1sec.

In fact, the SC was a rather interesting hybrid of the other Continental models in several areas. Crewe claimed that it had been built on the short wheelbase of the Continental T because that offered greater body rigidity, but it was also true that the short wheelbase helped to draw the eye away from the fixed-roof rear section and made it focus on the open front seats – and that, as already noted, was the real purpose of the car. The car had the Continental T's suspension and 285/45 Pirelli P Zero tyres, but the suspension bushes were softer and the electronic dampers were differently programmed.

There were other special external features. The wings had been slightly restyled, and so had the bumpers. The front had a more aggressive air dam, which contained extra driving lamps, and the sills were heavily flared. Crewe claimed this was a way of restoring the visual balance when the front roof sections were removed, but there was no denying the visual link to the style seen on BMW's high-performance M3 model of the time. There were also new 18in five-spoke alloy wheels, which could be ordered with chrome plating for the ultimate in attention-grabbing. Last but not least, the winged B motif on the grille had a red background to distinguish it from other Bentley models of the time, and the boot lid carried a plate badge with red lettering reading 'Continental SC'. This was a car to be seen in and to be recognized for what it was.

Inside, however, the car had few special features. There was a switch that locked the roof panels into place electrically when they had been manually located. Otherwise, the seats had the latest style of curved panelling and the pedals were the latest drilled variety.

THE BENTLEY 'LABELS'

It was part of the enduring Bentley myth that the company's products in the vintage years of the 1920s had been given different coloured grille badges to distinguish one variant from another. There was an element of truth in this, but the principle was never applied rigidly, and those who worked for Bentley Motors at the time have confirmed this.

Nevertheless, when the Continental SC with its red badges was released in 1998, Crewe felt it necessary to explain the colour-coding that it was using on its badges. The four colours were the same as those associated with the vintage models, although their supposed meanings were rather different. At the end of the 1990s, then, they were:

Black	representing 'daring'. Used on the Continental T.
Blue	representing 'glorious'. Used on the Azure convertible.
Green	representing 'thoroughbred'. Used on the Continental R.
Red	representing 'passion'. Used on the Continental SC.

The Continental SC had the distinction of being the last Bentley commissioned and designed before the Bentley marque was bought by Volkswagen. Final production approval actually came from VW boss Ferdinand Piëch. Some later examples were built as SC Mulliner models with special custom-ordered features.

1999 – THE CONTINENTAL R MULLINER AND CONTINENTAL T MULLINER

Following no more than six months after the Continental SC came yet another set of options for the Continental models, this time widening the customer's choice even more. The idea this time was to introduce an exclusive personalization

■ CONTINENTAL RENAISSANCE

The Continental R spearheaded the move towards a more bespoke product from Crewe, and the Personal Commission service from the company's Mulliner division became more and more popular. Each bespoke creation would be preceded by sketches, to ensure that the proposed combination of features worked visually.

service that allowed the buyer to tailor the car's features to his or her personal taste. The new bespoke service enabled buyers to feel that they had a direct and personal involvement in the creation of their own vehicles, and they were encouraged to discuss details of the specification with engineers and designers from Crewe. The whole system was rather like visiting a top-class tailor to get a special suit made – and of course the cost was dependent on the number of special features incorporated. Bentley gave the new service the name of Mulliner, which was of course the name of the Rolls-Royce and Bentley bespoke coachbuilding division.

Many earlier Continental models had of course been built

CONTINENTAL RENAISSANCE

RIGHT: **This striking bright yellow Continental T was built as a Motor Show car to demonstrate some of the possibilities available from the Mulliner bespoke service. Colour-matched mirror bodies, wing vents and a special apron with side and indicator lights in their own pods are all features that were not part of the standard specification.**

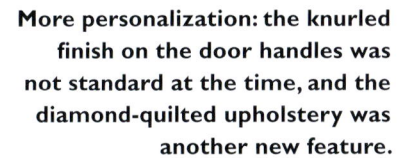

More personalization: the knurled finish on the door handles was not standard at the time, and the diamond-quilted upholstery was another new feature.

75

■ CONTINENTAL RENAISSANCE

LEFT: **The Mulliner features quickly became popular. This car has bright-finish mirror bodies to match the chromed alloy wheels.**

BELOW: **Yet another take on the interior possibilities, this car combines wood trim on the waist-rail with engine-turned aluminium for the dashboard and a two-tone leather gear lever grip in the standard gate.**

76

CONTINENTAL RENAISSANCE

This was a Personal Commission Continental T for the Detroit Show in 2001. Here, the mirror bodies are in the body colour, and there are different front wing vents. Running-lights are incorporated in the front and rear bumper wraparounds. The quilted leather luggage was a special touch.

Inside the Detroit Show car, diamond-quilted upholstery was matched to wood-veneer waist rail trim, and the rear seats were replaced by a platform for more matching luggage.

The rear luggage-platform option is seen here in more detail on another Continental T ordered under the Personal Commission scheme.

■ CONTINENTAL RENAISSANCE

to special order, but there were some variations that Crewe simply could not accommodate. The new service removed most of these restrictions, and also added some special features not normally available on the standard production models. The thinking here was that new features could in effect be market-tested by making them available through the personalization service. Those that proved popular could then be absorbed into the mainstream of production later on.

There was nothing radically new in this approach, which had also been adopted by other luxury car manufacturers. Land Rover had had its Autobiography service since 1993 and Mercedes-Benz its Designo service since 1998. Other makers would follow later. It did give rise to some quite uniquely specified cars, although there were of course not many of them. Figures currently available suggest that no more than forty-six Continental R Mulliner models were built between 1999 and 2002. The numbers of Continental T Mulliner cars are not known.

A typical Continental R Mulliner specification might add the 420bhp Continental T engine to the long-wheelbase car, together with that car's stiffer suspension and 285/45 tyres on 18in wheels. There might be an unusual paint colour and an unusual choice of upholstery colour, too. An example tested by *Autocar* magazine in its issue dated 21 July 1999 had the 420bhp engine, giving 0–60mph in 6sec. It had a more sporting suspension set-up (probably from the Continental T) with 18in wheels running on 285/45 Pirelli P Zero tyres. The steering ratio was described as 20 per cent quicker than standard, with just 2.74 turns lock-to-lock, and there was a different front air-dam with mesh inserts. This car was priced at £225,000.

As for the Continental T Mulliner, the bespoke car displayed at the Birmingham Motor Show in early 2001 was certainly representative. It was sufficiently eye-catching for both *Evo* and *Autocar* magazines to request loans for evaluation, the first magazine publishing its findings in the March 2001 edition and the second in its issue of 2 May 2001. Its cost was simply eye-watering, and was given as 'over £300,000'. The car was, said *Evo* magazine, 'almost certainly the most impressive, gloriously ostentatious car in the world'.

Bold Monaco Yellow paintwork ensured that this car would be noticed wherever it went. Its special front end details, picked from the Mulliner special options list, gave it an even more individual appearance. The indicators had been moved down into the air scoops of a deeper front bumper, and there were special headlamp surround panels to compensate for their absence. The front wings had 'power vents' (which were of course purely cosmetic) and the sills and rear bumper also differed from standard.

Inside, the seats and interior trim were in quilted black

This later Continental R has multi-spoke alloy wheels, colour-matched mirror bodies and the red badges by this stage associated with the model.

CONTINENTAL RENAISSANCE

leather, a style that was quickly copied by other bespoke manufacturers. The quilted leather even extended to the boot trim, and was complemented by silver-grey stitching, which was also used for the winged B logo on the front seat headrests. Other small details demonstrated the amount of care that had gone into creating this individual car: there was a criss-cross knurling on the undersides of the outer door handles and on the interior lock buttons, and this gave both an illusion of depth and a special tactile sensation to anyone using those items.

As production of the Continental range neared its end, Mulliner editions appeared. The dark car shown here is a Continental R Mulliner, with triangular wing vents. The silver car is a Continental T with four exhaust outlets but, in this case, no wing vents.

■ CONTINENTAL RENAISSANCE

2000 – THE MILLENNIUM EDITION

The start of a new century was not a marketing opportunity to be missed, and Bentley, like several other motor manufacturers, seized on it to deliver a Continental R Millennium Edition. There were just ten of these built.

They featured the wide wheelarches associated with the Continental T, a green starter button, a matrix grille and 18in wheels. Needless to say, their exclusivity came at extra cost: in the USA, they cost $20,000 more than a standard Continental R.

2001 – THE LE MANS MODELS

The Mulliner bespoke commissioning system allowed Bentley to produce special limited editions of the Continental very quickly to celebrate the marque's third place with the EXP8 car at Le Mans in spring 2001. They sold well, too: although there were only ever five Continental T Le Mans cars, the original plan to build just fifty Continental R Le Mans gave way to market demand and, in the end, 131 examples were made. These cost £230,900 each, before extras.

The Continental R Le Mans was distinguished externally by front wing vents, the wider wheelarches associated with the Continental T, and by a so-called sports bumper package. It also had red-painted brake callipers in the fashion of the time (they were, of course, visible through the spokes of the alloy wheels), and four exhaust tailpipes. The engine was the 420bhp 6.75-litre V8.

Interior features included a tasteful chrome-and-leather gear selector lever, green-faced instrument dials, and a number of winged B motifs inlaid on the woodwork. The ashtray ahead of the gearshift also bore the legend 'Le Mans Series' inlaid into its wooden face next to a Bentley logo.

THE AZURE, 1995–2003

It was no surprise that Crewe should develop a convertible version of its hugely successful two-door Continental R. The marque's existing two-door convertible, latterly also wearing Continental badges (see Chapter 2), had been introduced as long ago as 1967 and was now rather long in the tooth even if its timeless styling was just as acceptable as ever. So Project P100 was set in motion some time around 1993 under the leadership of Tony Gott, with the aim of delivering a replacement model based on the Continental R. The new car was given the name of Azure when it was announced in March 1995, a superb choice, which deliberately suggested blue skies and clear seas and also hinted at the Côte d'Azur in France

Last of the line were the Continental Le Mans Series, issued to capitalize on the Bentley third place at Le Mans in spring 2001. This factory sketch shows the key features of the more numerous Continental R version.

CONTINENTAL RENAISSANCE

Though based on the Continental, the Azure had a number of important structural differences to compensate for the absence of a fixed roof. None were visible, of course, and this shot pictures the car in the landscape for which it had been designed.

Open or closed, the Azure remained an elegant creation in the very best tradition of the large Bentley convertible. This was an early car, pictured in March 1996.

■ CONTINENTAL RENAISSANCE

TOP LEFT: **The interior of the Azure was essentially the same as that of the Continental R but, as is clear in this picture of an early car, the rear side panels tapered inwards to allow for the hood mechanism.**

TOP RIGHT: **The interior of the Final Series featured exquisite detailing from the Mulliner division. The elegant juxtaposition of chrome, wood-veneer and stitched leather said everything about what a Bentley could be – and the drilled pedals were a reminder of its huge performance.**

MIDDLE & BOTTOM: **There were some striking touches to characterize the Azure Final Series in 2003, possibly the most effective being a reversion to the chromed grille surround of earlier times. Chromed wheels and detailing, a painted coachline and a Mulliner badge on the tail completed the picture.**

where the car was likely to find many of its customers. It was also a name that distanced the new model from its predecessor and give it an identity separate from that of the Continental R on which it was based.

The new body structure was developed with the aid of leading Italian design house Pininfarina, and in fact Pininfarina would retain an involvement with the new car throughout its production life, as the bodies were partially constructed in Italy. At the time of the car's announcement in March 1995, Crewe claimed that it had looked at working with body specialists in the UK but had decided that the Italian company had the most to offer.

At first glance, most people found it hard to imagine how Crewe had managed to spend $30 million on developing this car from the Continental R, which it resembled so closely. However, an enormous amount of work had been necessary to provide the new model with the refinement it needed as the new Bentley flagship. A key element in the car's 414lb (188kg) weight increase over the coupé was heavy reinforcement of the underframe to compensate for the torsional rigidity lost with the removal of the fixed roof. Crewe claimed that the new convertible's static torsional rigidity was 25 per cent better than that of the Continental convertible it replaced, although road tests when the car was new did report that it was not entirely free of scuttle-shake. The windscreen was also more steeply raked than its coupé equivalent, and was now carried in a massively stiffened frame, which was capable of taking the full weight of the 2.5-ton car in a rollover accident. Some commentators suggested that the windscreen pillars now seemed uncomfortably thick from inside the car. Then the line of the boot had been raised very slightly to allow it to blend more smoothly with the rigid hood cover behind the rear seats.

As for the interior, there were new front seats with integral seat belts that emerged through outrigger panels alongside the headrests and were based on the seats used in the BMW 850 coupé. The rear seats were narrower than those of the Continental R, thanks to the need to accommodate the hood mechanism behind the rear side trim panels, but there was still an impressive amount of room in the back. The rest of the interior broadly followed the lines of that in the coupé, as was only to be expected. The end result was what Crewe claimed, with some justification, to be the only full four-seater convertible in its class.

The new convertible top was a delight in itself, and was completely concealed when the car was open, stowing away under three metal covers that were trimmed to match the seats. When called into action by a button on the centre console, electric motors and hydraulic rams embarked on a smooth and fully automated sequence of events. First, the hood cover opened and the hood itself began to emerge. Then the two additional cover panels, one on each side, opened to allow the frame to follow. Once the front of the hood had locked itself into position on the windscreen header rail, the rear section folded back and locked home onto the body.

The hood itself consisted of five separate layers, which made the inside of the car almost as sound-proof as the inside of the parent Continental coupé. The only disappointment was that there had not been enough room to provide a glass rear window, so a traditional Perspex type had been used. However, it did have its own dedicated demister outlet behind the rear seats, which was almost as good as having the embedded heating elements of a glass window.

Early pre-production cars were used for the press launch, and these had the 360bhp version of the V8 engine. However, production models had the 385bhp version, with single Garrett turbocharger and 553lb ft of torque. The car was claimed to reach 60mph from rest in 6.3sec and to have a governed maximum speed of 150mph (242km/h). The gearbox was the same four-speed GM type as in other Bentley models, but the suspension had softer settings than in the Continental R, with different adaptive damping characteristics, more compliant anti-roll bars and softer 255/55WR17 tyres. One reason for these changes was to minimize body shake over rough surfaces, and one result was that the car handled rather less crisply than its coupé parent.

Nevertheless, the American *Car & Driver* magazine reported in its June 1995 issue that the Azure had 'surprisingly taut handling', and that 'it positively relishes fast sweepers on the highway, the dampers firming up as the car responds to the nicely-weighted and high-geared power steering'.

The build sequence for the Azure was every bit as complicated as it had been for the convertible that preceded it, and went some way towards explaining its huge cost – £215,000 in its home market and $347,645 in the USA when it was introduced in 1995. The floorpan was made in the Rover Group factory at Cowley, which had once been the Pressed Steel works and, as also happened with the coupé, was then shipped to Park Sheet Metal in Coventry. Here, the front section of the car as far back as the B-pillars was assembled on to the floorpan, and then the half-completed bodies were shipped to Pininfarina in Turin. Pininfarina's task was to fit the rear body panels and the mechanism for the convertible top. In this state, the bodyshells then returned to Crewe for paint

■ CONTINENTAL RENAISSANCE

and final assembly. The whole process added about three weeks to the twelve-week build cycle of a Continental R.

Like the Continental coupé, the Azure was made available from 1999 in Mulliner trim, with the 420bhp engine that delivered 875Nm of torque. The Azure Mulliner had additional visual features, such as front wing power vents, and of course customers could personalize fittings and equipment on their cars. As a result, probably no two cars in these last four years of the model's production were exactly alike. The Azure ended production in 2003 with a special run of Final Series models, which featured a number of options from the Mulliner programme as standard plus, to striking effect, a chrome-plated radiator shell, which recalled the days before painted shells had taken over at Bentley. Though no-one outside Crewe knew it at the time, the chrome grille surround would be a feature of the Azure's replacement when it entered production in 2005 (see Chapter 10).

Production levels for the original Azure were always low, and just 1,308 examples of the Bentley convertible were delivered in eight years – an average of approximately 164 cars a year, or just over three cars a week. By Bentley standards, that was a huge success, as was the fact that 709 of those cars were sold in the USA, where the Azure had gone on sale in autumn 1995.

As an interesting footnote, the Azure formed the basis of a new Rolls-Royce model introduced in 2000 with the Corniche name. This car was the only new Rolls-Royce model developed during the marque's period of ownership by Volkswagen and its production ended in 2002, just before Rolls-Royce passed into BMW ownership in 2003. Just 374 examples were built, all of them with a lower-performance version of the V8 engine than was used in the Azure. The cars all had front end panels and other styling elements that linked them to the latest Rolls-Royce Silver Seraph saloons and, despite a very close resemblance to the Azure, in fact shared only two minor body panels with the Bentley.

SPECIAL DEALER EDITIONS

As happened with other Bentley models of the time, some dealers created their own exclusive editions of the Continental and Azure. The known ones are listed below, but there may have been others.

Chatsworth Continental R.
Chatsworth Continental T.
Concours Beverley Hills Continental R.
Cornes Continental R.
Jack Barclay Continental R: ten examples; flared wheelarches, 18in five-spoke wheels; chromed radiator grille and surround; Azure-pattern seats with ruched leather; turbo boost gauge.
Jack Barclay Platinum Anniversary Azure: ten examples for the 70th anniversary of Jack Barclay Ltd in 2001; ruched leather and special 'starburst' walnut veneers.
RSE Special Edition Continental R.
Stratton Continental R.
Symbolic Continental R.

CHAPTER FIVE

ARNAGE

The project for a new saloon to replace the SZ range, which had arrived in 1980 as the Rolls-Royce Silver Spirit and Bentley Mulsanne, began to take shape in 1994. By that stage, it was very clear at Crewe that its manufacturing processes needed modernizing if its two marques were not to become quaint anachronisms, but the key difficulty would be in maintaining enough of the qualities associated with traditional hand-finishing, while adding the precision and speed that were now available from modern methods. There was another major problem: finance was not unlimited.

During 1994, it became clear that the company could not afford to invest in both a new assembly plant and in the development of a new engine to replace the long-serving V8 that had first been seen in 1959. The decision more or less made itself, and the company chose to go for the new plant at Crewe. This automatically meant buying-in an engine, or more than one engine, from an outside supplier. Those evaluated included a Mercedes-Benz V8 and the General Motors Northstar V8, but in December 1994 a contract was signed with the German BMW company for the supply of engines to go into the next range of new cars from Crewe.

Although news of the deal was made public, its details remained secret. What would not become clear until the new cars were announced, in the second quarter of 1998, was that different engines would be used in the same bodyshell to help distinguish Bentley from Rolls-Royce and to give the two versions of the new car very different driving characteristics.

The project for the new saloons was known internally as P3000, and was run by Tony Gott. In order to meet a tight development schedule, Crewe employed a number of engineering consultants (a practice that was then on the increase in the motor industry as a way of containing development costs), as well as some new practices, which included a version of the 'simultaneous engineering' that had been employed at Land Rover in the 1980s to deliver the Discovery in a record-breaking three years from scratch. Under this system, teams from different disciplines worked on areas of the design together rather than in sequence, as was the old way.

So although the style of the new body was created by Crewe's chief designer, Graham Hull, the body engineering was largely done by Mayflower, who also designed the new body plant where it would be built. BMW were to supply the powertrain and several other sub-systems, while the suspension was designed by Lotus and further developed at Crewe. Other consultancies who worked on P3000 included Randle Engineering Solutions, Hawal Whiting and MSX. When the cars were introduced, parent company Vickers quoted the figure of £200 million as having gone into them, although this broke down as £160 million for the cars themselves and £40 million on the new assembly facilities at Crewe where they were built.

Grilles and badges apart, the key difference between the two cars lay in their different engines. The focus for the Rolls-Royce was on refinement, and so the engine chosen was the BMW 5.4-litre V12. For the Bentley, however, the focus was on performance, and so a special derivative of the BMW 4.4-litre V8 was developed. This engine had twin turbochargers. The main development was done by Cosworth Engineering, which was owned by Crewe's masters at Vickers, but there is some reason to suspect that BMW-favoured tuners Alpina may also have been involved: a twin-turbo V8 was certainly seen on bench test at their premises at around the right period.

The turbochargers chosen were low-inertia water-cooled types, and their housings were cast into the exhaust manifolds themselves in order to minimize turbo lag. Low-compression pistons were specified, to reduce the risk of detonation associated with high-compression ratios in forced-induction engines.

The results were 350bhp as against the 286bhp in BMW's 540i saloon, with torque of 413lb ft at just 2,500rpm compared to 310lb ft at 3,900rpm in the BMW installation. The engine was mated to the same five-speed ZF automatic gearbox that BMW used in their cars, which had a switchable

■ ARNAGE

Sports mode that re-programmed the electronic control system to hold on to gears longer to give maximum acceleration. The gearbox was also an adaptive type, which meant that its electronic control system would 'learn' the driver's style and program the upshifts to match this.

The bodyshell was new from the ground up, and was the first one ever to be manufactured completely at Crewe – thanks to the all-new body plant that had been built there in the mid-1990s. Crewe claimed its torsional stiffness was 65 per cent better than that of the SZ range. Even though it was actually slightly longer than that of the standard-wheelbase cars it replaced, it looked quite a lot smaller. It was indeed very slightly lower, but the size illusion was brought about by the styling, which was recognizably Crewe and was as imposing as ever, if in a more subtle way than before. When the new models were announced in 1998, some onlookers admitted to mild disappointment, and it was true that the new saloons were perhaps more bland than the ones they replaced. At this stage, there were only standard-wheelbase cars, and no replacement for the long-wheelbase SZ models was mentioned.

The Rolls-Royce was introduced first as the Silver Seraph in March 1998, and the Bentley followed as the Arnage in June. The name once again reflected Bentley's determination to mine its heritage, as Arnage is the name of one of the corners of the Le Mans circuit where the Bentley sporting reputation had been forged in the 1920s. There were several visual differences between the Silver Seraph and the Arnage, the most obvious being the Bentley's more discreet grille with its honeycomb mesh and body-coloured surround surmounted by the winged B emblem against a green background. Arguably, it suited the shape more than the Rolls-Royce grille, which somehow appeared rather grandiose with the new body shape. But there were other important differences, too. The Bentley had a deeper front air-dam than the Rolls-Royce; it had less chrome trim on its bumpers and had a body-coloured rear number-plate surround rather than the chromed one of the Rolls-Royce; and its paired headlamps were set against a black background rather than the chromed one of its sister car.

The traditional peerless combination of wood and leather made potential customers feel instantly at home in the interior, and the Bentley shared with the Seraph its electrically adjustable rear seats. However, there were important differences elsewhere. The Bentley had a more sweeping centre console and the faces of its instruments were cream rather than black. It also had a rev counter instead of the combined-instrument dial of the Silver Seraph, and the three displaced instruments made the number of smaller dials on the Bentley dash up to five. Where the Seraph had a column-mounted

The original Arnage made its debut in 1998 and featured the discreet styling so characteristic of the Rolls-Royce era. Yet underneath that elegant bonnet was a twin-turbocharged BMW V8, with a high-revving character quite unlike that of earlier Bentley engines.

ARNAGE

RIGHT: **The second tail-light group on either side of the number-plate was one of the less successful features of the Arnage's styling. The car tended to look smaller than it really was – no bad thing in a period when fuel consumption and associated emissions were again becoming a preoccupation in some social circles.**

BELOW: **The Arnage's interior contained no real surprises, although the upturned rear to the centre console was new. Otherwise, wood, leather and impeccable workmanship reigned in their familiar way.**

transmission selector, the Bentley had its selector mounted on the centre console to give a more sporty ambience.

Like the Rolls-Royce, the Arnage had a flip-up panel on the dashboard to conceal the standard Alpine ICE system, together with traditional chromed ball-type air vents, but these were now made of aluminium rather than brass as in earlier models. The two cars also shared switchgear, but a good deal of this had come straight from the BMW parts bins, and many commentators were quick to note that its quality was not up to Crewe's traditional standards. The BMW air-conditioning system, if as efficient as buyers could wish for, also lacked the controls of the earlier Rolls-Royce type, which had been such a pleasure to handle.

Underneath the bodyshell, the suspension was once again carried on separate front and rear sub-frames, which were mounted to the shell with insulating rubber bushes. But this time, the engine and differential were mounted directly to the bodyshell with their own rubber bushes, so that the mountings between bodyshell and sub-frame could be more effectively tuned to alter the handling characteristics – as indeed would occur in later iterations of the Arnage. The rack-and-pinion steering, with power assistance of course, was mounted directly to the front sub-frame for similar reasons.

Both Seraph and Arnage had the same basic system of independent double wishbones with coil springs on all four wheels, supplemented by adaptive hydraulic dampers all round. The adaptive ride control had been further revised for the new saloons, and was now able to respond faster than in its SZ incarnation; Crewe claimed reaction times of 1/100th second. However, the Seraph's suspension was tuned for comfort, to give the wafting ride expected of the Rolls-Royce marque. By contrast, the Arnage had springs that were 40 per cent stiffer, and dampers to match. The Bentley also had bigger brakes, and to accommodate these it had 17in wheels rather than the 16in wheels of the Rolls-Royce. They were shod with low-profile tyres, to a 255/55ZR17 size. Both models were fitted with a BMW-sourced Automatic Stability Control system,

ARNAGE

which operated through the standard ABS brakes, but this could be turned off by a switch on the dashboard.

Initial road tests of the Arnage were enthusiastic. 'This is a proper sports car,' said *Car* magazine in its June 1998 issue. *Motor Sport* for the same month thought that the steering was 'boldly heavy and admirably precise, though… lacking the feel that has now been exorcised from… every large car on sale'. Criticisms included rear legroom, which was in fact an inch less than on the outgoing saloons, and a modicum of body shudder over poor surfaces. Generally, the Arnage got far better reviews than the Seraph, which probably did not harm sales of the Rolls-Royce one bit but may have helped boost interest in the Bentley.

2000 MODELS – THE ARNAGE RED LABEL

Yet despite the very positive reactions to the new Arnage, there was a feeling in some quarters that all was not as it

---

SPECIFICATIONS FOR BENTLEY ARNAGE MODELS

Years of manufacture 1998–2010

Build quantity
- 1,123 — Arnage 1998–99
- 59 — Arnage Green Label
- 2,273 — Arnage Red Label

Engine

Arnage and Arnage Green Label:
- 4398cc (92mm × 79mm) V8 with four overhead camshafts and four valves per cylinder
- Bosch engine-management system; twin Garrett GT 17 turbochargers with intercoolers
- 8.5:1 compression ratio
- 350bhp at 5,500rpm
- 413lb ft from 2,500 to 4,200rpm

Arnage Red Label:
- 6750cc (104.14mm × 99.1mm) ohv V8
- Zytek EMS 5 engine-management system
- Garrett T04E turbocharger
- 8.0:1 compression ratio
- 400bhp at 4,000rpm
- 616lb ft (835Nm) at 2,150rpm

Arnage R:
- 6750cc (104.14mm × 99.1mm) ohv V8
- Bosch ME 7.1.1 engine-management system
- Twin Garrett T3 turbochargers (with air-to-water intercoolers)
- 7.8:1 compression ratio
- 400bhp at 4,100rpm
- 616lb ft (835Nm) at 3,250rpm

Arnage T:
- 6750cc (104.14mm × 99.1mm) ohv V8
- Bosch ME 7.1.1 engine-management system
- Twin Garrett T3 turbochargers (with air-to-water intercoolers)
- Twin Mitsubishi turbochargers, from September 2006
- 7.8:1 compression ratio
- 450bhp at 4,100rpm
- 507bhp (500PS) from September 2006
- 645lb ft (875Nm) at 3,250rpm
- 738lb ft (1,000Nm) from September 2006

should be. The new twin-turbo BMW V8 engine was all very well, but it simply did not provide the massive wave of torque that had been available from the old Bentley Turbo R. It was a feeling shared by customers and Crewe's engineers – and when VW took over at the helm of Bentley, it was a feeling shared by the new top management as well.

When BMW had signed the engine supply deal in 1994, they had agreed to continue providing engines for between one and two years after Rolls-Royce and Bentley were sold to another owner, even though the sale of the two marques was not on the cards at that stage. As a contingency plan, Crewe's engineers had done some preliminary work on fitting their own 6.75-litre V8 engine into the car, just in case the supply of engines was terminated at some inconvenient point in the future. It was just as well that they had, because VW were not keen on continuing to use BMW engines after they took over, and BMW were unlikely to be very keen on prolonging the deal to supply them.

VW actually wasted no time in deciding how they would proceed with the Bentley marque once it was in their hands.

Transmission
Arnage Green Label:
Five-speed ZF automatic gearbox with torque converter.
Arnage Red Label, Arnage R, and Arnage T to August 2006:
Four-speed GM 4L80-E automatic gearbox with torque converter; switchable Sports mode and converter lock-up on top gear.
Arnage R and T (from September 2006), and Final Series:
Six-speed ZF 6HP26 automatic gearbox with torque converter and mode control.

Suspension
Independent front suspension with coil springs, twin wishbones, anti-roll bar and electro-hydraulic dampers.
Independent rear suspension with coil springs, twin wishbones, anti-roll bar and electro-hydraulic dampers.

Steering
Power-assisted rack-and-pinion steering.

Brakes
Ventilated disc brakes on all four wheels, with 13.1in (334mm) diameter at the front and 12.9in (328mm) at the rear (Arnage and Arnage Green Label); 13.7in (348mm) at front and 13.5in (345mm) at rear (Arnage Red Label and Arnage T). Four-channel ABS standard.

Wheels and tyres
Arnage and Arnage Green Label: 17in alloy wheels with 255/55R17 tyres.
Arnage Red Label: 18in alloy wheels with 8in rims and 255/50ZR18 tyres.
Arnage Final Series: 20in five-spoke two-piece Sports alloy wheels with 8.5in rims and 255/40ZR20 tyres.

Vehicle dimensions
Wheelbase	122.6in (3,116mm)
Overall length	212.2in (5,389mm)
Overall width	76in (1,930mm)
Overall height	59.6in (1,514mm)
Weight	5,079lb (2,304kg) kerb weight (Arnage Green Label)
	5,556lb (2,520kg) kerb weight (Arnage Red Label)
	5,699lb (2,585kg) kerb weight (Arnage T)

Performance
Max. speed	150mph/242km/h (Arnage and Arnage Green Label)
	155mph/250km/h (Arnage Red Label; electronically limited)
	179mph (288 km/h) (from September 2006)
0–60 mph	6.2sec (Arnage Green Label)
	5.9sec (Arnage Red Label)
	5.2sec (Arnage T from September 2006) and Final Series
Fuel consumption	17mpg (14ltr/100km)

■ ARNAGE

Good though the Cosworth-developed BMW V8 may have been, it was no Bentley engine. So the return of the 6.75-litre V8 in 2000 was greeted enthusiastically by observers and customers alike.

Vickers had not wanted to spend any more money developing the old Rolls-Royce V8 engine in the mid-1990s, and that was one reason why it had been sidelined for the P3000 project. However, VW did not yet have an engine of its own that would suit the Bentley range, and there was little doubt that it would be far quicker and far cheaper to re-engineer the 6.75-litre V8 to meet forthcoming emissions requirements and to deliver more power than to embark on the development of an all-new Bentley engine. The decision to do so was taken at a VW Board meeting in September 1998.

The fully re-engineered V8 was some three years away, however, and the Arnage needed some improvements before then. So an interim upgrade for the car was planned for autumn 1999 – barely a year in the future. This would incorporate a number of improvements to the specification that had been planned for the 2001 model-year but which could be brought forward and, most importantly, it would also see the Arnage re-engined with the existing single-turbo version of the trusty old V8.

The plan was executed in the cautious manner so typical of Crewe thinking. The overall package of improvements was introduced for all versions of the Arnage at the same time, but the 6.75-litre V8 was not to replace the BMW twin-turbo V8 completely just yet; instead, it would be made available in a companion high-performance model, which would be known as the Arnage Red Label, while the BMW-engined car would remain available for a time as the Arnage Green Label. It was also not hugely different from earlier production versions of the engine, although it was developed for installation in the Arnage with the codename of F1.

The Arnage Red Label appeared in November 1999, priced at £149,000 in the UK, which was £4,000 more expensive than the Green Label car. Both had a package of upgrades, which responded to customer criticisms of the first Arnage models. They had a bodyshell that was 24 per cent stiffer than before, thanks to stiffening plates welded to the transmission tunnel, extra swages in the floorpan and, above all, to a cast alloy engine bay brace. The bodyshells had also been altered at the rear of the passenger cabin, where the floorpan had been lowered and the rear seat re-located. This delivered an extra 50mm (nearly 2in) of headroom and an extra 25mm (just under 1in) of legroom to counter criticisms of restricted rear space in the early cars. The new cars also had a Park Distance Control radar system to aid parking, and an Alpine satellite navigation system, whose screen popped up in a rather ungainly fashion from the top of the dashboard. That was perhaps the least successful of the upgrades, and US road-testers even reported that it did not work reliably on early production cars.

The Red Label car, however, had that wonderful old

ARNAGE

The new Red Label car had red labels all over it – on the bonnet, on the boot lid and in the centres of its new six-spoke alloy wheels. Bentley missed no tricks with this publicity photograph, having the whole car in red plus a red flower in the model's hand.

engine – and it made a huge and exciting difference to the way the Arnage performed. *Car* magazine for November 1999 described the result vividly as 'an English stately home shacked up with a dragster'. The big single-turbo V8 was in much the same tune as in the Continental R coupé and the Azure convertible, with 400bhp and 616lb ft of torque, and it delivered the punch that the BMW engine so sadly lacked. Crewe claimed 5.9sec for the zero to 60mph time, and governed the top speed to 155mph (250km/h), but the Red Label's most salient characteristic was the wave of torque that was available from so low in the rev range.

All this was allied to the GM four-speed transmission, speed-proportional power steering, sub-frame changes to tauten the handling and stiffer front springs with revised damper settings. Those stiffer springs were needed partly because the single-turbo V8 put an extra 100kg of weight over the front wheels. To match the extra performance, Crewe had specified larger brake discs, and to make room for these they had to fit 18in wheels in place of the 17in types of the Green Label car. These ran on 255/50ZR18 Pirelli P-Zero tyres.

The final BMW-engined Green Label cars were built during 2000 and these, like all the 2000-model Arnage derivatives,

91

■ ARNAGE

A bit more Bentley, a bit less Rolls-Royce… note how the lighter colour and contrasting stitching really lift the interior of this Arnage Red Label as compared to the rather dull and conventional interior of the original car. However, that satellite navigation installation on the dash top was a mistake.

had plastic headlamp covers in place of the earlier glass type. The very last Green Label models were issued as a limited edition called the Birkin Arnage, in homage to Sir Henry 'Tim' Birkin, the creator of the original 'blower' Bentleys at the end of the 1920s. There is some dispute about the numbers of the Birkin edition. Some sources claim fifty-four were built, and others claim fifty. Beyond doubt is that UK-market cars had a numbered limited-edition plaque, which claimed a total of just twenty – but that was probably the total for the UK alone.

2001 MODELS – A LONGER WHEELBASE

With the Green Label model out of production, the Red Label then briefly remained the only variant of the original Arnage available until the new models with the redeveloped 6.75-litre V8 reached the market in early 2002. However, 2001 was not without interest, because it brought the announcement of not one but three new Arnage derivatives.

For 2001, a long-wheelbase Arnage finally joined the range. Only a close look revealed the extra length, which was all in the rear doors.

Noticeable by its absence when the original Arnage had been launched was a long-wheelbase variant. However, this had not been forgotten. A prototype long-wheelbase car was shown, supposedly as a concept, at the Paris Motor Show in September 2000. Reactions were favourable, and the car was introduced as a production model at NAIAS in Detroit in January 2001.

The actual increase in the wheelbase was 9.8in (250mm), which put the total up to 132.5in (3,366mm). As in earlier long-wheelbase derivatives of Bentley saloons, the extra length was accommodated simply by fitting longer rear doors. However, the new model – known as the Bentley Arnage RL – was soon made available with a choice of two additional wheelbase options. A 17.7in (450mm) stretch put the wheelbase up to 140.4in (3,566mm), and there was also a 28.7in (728mm) stretch, giving a wheelbase of 151.3in (3,844mm). The 151.3in version had an extra body section inserted between front and rear doors, and both this and the intermediate 140.4in car had a roofline raised by 3.9in (100mm) to maintain the car's good looks.

Not surprisingly, the potential market for these hugely expensive cars was small, and Bentley's intention from the beginning was that they should be made only to order, and should be fitted out by the Mulliner division as Personal Commission cars. One option available was full armour-plating to B6 standard, which was built into the bodyshells during the early construction stage.

Very early long-wheelbase cars had what was in effect a Red Label mechanical specification, with suspension and brakes modified appropriately to cope with the extra weight. However, the mechanical specification of the long-wheelbase cars kept pace with later developments in the Arnage range.

2002 MODELS – THE SERIES 2 CARS

The redevelopment of the V8 engine was funded by VW but was carried out primarily at Crewe and, by the time it was completed, some 50 per cent of the engine was new, while most of the rest had been re-engineered. The company claimed, when it was introduced in January 2002, that only around 15 per cent of the original 1959 engine now survived in its original form.

One of the primary drivers behind the re-engineering had been the need to make the engine meet new emissions regulations due in 2002, and at an early stage Project Manager Simon Clare settled on the most effective way of doing this as changing the single turbocharger for twin smaller turbochargers. So there were now two Garrett T3 turbochargers, their smaller size reducing inertia and allowing faster response to the accelerator. A further advantage of the new installation was that it allowed the catalytic converters to be located closer to the cylinder heads, where they would warm up more quickly.

■ ARNAGE

The Arnage T looked subtly different, with altered front and rear aprons and more aggressively sporting five-spoke alloy wheels. The Bentley badges now had black backgrounds.

There were new and less restrictive exhaust manifolds, too, now tubular fabrications rather than the old iron castings. On top of that, the cylinder heads had been modified to give better gas flow, and the valves themselves were new and lighter. A single auxiliary belt-drive at the front of the engine replaced the multiple belt-drives of the older V8s. Finally, the engine-management system was now a Bosch Motronic ME-7, which was able to work with a variety of other on-board electronic systems and in particular allowed the use of ESP (Electronic Stability Program) in place of the less sophisticated traction control system on earlier cars.

The new engine, coded F6 at Crewe, was introduced first in a new top model called the Arnage T, which Crewe described as the first of the 'Series 2' Arnage range. In this guise, it thundered out no less than 450bhp with a massive 645lb ft of torque, and would rev to 5,000rpm, which was 500rpm more than the older V8 could manage. The combination delivered a 5.5sec 0–60mph time, a 168mph (270km/h) top speed (Bentley had decided not to subscribe to the voluntary 155mph limit), and would power the car from 50 to 70mph in 3sec. That statistic, as one motoring magazine gleefully pointed out, made the car more than twice as quick as a

ARNAGE

BMW M3. For such a large car, the performance was simply breathtaking.

The Arnage T even boasted a taller final drive than the Red Label and Green Label cars. It had a lighter differential that was claimed to be capable of handling twice as much torque as the earlier type, and the standard 18in wheels could be replaced, if the buyer so wished, by 19in five-spoke wheels with fashionable split rims and 255/45ZR19 Pirelli P-Zero tyres. These wheels could be chromed to order. There were stiffer front and rear springs, while the front anti-roll bar had been stiffened and a rear anti-roll bar had been added. The result was roll stiffness improved by 57 per cent over that of the Red Label car. There were also stronger mounts for the steering rack, to sharpen steering feel and response.

The bodyshell had been developed further, too. Extra bracing in the roof and sills added 15kg (33lb) of weight but improved stiffness by a further 10 per cent. A deeper front air-dam contained integrated fog lamps and bigger air-scoops, which now had mesh inserts and were designed to get more cooling air to the brakes. A subtle spoiler had been engineered into the boot lid pressing, and there were curved highlight lines in the bumper apron above the twin exhaust outlets. The sills, too, were thicker, and there was now no chrome at all on the body. The winged B badges now had black backgrounds to indicate that this was the full-house performance version of the car.

Of course, there had been interior changes for the Arnage

TOP: **For the Arnage T came yet another contrast in interior ambience. The diamond-quilted upholstery and all-black colour scheme here make a striking contrast with Arnage interiors illustrated earlier.**

RIGHT: **The real transformation for the Arnage T was under the bonnet, where the 6.75-litre V8 now sported twin turbochargers.**

ARNAGE

T. The upholstery was in the latest quilted diamond-pattern with perforated leather, and the stitching was in a contrasting colour with an embroidered winged B motif. For those who wanted it, the standard walnut trim could be decked out by turned aluminium overlaps on the doors and around the instruments.

Black instrument faces replaced the earlier white ones, and the steering wheel had a thicker rim. The engine was now started not solely by the key, but by means of a large 'Start' button – a feature introduced by customer request. Side curtain airbags had been added to the safety equipment, and the gear selector had been redesigned with a large ball-like grip. The power-folding door mirrors, previously optional, were now standard. The satellite navigation system was a new DVD-based type, and the picnic tables were covered in Kevlar. And, matching moves elsewhere in the motor industry, all the Series 2 cars came with ISOfix child-seat mounting points in the rear.

All this, of course, came at a price. The new Arnage T cost £166,500 in its home country, and $242,277 in the important market of the USA, which was expected to take large numbers. It was no coincidence that the car had been introduced at the Detroit Motor Show, usually known as NAIAS (North American International Auto Show).

2003 MODELS – THE ARNAGE R

The Arnage T pioneered the use of the 6.75-litre V8 in the Arnage bodyshell, but it would not be alone for long. The plan was to upgrade the less expensive Arnage model as well, and the 2002 model-year was the last for the Red Label Arnage. Its replacement, the new 2003-model Arnage R, was announced at the Geneva Motor Show in March 2002.

This new model cost just £151,500 and offered very nearly as much performance as the Arnage T – certainly enough for most buyers. It had a slightly less powerful version of the twin-turbo 6.75-litre V8 engine, with the same 400bhp and 616lb ft of torque as the single-turbo engine in the Red Label; the progress, however, was that it would meet the latest emissions regulations, whereas the older engine would not. The engine-management system was also different, being a Motronic ME7.1.1 type, and the car was more softly sprung and damped than the Arnage T.

Even so, it was an impressive machine. *Evo* magazine for October 2002 enthused: 'There are quicker cars than the Arnage R, but there's nothing quite like experiencing first-hand the forces summoned to hurl this great mass forward with such vigour... there's such a deep well of mid-range torque you're rarely left thirsting for more'. Most important, perhaps, was that 'there's a cohesion about the whole dynamic package that hasn't been evident in earlier turbocharged Bentleys'. Crewe claimed 155mph (250km/h) and 5.9sec for the 0–60mph sprint, the same as for the superseded Red Label model. This no doubt was planned so that recent buyers of Red Label models would not feel too upstaged by the new Arnage R – but few people can not have imagined that there would be more to come in the future.

2004 MODELS – THE ARNAGE T-24

Bentley's win at Le Mans in summer 2003 had been all about publicizing the marque, and the company was not slow to follow up with a special edition of the Arnage T named after it. Sold as a 2004 model-year car, the Arnage T-24 was built in very limited numbers, with twenty-four cars destined for the USA and only 'a handful' (according to Bentley press releases) for the UK and continental Europe. The number twenty-four was of course chosen to refer to the twenty-four hours of the Le Mans race, and each car was individually numbered.

The T-24 was drawn up by the bespoke Mulliner division, with the aim of giving the Arnage T a yet more sporting appearance. In this, it also tested the water for acceptance of the more aggressive design features that inevitably accompanied such an aim. Bentley also claimed that the car was designed to have clear visual links to the Speed 8 racing cars that had dominated Le Mans in 2003.

So there were front wing vents, supposedly designed to recall the distinctive louvres over the front wings of the Speed 8. Above each vent was located a simple Union Flag badge with the number '24', in the same style as the 24 used on the Le Mans winners' trophy. The split-rim 19in wheels were highly polished versions of the wheels otherwise available only as options on the Arnage T. Then body-coloured inserts replaced the chromed front and rear lamp bezels, and four exhaust outlets below a redesigned rear bumper made the T-24 distinctive from the rear.

Inside the passenger cabin, the kickplates beneath the doors read 'T-24 Mulliner', and the demister ducts and interior mirror surround matched the colour of the leather upholstery. Carbon-fibre inserts replaced aluminium for both the waist rails and the facia, and the same material covered the rear

ARNAGE

The Le Mans win in summer 2003 gave Bentley an excuse to try several Mulliner ideas for the Arnage on a limited-edition model. Called the T-24, it was sold mainly in the USA.

picnic tables as well. Bentley's press material insisted on the connection between this finish and the carbon fibre used in the construction of the Speed 8 Le Mans winner.

Spectacular though the 2003 Le Mans win may have been, it was not the only thing on Crewe's collective mind that year. It was in 2003 that Bentley and Rolls-Royce once again became rivals, after more than seventy years when they had been two brands owned by the same parent company. That was the year when Bentley showed its future direction with the Continental GT (see Chapter 7), and also the year when Rolls-Royce nailed its colours to the wall with the gargantuan Phantom limousine. While there was no chance that Rolls-Royce would produce a direct competitor for the overtly sporting Continental GT, Bentley Motors did intend to continue competing at the top end of the limousine market.

A direct result of this was the appearance at the Geneva Show in March 2004 of an Arnage Limousine, officially at this stage a concept, but in fact intended for limited production. It was, of course, a flag-waving exercise, but no less serious for all that. That the show car should be finished in an attractive two-tone colour scheme of claret over black was clearly no coincidence, either: two-tone schemes were available on the Phantom.

The Arnage Limousine was based on the existing long-wheelbase Arnage platform with its 140.4in wheelbase, 17.7in (450mm) longer than that of the standard car and conveniently close to the 140.6in (3,571mm) of the Rolls-Royce Phantom. In those dimensions, it was not new, but the body had been heavily re-worked to improve the visual balance and

97

■ ARNAGE

The Arnage Limousine shown at Geneva in March 2004 was a deliberate counter to the new Rolls-Royce Phantom. Crewe was particularly proud of the new D-pillar, which allowed the rear seat to be recessed for occupant privacy.

add distinction. There was nearly 8in (200mm) of sheet metal on the D-pillar behind the rear doors, where the Arnage RL had none. The rear doors themselves were extended by 8in (200mm), and 2in (50mm) went into the front doors. The widened D-pillar provided greater privacy for the rear seat passengers, whose seat was hidden behind it. A smaller rear window increased the privacy available, ensuring that rear-seat occupants could not easily be seen from outside the car.

2005 MODELS – A FACELIFT, THE PRODUCTION LIMOUSINE AND A CONCEPT

With other, more pressing projects out of the way, Crewe was now able to make the Arnage more Bentley and less Rolls-Royce in appearance. So for 2005, the cars were facelifted, with twin individual headlights and a raised bonnet line that made them look much more like the Continental R. Invisibly, and perhaps of interest only to those with a sense of history, revisions to the engines for the 2005 model-year made them the first ones to have no common components at all with the original 1959 Rolls-Royce V8.

The interior was freshened up, too, with a revised centre console incorporating new switchgear for the air-conditioning controls and relocated switches for the electric windows and seat and mirror adjusters. The satellite navigation system, always something of an eyesore on the early Arnage, was also better integrated into the top of the dashboard.

This was also the year in which Crewe made clear that it had plans for the Arnage platform, and an Arnage convertible concept car was shown at the Los Angeles Auto Show that opened on 17 January 2005. That car was later confirmed for production as the new Azure (*see* Chapter 8). Meanwhile, in December 2004, the company announced (to nobody's great surprise) that the Arnage Limousine shown at Geneva earlier in the year would go into limited production. 'Such has been the demand following its unveiling,' read the press release, '20 individually numbered, bespoke Arnage Limousines will be commissioned for customers looking to own a truly luxurious car that provides extraordinary levels of comfort and craftsmanship as well as valuable privacy'.

Those numbers were not great, and the Limousine really was a bespoke creation. Customers were able to get involved in the design of their own car by having direct access to a designer and account manager from the Bentley Mulliner division. Bentley spoke of a 'blank canvas' on which each customer could create an individual car, with the result that no two Arnage Limousines would be exactly alike. It was, they claimed, a return to the great days of the coachbuilt Bentleys of the 1920s and 1930s. 'The scope for personalization is as wide as the customer's imagination,' read the press release, 'and whilst the concept is still in the virtual world of computer-aided design, styling sketches and renderings, Bentley Mulliner can be as flexible and creative as that vision demands'.

The Geneva Show car in March 2004 had in fact previewed the facelifted 2005-season front end, and of course all the production models had this as well. Split rear seats were standard, although the Geneva Show car had featured a bench. Electrically adjustable rear footrests were optional, and a rear DVD entertainment system was standard, with a 12in screen mounted in the back of each front seat. All Arnage Limousines also had uprated 8-cylinder front and 4-cylinder rear brake callipers operating on ventilated alloy brake discs.

2006 MODELS – THE DIAMOND SERIES

For the 2006 model-year, Bentley's main promotional effort was behind the new Azure convertible (*see* Chapter 9), but a special edition provided interest for the Arnage range. This was the Arnage Diamond Series, of which just sixty were made. The figure was linked in publicity material to the sixty years of Bentley manufacture at Crewe – which was accurate if the post-war resumption of production in 1946 was considered as the start date, but not if the actual start in 1933 was taken into account!

Still recognizable as the car that had been launched in 1998, but only just, this was the facelifted Arnage that became available for 2006. The front end was now much more like that of the Continental R and Azure, while the front wing vents and four tailpipes added to the sporting appearance. Note the aerial for the satellite navigation system and telephone on the roof – not an attractive feature, and one that the company would eliminate on the new Mulsanne in 2010.

■ ARNAGE

Another welcome return was the winged B bonnet mascot, which in this case was designed to retract under impact in order to meet safety regulations. It was an option.

Crewe put a huge amount of effort into the redevelopment of the 6.75-litre V8, and the twin-turbocharged version used in the 2006 model-year cars had no components at all in common with the original 1959 engine – although it was recognizably the same design.

ARNAGE

ABOVE AND RIGHT: **The Arnage ended production with a Final Series that had an array of the special features so beloved of Bentley customers.**

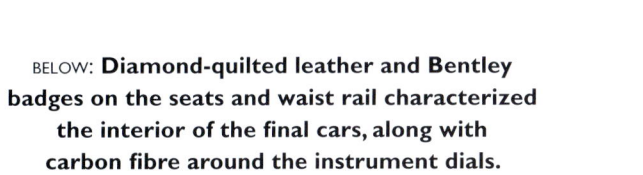

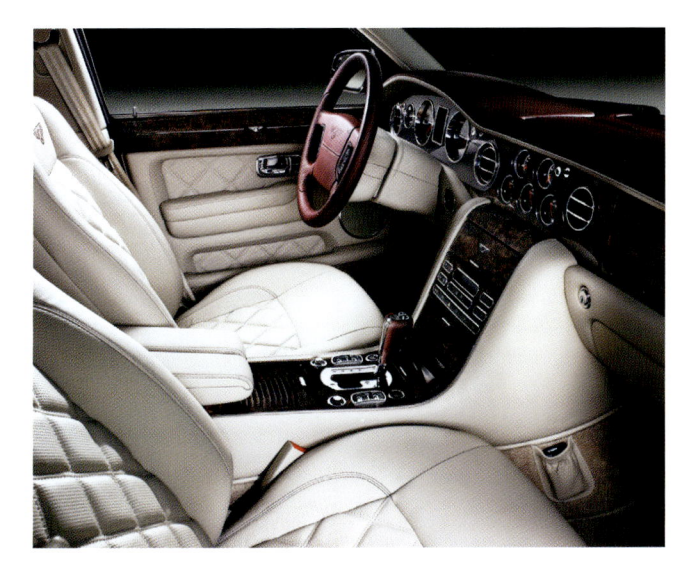

BELOW: **Diamond-quilted leather and Bentley badges on the seats and waist rail characterized the interior of the final cars, along with carbon fibre around the instrument dials.**

■ ARNAGE

The special features of the Diamond Series were 19in alloy wheels, a stainless steel front bumper, and Union Flag badges on the front wings. Inside, the distinctive quilted leather was standard, with diamond inlays in the wood. Most of these cars seem to have been sold in the USA.

2007 MODELS – SIX SPEEDS AND LIGHTWEIGHT TURBOCHARGERS

There was more of interest for the 2007 model-year Arnages, which were announced in September 2006. Continuing engine development had led to a change from the original Garrett turbochargers to a pair of Mitsubishi units, adopted because of their lighter weight and lower inertia, which gave faster reaction times. A re-profiled camshaft with an all-new roller tappet system gave revised valve timing and substantially improved refinement. These changes also delivered more power and enhanced durability. From a legislative point of view, they also ensured that the engine would comply with European EU IV and US LEV II emission standards. Interestingly, some publications at this time began to quote the swept volume of the V8 as 6761cc, although there appears to have been no actual change, and the figure of 6750cc soon reappeared in Bentley literature.

This latest version of the V8 engine was allied to a new six-speed gearbox from ZF, with the usual three transmission models of Drive, Sport and Semi-Automatic. This promised even smoother gearchanges than before and, because of the larger number of ratios, more appropriate gearing for all circumstances. The combination of the two upgrades allowed Bentley to advertise the 2007 Arnage as being capable of 179mph (288km/h).

One smaller change for the 2007 model-year cars was the addition of a tyre-pressure monitoring system, which warned the driver if one or more tyres lost pressure.

2009 MODELS – THE FINAL SERIES

There were no important changes for the 2008 model-year, but the 2009 model-year was destined to be the last one for the Arnage and Bentley decided to offer a tempting carrot for customers who might have been planning to wait for the replacement model before placing an order – or, worse, gone elsewhere for their new cars.

The carrot was another limited edition model, this time called the Final Series. True to form, Bentley publicity linked it to the marque's heritage, claiming that it celebrated ten years of the Arnage, fifty years of the V8 engine and ninety years of the Bentley marque itself. The model was announced in September 2008 for the 2009 season.

The uniqueness of the Final Series was assured by combining the 500bhp Arnage T engine with the refinement of the Arnage R, plus a few design elements from the Brooklands coupé, the limited-volume two-door fixed-head model derived from the Arnage (*see* Chapter 8). There were to be just 150 examples of the Final Series, and the very last cars were not built until early 2010.

The Final Series had its own exterior recognition features. Most obvious, perhaps, were the 20in five-spoke two-piece alloy wheels and the Le Mans lower wing vents introduced on the Brooklands coupé. A closer look would reveal body-coloured headlamp bezels, dark-tinted upper and lower grille matrices, a retractable winged B bonnet mascot, a 'jewel' aluminium fuel filler cap, a 'Final Series' badge on each front wing, and twin exhaust tailpipes.

There were special touches in the cabin, too. The front doors had polished stainless steel treadplates with 'Final Series' logos, and the wood-veneer waistrails had an inset chrome strip and recessed Bentley marque badges. The brake and accelerator pedals were drilled to give a sporting look, and there was a large-display ICE head unit with an SD memory card slot instead of the single CD slot. Rear passengers had their own delights, which began with removable cup holders in the rear centre armrest. Two picnic tables were available in a range of three unbleached veneers, and there was a cocktail cabinet with document stowage, all trimmed in leather. Inside that cabinet came a stainless steel flask and a set of shot glasses, all bearing the Final Series logo. In the boot were stowed four Bentley umbrellas with wooden handles, and the boot rail itself was trimmed in leather.

Then, of course, there were options. Although the range available through the Bentley Mulliner system was almost limitless, there were some listed options. These were an iPod interface, a remote control that enabled rear passengers to operate the infotainment system, and an 1,100W Naim for Bentley audio system. Also promoted was the carbon-silicon carbide high-performance braking system.

Even so, Bentley did recommend just six colour and trim combinations, which, they said, would 'help customers

ARNAGE

finalize the specification of their Arnage Final Series'. These were Titan Grey (with Anthracite interior), Royal Ebony (with Beluga), Windsor Blue (with Windsor Blue), Meteor (with Imperial Blue), Burnt Oak (with Burnt Oak) and Black Velvet (with Burgundy).

Individual drinks cabinets, special kickplates and a rack of umbrellas in the boot were among the special details of the Final Series cars.

NAIM FOR BENTLEY

In February 2008, Bentley announced the availability of an optional new premium sound system for its cars. This had been designed by British specialists Naim Audio, was exclusive to Bentley, and was claimed to be the most powerful in-car stereo system in series production.

The first version of the 'Naim for Bentley' system featured an 1,100W amplifier. It was made available progressively across the Bentley range during 2008, powering ten speakers in the Arnage, Azure and Brooklands models and fifteen speakers in the Continental GT, GTC and Flying Spur. The system featured the latest Digital Signal Processing (DSP) technology for the radio, dynamic equalization, speed-dependent volume control and could be integrated with telephone and satellite navigation systems as well. Later systems went on to become even more powerful, and by the time of the new Mulsanne in 2010 the amplifier was putting out 2,200W through no fewer than twenty speakers.

CHAPTER SIX

VOLKSWAGEN AND LE MANS

The story of how Bentley Motors, that most British of car manufacturers, ended up in foreign ownership at the end of the 1990s is a complicated one. But for anyone who doubts whether the Volkswagen Group, who eventually claimed ownership, were to be worthy custodians of the marque, the story of Bentley's return to Le Mans, its triumphs there and the new cars built under Volkswagen ownership should tell their own tale.

As Bentley's revival proceeded apace during the 1990s, it became increasingly obvious that there was a limit to what could be achieved in the existing factory at Crewe. Thoroughly modern luxury cars, such as Bentleys were now, need thoroughly modern production facilities, and Pyms Lane did not have them. If production were to be expanded to meet the obvious demand, the whole factory would have to be modernized. So, between 1995 and 1998, a vast modernization programme brought a new body plant, a new production line and a new paint shop – all equipped to deal with more modern manufacturing processes and considerably higher production volumes than their predecessors.

In September 1997, the owners of the Bentley and Rolls-Royce brands decided the time had come to sell them. Vickers plc had owned the two brands since its 1980 acquisition of Rolls-Royce Motors, and the two were still so closely intertwined – not least because of their common engineering and manufacturing base in Crewe – that they were to be sold together.

The widely-held assumption at the time was that the two marques would go to BMW, who were in expansionist mood and were already supplying engines for both Bentley and Rolls-Royce cars. BMW did indeed bid for the car manufacturers, offering £340 million at the end of March 1998, and at the end of April, Vickers accepted the BMW bid. It then became clear that there was a rival bidder who was offering more. The Volkswagen Group, also in expansionist mood, had bid £430 million. So, a week after announcing that Bentley and Rolls-Royce were to go to BMW, Vickers found itself announcing that Volkswagen had in fact won the bidding.

From this point on, a complicated series of negotiations over the Rolls-Royce name ensued. That Bentley would now belong to the Volkswagen Group was never really in dispute, but BMW were determined to fight hard over the Rolls-Royce brand. One of their first moves was to point out that their existing engines' contract with the old Rolls-Royce Motors had a twelve-month notice clause. In effect, this was a threat to cut off engine supplies within a year, which would not give Volkswagen enough time to re-engineer the existing production Bentley models, much less design a new one from scratch.

BMW swiftly reinforced their position through another deal. The small print of the sale required that, if the Rolls-Royce car division was sold, the associated aero-engine division (Rolls-Royce plc) should retain ownership of the essential trademarks of the Rolls-Royce name and logo. BMW exploited the existing strong relationship between their own aero-engine division and the Rolls-Royce aero-engine division, and negotiated a £40 million deal with Vickers, which allowed them to use the Rolls-Royce name on cars.

Discussion between the two companies eventually found a way out of the deadlock in July 1998. Broadly speaking, from 1 January 2003, full rights to manufacture Rolls-Royce cars would belong to BMW, and full rights to manufacture Bentley cars would belong to Volkswagen. This arrangement put a lot of pressure on BMW to develop a new Rolls-Royce and build the factory to assemble it within the remarkably short period of three and a half years. It is to their credit that they achieved both targets, the new factory being erected at Goodwood and the new Rolls-Royce Phantom reaching the showrooms during 2003.

As an interim arrangement, the existing Bentley and Rolls-Royce models would continue to be built at the VW-owned factory in Crewe.

BMW agreed to continue supplying engines for the cars

BENTLEY MULLINER

The Bentley Personal Commission service was established during the 1990s to reintroduce the element of personalization to the Bentley marque. In 2002, just before the formal split between Bentley and Rolls-Royce took place, agreement was reached that the names associated with the Mulliner Park Ward coachbuilding division (established in 1959) should be divided between the two marques. The Mulliner name went to Bentley, where it effectively replaced the Personal Commission service, and the Park Ward name stayed with Rolls-Royce.

The element of personalization was an important one in Bentley's twenty-first century strategy, and the activities of its Mulliner division were expanded appropriately. During 2003, Bentley Mulliner increased its turnover by 105 per cent and 60 per cent of all Arnages ordered came with some form of Mulliner personalization. By 2008, up to 80 per cent of Arnage customers specified Mulliner features.

'Bentley Mulliner has one purpose – to provide our customers with the Bentley that they want, not the Bentley we want to sell them,' explained Bentley Mulliner brand director Derek Davies in 2004. 'Many of our customers are used to a certain level of service from other car companies, but without fail they are amazed by what we can do to meet their needs. Other carmakers may claim to offer thousands of choices but Bentley Mulliner's option list is genuinely infinite – we will do whatever it takes to provide the bespoke car. Put simply, no two Bentley Mulliner cars are the same because no two customers are the same.'

In 2004, Bentley Mulliner employed around 130 specialist coachbuilders, trimmers, cabinet makers, electronics specialists and fitters. All worked in a dedicated workshop within the Crewe factory that included its own wood and trim shops, as well as steel fabrication and tool-making areas. A limited number of features could be installed in the main factory as cars passed through the standard production process. More commonly, though, a car destined for the Mulliner treatment was assembled as a basic structure and then passed to the Mulliner workshop for completion.

The time taken to create a Mulliner Bentley obviously depended on the extent of the customer's wish list. Some owners simply wanted a few small touches to personalize their car and to put their own signature on them. However, an Arnage Limousine with a high level of unique cabinetry and technological infrastructure could easily take upwards of 6,000 man-hours to complete – up to a hundred times longer than a mass-produced limousine from a mainstream manufacturer.

---

and would allow use of the Rolls-Royce name on cars built at Crewe. Volkswagen, meanwhile, were determined not to be upstaged by the announcement of a new Rolls-Royce in 2003. So they too began work on a new car for announcement that year. That car is discussed in Chapter 7 – and in the meantime, the company embarked on a programme to replace the BMW engines in its cars and so to disentangle itself from involvement with that company by 2003. That, more than anything else, explains the huge investment that went into re-engineering the existing V8 engine for high-performance Bentleys in the first years of the twenty-first century.

In fact, Volkswagen poured enormous amounts of money into its new acquisition in the years immediately after the take-over, and the quoted figure of £500 million is considerably more than the VW Group actually paid for the company in the first place. Most important was a further increase in production capacity, which was dramatically increased from around 2,000 cars a year to a claimed 9,000 a year. The Crewe workforce more than doubled from the 1,500 employed there in 1998 to some 3,500 by 2010. Other reports have clamed that Volkswagen invested a total of nearly $2 billion in re-inventing the Bentley marque for the twenty-first century.

However, that re-invention drew heavily on the past. The VW Group were under no illusions about the value of the Bentley heritage – indeed, that was really what they had spent their initial £430 million to acquire. At an early stage, they identified their aim that the Bentley brand should represent both high performance and high quality, and that it should also embody both the extraordinary and the bespoke in order to give it appeal to those who were able to purchase cars at the most expensive end of the market. Yet these were not to be conventional supercars, useful only for summer weekend trips. These were to be thoroughly practical machines, capable of everyday, all-weather use as well.

■ VOLKSWAGEN AND LE MANS

GUIDING LIGHTS

With the transfer of Bentley into Volkswagen Group ownership, a number of new people were appointed to senior positions. The key figures have been those listed below.

Dr Franz-Josef Paefgen
Franz-Josef Paefgen held several positions at Ford and was also Chief Executive Officer of Audi before becoming CEO of Bentley Motors (and of Bugatti, also owned by Volkswagen). He retired at the end of January, 2011, and was succeeded by Wolfgang Dürheimer.

When the Volkswagen Group took over the Bentley marque, Dr Franz-Josef Paefgen was appointed as Chief Executive Officer. He served until early 2011.

Wolfgang Dürheimer
Dürheimer took over from Franz-Josef Paefgen as Bentley's CEO at the start of February 2011. He had been chief of Research and Development at Porsche since 2001, and had been responsible for the Porsche Cayenne SUV programme. He publicly favoured the idea of a Bentley SUV when he was appointed as the brand's CEO, and it may well turn out that development of such an extension to the range was the main reason why he was put in charge of Bentley. There is every chance that a future Bentley SUV would share major components with future large SUVs from other Volkswagen brands, particularly Porsche and Audi.

Paefgen's replacement as CEO in 2011 was Wolfgang Dürheimer. His appointment was widely expected to be associated with Bentley's plans to produce an SUV model some time around 2014.

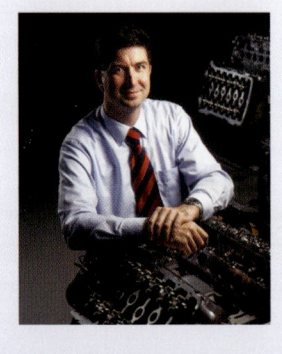

Dr Ulrich Eichhorn
Ulrich Eichhorn joined the Volkswagen Group from Ford, where he had been responsible for the programme to produce the first Ford Focus. VW were deeply concerned that the car outclassed their own Mk IV Golf, and appointed Eichhorn as their Director of Research in 2000. In 2003 he was appointed to the Bentley Board as Engineering Director.

Dr Ulrich Eichhorn was appointed as Bentley's Engineering Director and remained in that job as this book went to print.

Dirk van Braeckel
Belgian-born Van Braeckel initially worked for Ford in Germany before joining Audi in 1984 to work on exterior design. He then moved to the Volkswagen Group's Skoda division, where he oversaw a complete revision of the model line-up. He then became chief designer for Bentley under Volkswagen, with particular responsibility for creating the less expensive Bentley that materialized in 2003 as the Continental GT.

THE TWENTY-FIRST CENTURY STRATEGY

The Volkswagen strategy for developing Bentley was quite different from the one that BMW adopted for developing the Rolls-Royce marque. BMW chose to begin by launching a large limousine, the Phantom, in 2003; they then expanded the range with smaller and less expensive models. At Bentley, the plan was initially to replace the BMW engines in the existing Arnage models, and then to introduce a smaller and less expensive Bentley, which would both broaden the appeal of the Bentley brand and provide a platform for a new range of cars.

So it was that the venerable Rolls-Royce V8 engine, first introduced in 1959 but now owned by Bentley as a member of the Volkswagen Group, underwent a major re-development to emerge in twin-turbocharged form for the Arnage in 2002. That engine went on to have a remarkable revival as a Bentley power unit, and over the next few years it was gradually developed to become the world's most powerful production car V8, as well as to meet increasingly stringent emissions regulations. By 2009 it had been completely re-engineered with an alloy cylinder block, variable camshaft timing and even a cylinder shut-off system, but was still fully capable of delivering the massive power and torque that Bentley cars needed, and was still recognizably the same engine that had been designed at the end of the 1950s, half a century earlier.

The Volkswagen strategy for Bentley was to have two basic platforms in production at the same time. So it was that the Arnage platform was used as the basis of the Azure convertible from 2005 and the Brooklands coupé from 2008. These were the 'grand' Bentleys, and were priced accordingly. They were replaced in 2010 by an all-new platform developed under Volkswagen but still featuring the original V8 engine in its latest incarnation. This new model was called by the same Mulsanne name that had been given to the Bentley version of the Rolls-Royce SY car.

The second platform was newly developed and appeared first in 2003 as the Continental GT, a smaller two-door coupé powered by a W12 engine from the Volkswagen Group stable. This platform was then developed to deliver the Continental Flying Spur saloon in 2005, the Continental GTC convertible in 2006, the GT Speed model in 2007, the GTC Speed and Continental Supersports in 2009, and finally the Continental Supersports convertible in 2010. It was then given a major overhaul in 2010 to deliver a facelifted Continental GT range, which featured a new Volkswagen Group V8 engine as an option alongside the older W12. Interestingly, the official line, as conveyed on the Bentley Motors' website, was that the revival of the marque was completed in 2006 with the arrival of the Continental GTC convertible.

Bentley's marketing strategy also had a profound impact on the cars it produced in the twenty-first century. By the end of the 1990s, the massive 'wave of torque' associated with the turbocharged V8 engine had become one of the key characteristics of the marque, and Bentley's new owners built on this as they developed new and existing engines. Also becoming important was the increasing readiness of the company to personalize its cars through the Personal Commission scheme operated by its Mulliner division. This had come about partly as a way of securing sales at a difficult time for the marque, but under Volkswagen it was elevated to an art form.

The first decade of the twenty-first century saw a vast increase in the individualization options available through Bentley Mulliner, with the aim of ensuring that no two Bentleys ever needed to be identical. In addition, the liberal creation of special editions ensured that the limited number of basic models in production always seemed fresh and exciting. There were many special-edition models, too, and although initially these mainly commemorated events associated with the Bentley marque, by 2009 the company was also creating market-specific special editions to suit tastes in its major overseas markets. Each of these special editions could be individualized, too, while retaining the key features common to others of its kind. The result was that no customer ever needed to visit a Bentley agent to buy 'a new Bentley'; instead, each customer was able to feel that he or she was buying 'my new Bentley'.

Lastly, Bentley marketing relied very heavily on the Bentley marque traditions. The sporting heritage proved a rich source of inspiration for new model variants and new model names, and in early 2011 the company put on an exhibition, which it called 'The Unbroken Line', showing how modern Bentley design drew on the marque's past and developed it further.

BENTLEY AND THE EVIRONMENT

At the opening of the Geneva Show in March 2008, Bentley CEO Dr Franz-Josef Paefgen announced a three-stage environmental strategy, which he stated would be implemented on new Bentley models between then and 2012. He said that the

■ VOLKSWAGEN AND LE MANS

During 2011, Bentley Motors organized an exhibition called the Unbroken Line, which demonstrated how the Bentley tradition has been carried through from the 1920s to the present day. Here with one of the exhibits, the Bentley Coupé with which the company's then chairman was for many years thought to have raced the famous Blue Train from Nice to Paris, are three key members of the design team. On the left is Chief Designer Dirk van Braeckel; in the centre is Robin Page, chief of interior design; and on the right is Raul Pires, chief of exterior design.

plan would help Bentley as a corporation to address the twin global issues of carbon dioxide emissions and longer term fuel availability, as part of its corporate social responsibility. 'This is a major step in the history of Bentley,' he said, 'reflecting the increasing expectation from our customers around the world for performance motoring with fuel efficient engines. We will set a benchmark in our segment of the industry by making every engine capable of running on renewable fuels, reducing emissions and improving fuel efficiency throughout our fleet.'

The Bentley strategy was described as being based on a long-term vision and as following years of engineering studies and intensive product development, exploring alternative environmental technologies in depth. Paefgen claimed that the renewable fuel programme reflected Bentley's commitment to the environment while maintaining vehicle performance.

The first stage in the strategy would be to apply innovative technology to the Bentley V8 and W12 engines, and to achieve at least a 15 per cent reduction in carbon dioxide emissions by 2012. The second stage of the strategy would be to introduce a new powertrain by 2012, delivering a 40 per cent reduction in fuel consumption, while maintaining current levels of performance. The third stage was to make all Bentley engines compatible with the use of renewable fuels by 2012, with the initial rollout promised for 2009.

As this book went to press, some of those targets were still in the future. However, the arrival of the re-engineeered

V8 for the new Mulsanne in 2009 was the first step in reducing carbon dioxide emissions, and the car did indeed promise 15 per cent lower emissions than its Arnage predecessor. A new and smaller-capacity engine in the Continental GT during 2010 also contributed to this aim. As for the use of renewable fuels, Bentley initially pinned their hopes on the use of second-generation biofuels, and in fact the first FlexFuel models, capable of running on ethanol-based fuels, were available before the global infrastructure for delivering such fuels was very far advanced. 'By preparing our engines at an early stage for these fuels, we believe we will help accelerate their adoption, as the supply and market for them develop,' said Paefgen in 2008. 'Taken together, the measures we are announcing will make the entire Bentley fleet capable of delivering less than 120g/km by 2012.'

THE RETURN TO LE MANS

Despite the rediscovery of Bentley's sporting heritage since the arrival of the Mulsanne Turbo models in the mid-1980s, the Bentley marque was not really considered in the supercar bracket at the end of the 1980s. Expensive and exclusive, yes; capable of much greater performance than appearances would suggest, certainly; but the marque's sporting achievements had been made some seven decades earlier and, with the best will in the world, were now fading into mere legend. What was needed to reinforce the appeal of the rejuvenated brand under its new ownership was a racing programme.

The nature of that programme needed careful scrutiny, however. Touring-car events were of limited interest – the British and German championships, for example, having legions of fans in Europe but few elsewhere. Besides, these events were dominated by marques such as Ford, Alfa Romeo and BMW, which were not really in the same class as Bentley. To gain maximum publicity, and of the right kind, Bentley needed to compete in an event of world-wide interest. There was an obvious choice. Bentley had made its name at the Le Mans 24h event, and it would be perfectly fitting to try for Le Mans honours again.

However, Le Mans was not at all the same type of event as it had been in the 1920s. Back then, entering a race-prepared version of a regular production model had been quite normal. By the late 1990s, Le Mans cars had become special race-bred machines with only the vaguest of resemblances to the production cars from the manufacturers that entered them. So there was no chance of putting a Bentley Continental into the fray and expecting success, despite its giant-killing performance. Bentley Motors would have to develop a special Le Mans racing car for the job.

There was, however, a complication. Bentley's stable-mate in the VW Group, Audi, was already fielding a successful Le Mans car, which looked good enough to be a potential winner in 2000. There was no point in allowing the Bentley entry to undermine the Audi effort, so the timing had to be carefully arranged. Nor was there any point in unnecessary and expensive duplication of resources. So, although the plan was always to run the Bentley racing operation independently of the Audi one, it was inevitable that there should be some cross-fertilization between the two.

The open-cockpit Audi R8 achieved a one–two–three finish in its first outing at Le Mans in 2000, and this stunning success helped Volkswagen to decide on an overall racing strategy. Audi should be given the opportunity to achieve more wins at Le Mans, while the new Bentley car found its feet. In the light of Audi's success or otherwise, the Bentley racing strategy would evolve. In an ideal world, Audi would win again in 2001 and claim a hat-trick of wins in 2002. By then, the Bentley car would have been sufficiently developed to be capable of winning in 2003. It was a bold, ambitious and even somewhat arrogant strategy, but the VW Group were confident of success. So after the Audi victory at Le Mans in 2000, Volkswagen announced a three-season racing programme for Bentley. If things did not go according to plan, the opportunity existed for the programme to be extended. In practice, it all worked perfectly: Audi got their hat-trick of Le Mans wins, and Bentley won Le Mans in 2003, making four victories in a row for the VW Group.

Audi had already worked with the British specialist RTN (Racing Technology Norfolk), and so the contract for the design and development of the new Bentley went to them. However, largely to ensure that the Bentley was suitably different from the Audi, RTN appointed a different team of engineers to work on the Bentley project. At its head was designer Peter Elleray, and his brief was to deliver a car for the closed-cockpit LMGTP (Le Mans GT Prototype) class. That Audi were at this stage competing in the open-cockpit LMP (Le Mans Prototype) class again differentiated between the projects.

The first iteration of the Bentley came together in 2000, and two test-bed cars were built. As was typical of Le Mans cars at the time, they had monocoque bodies made of carbon fibre and aluminium honeycomb to give maximum strength with minimum weight, and had a carbon rollover

VOLKSWAGEN AND LE MANS

hoop integrated with the roof structure. The engine was mounted longitudinally in the middle of the car, to give the best possible weight distribution. In the early stages, the team considered using a naturally aspirated engine, and the first prototype car (number 001) was initially tested with an engine built by Cosworth, the race engineering company formerly owned by Vickers, which had passed along with Bentley into the hands of the VW Group.

However, the eventual choice fell on the twin-turbocharged 3.6-litre engine that had powered Audi's 2000 Le Mans winner. The plan, though, was for the Bentley and Audi racing teams to develop their own versions of the engine independently; this would both ensure differentiation and encourage different approaches, which might be beneficial to both teams in the long run. For even further differentiation, the Bentley team developed a special six-speed gearbox in conjunction with Xtrac, rather than relying on the Ricardo type used in the Audi R8. The differences between the LMP 900 regulations that governed the Audi and the LMGTP regulations that governed the Bentley also led to a difference in tyre width between the two cars; this gave another opportunity for differentiation, as the Bentley team decided to use Dunlop tyres, rather than the Michelins that Audi favoured.

The new car was known as the EXP Speed 8; EXP referred to its experimental status, while the Speed 8 designation both hinted at the Speed Six designation of the cars that had won Le Mans in 1929 and 1930, and indicated that the new Bentley had an 8-cylinder engine. Chassis and suspension were both developed from scratch, and the original flat front-end had been changed to incorporate a raised crash box at the nose, with additional bodywork to shroud the front suspension arms. The cockpit was also tapered to give better airflow over the rear wing. In addition, the Bentley team switched for 2003 to the Michelin tyres formerly used by Audi. Maximum speed of the EXP Speed 8 was said to be over 220mph (322km/h), with 105mph (169km/h) available in first gear. Weight, to meet the LMGTP regulations, was just on 900kg (1,984lb).

The lessons learned from the prototype cars were brought together in the first full Le Mans cars. Both were painted in British Racing Green with silver accents, and a team of top drivers was engaged. The car, which wore number 7 in the race (chassis number 004), was crewed by Martin Brundle, Guy Smith and Stéphane Ortelli, and the car that wore number 8 (chassis number 003) by Andy Wallace, Butch Leitzinger and Eric van der Poele. The cars were run at the circuit by Apex Motorsport.

Le Mans in 2001 saw some of the worst conditions ever experienced for the race, and the number 7 car failed to finish; after running strongly in the torrential rain, it caught fire and had to be abandoned. The number 8 car fared much better,

LEFT AND TOP OPPOSITE: **The Bentley EXP 8 was entered for the Le Mans 24h race in June 2001. Car number 8, crewed by Wallace, Leitzinger and Van der Poele, is seen here during a night-time pit stop on 16 June and at speed on 17 June.**

though. It ended the race with a class win (inevitably, as the Bentleys were the only LMGTP entries that year) and in third place overall, behind two Audis.

This was very encouraging indeed, and out of the public view further development went ahead on the Bentley in preparation for the 2002 Le Mans. Most importantly, the team decided on a larger engine, this time a 4.0-litre derivative of the existing V8, which developed some 600bhp. This new engine was better suited to the EXP Speed 8 and to the restrictors it required to meet the Le Mans regulations, but in the event only a single car was entered for the 2002 Le Mans event. The official reason was that an economic downturn had obliged the VW Group to restrict its motorsport activities, but there were some who wondered whether entering only a

The EXP Speed 8 was modified for the 2002 Le Mans and fitted with a larger engine. However, just one car was entered for that year's event, and finished fourth behind the works Audis.

■ VOLKSWAGEN AND LE MANS

The 2002 Le Mans entry was driven by the team that had come third in the 2001 event. From left to right, Butch Leitzinger, Andy Wallace and Eric Van der Poele are seen with the 2002 car.

single car gave the Audi team a better chance of winning. That single car, chassis number 006, wearing race number 8, was driven by the successful 2001 team of Andy Wallace, Butch Leitzinger and Eric van der Poele. After an almost trouble-free run, it finished in a very creditable fourth place behind the three 'works' Audis. Inevitably, it also won the LMGTP class.

The Audi team announced an end to its racing activities in 2002 (although it did return to Le Mans a couple of years later), leaving the field open to Bentley. The car was extensively redesigned for the 2003 event, and was now known simply as the Speed 8. It had new bodywork, designed specifically to improve airflow over the body and especially to the rear wing. So the external cockpit area was reduced (although the cockpit was actually more roomy inside), and the turbocharger air intakes of the EXP Speed 8s were replaced by snorkel intakes on the sides. The results were much greater downforce than

Clear in this picture is the redesigned front end of the Speed 8 for the 2003 Le Mans. This time, Bentley fully expected to win, and in the event carried off a 1–2 finish.

112

VOLKSWAGEN AND LE MANS

A highly-trained pit crew is always essential to racing success, and here the Bentley team works on the number 8 car that would come second at Le Mans in 2003.

on the earlier car and a more consistent aerodynamic performance under all conditions. The designers also created a special 'sprint' aerodynamics package for the car, designed to provide greater downforce and allow the Speed 8 to race at tracks other than Le Mans.

The twin-turbocharged V8 engine was meanwhile re-engineered around the new Le Mans regulations for 2003 that required a 10 per cent reduction in engine restrictor size. Many internal engine components had to be redesigned as a result, and a new electronics strategy was needed to minimize the drop in power caused by the restrictor changes. In the end, the 4.0-litre V8s were putting out around 615bhp, with more than 590lb ft of torque at 7,500rpm. In a car weighing just 916kg (2,019lb), performance was quite sensational.

The decision was also taken to go with Michelin tyres as earlier used by the Audi team, and this change required additional work on the suspension. Torsion bar springs were used at the rear, and all the geometry had to be changed, including the mounting points for the rear suspension on the gearbox. This, in turn, required a new gearbox casing.

Four cars were built with the new specification, although the plan was for a two-car entry to Le Mans. Two were entered in March for the Sebring 12h race in the USA, as a warm-up race. Although a rules infraction during the qualifying laps saw the two Bentleys relegated to the back of the starting-grid, despite times that would have placed them in the first two positions, they quickly made their way up through the field to claim third and fourth places behind a 'works' Audi R8 and a privately-entered similar car. Bentley number 8 (chassis 009), driven by Johnny Herbert, David Brabham and Mark Blundell finished third, and car number 7 (chassis 007), driven by Tom Kristensen, Guy Smith and Rinaldo Capello, came in behind it.

113

■ VOLKSWAGEN AND LE MANS

The number 7 car for 2003 had deep side plates on its rear wing. At Le Mans, it was driven to first place by Tom Kristensen, Guy Smith and Rinaldo Capello.

MIDDLE LEFT: **In the heat of the action, the eventual Le Mans winner is seen at speed during the night-time element of Le Mans.**

BELOW LEFT: **The Le Mans winning team, from left to right Kristensen, Capello and Smith.**

BELOW RIGHT: **Bentley Boys, too: the number 8 car finished second and was driven by David Brabham, Mark Blundell and Johnny Herbert.**

114

VOLKSWAGEN AND LE MANS

WEIGHTS AND MEASURES

The 2003 cars had the following specification:

Carbon-fibre monocoque
4.0-litre twin-turbocharged 90-degree V8
Approx 615bhp and over 590lb ft at 7,500rpm
Six-speed sequential manual gearbox, with Megaline pneumatic actuation

Length	183in (4,650mm)
Width	78in (1,990mm)
Height	39in (990mm)
Wheelbase	108in (2,740mm)
Weight	2,019lb (916kg)

Capello and Kristensen had formerly raced the 'works' Audi R8s.

At the Le Mans test day in May, the Kristensen/Capello/Smith team again used their Sebring car, chassis 007, although this was kept in reserve for the event in June. The Herbert/Brabham/Blundell team stuck with their Sebring car, number 009. It was a promising start: the Bentley teams finished the day with first and third fastest times.

For Le Mans, one Bentley was run by Joest Racing, who had run the successful Audi assault on the circuit in recent years, while the other was run by RTN. Right from the beginning, it was clear that the Speed 8s would do well, and some commentators have suggested that their dominance was such that the race was relatively unexciting to watch. During qualifying, Tom Kristensen set an unbeatable target with a lap of 3min,

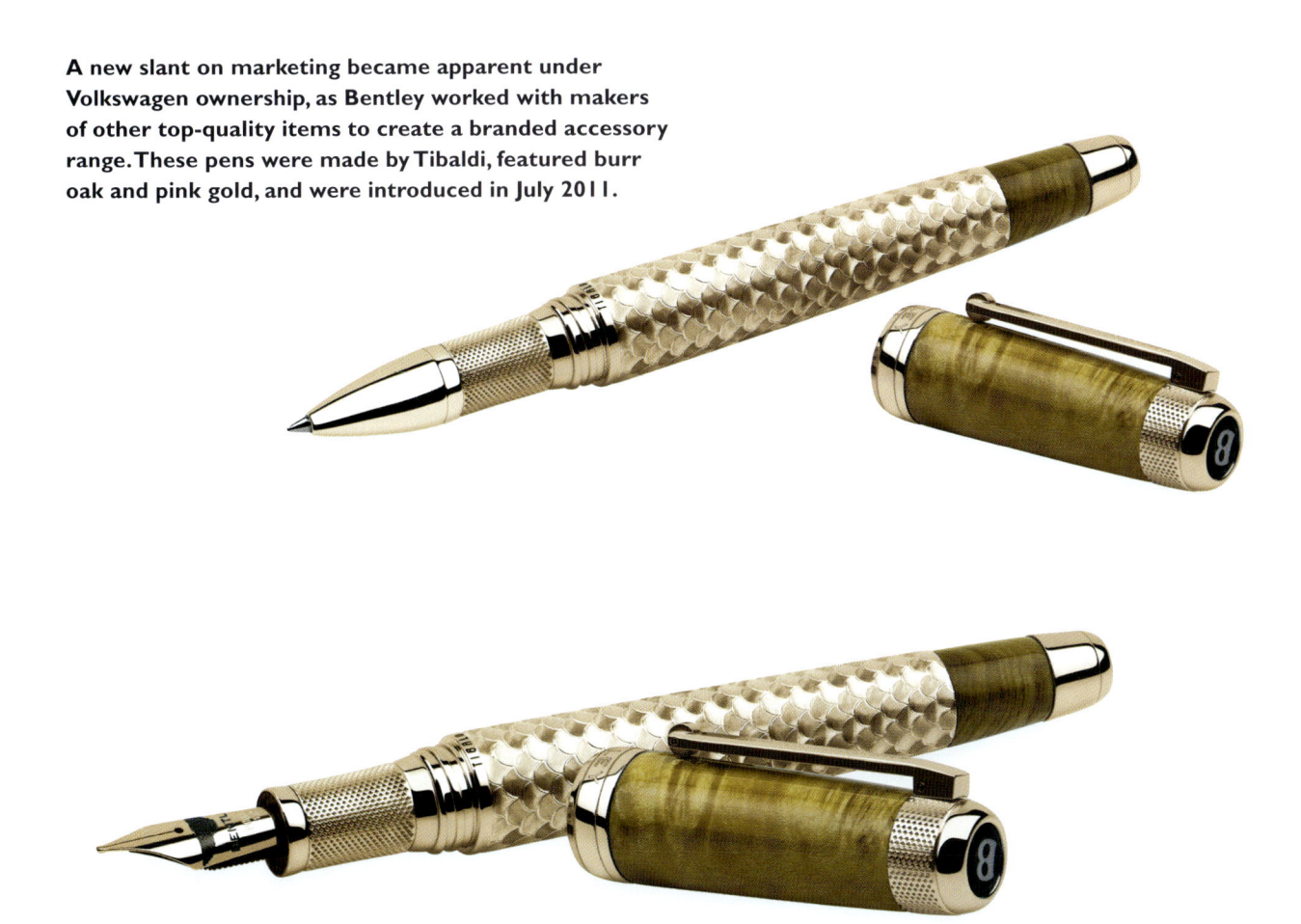

A new slant on marketing became apparent under Volkswagen ownership, as Bentley worked with makers of other top-quality items to create a branded accessory range. These pens were made by Tibaldi, featured burr oak and pink gold, and were introduced in July 2011.

115

■ VOLKSWAGEN AND LE MANS

31sec in the number 7 car (chassis 011, distinguished by deep end-plates on its rear wing), and the number 8 car (chassis 009, run by RTN) achieved second slot on the starting grid.

The two Bentleys took an early lead, and those who witnessed the event say that they were never under any serious pressure. Johnny Herbert set the lap record for the race on the Sunday. At the end of the twenty-four hours of racing, car number 7 stormed home in first place after 377 laps of the French circuit, with Guy Smith at the wheel. Car number 8 finished just two laps behind it in second, with David Brabham in the driver's seat. It was the one–two victory that Bentley had worked so hard to achieve, and for the Bentley marque it was a sixth Le Mans win, resuming the glory achieved back in the 1920s. That, however, was enough. Bentley had made their point, and now withdrew from Le Mans competition to make way for a return by their stable-mates, Audi.

Sharp-eyed readers may have spotted that there has been no mention of three of the cars, chassis numbers 005, 008 and 010. The first two were both written off during testing, number 005 at the Paul Ricard circuit in France and number 008 at Jerez in Spain. As for car number 010, it was never raced, but was used for promotional purposes during 2003. Car number 004 was modified to 2002-specification and was also used for shows. One car (number 003) was sold to a Japanese collector and subsequently moved to the USA. Four cars were retained by RTN, these being numbers 006 (Le Mans 2002), 007 (Sebring 2003), 009 (Sebring and Le Mans 2003) and 011 (the 2003 Le Mans winner).

THE ROAD TO SUCCESS

The 2007 calendar-year saw Bentley achieve its highest-ever global sales, and its fourth consecutive year of growth. A total of 10,014 cars were sold world-wide, and overall volume grew by 7 per cent, with increases in almost all major markets. In the UK, a record 2,079 cars were sold, and in North America – the brand's largest market – there were 4,196 sales. Export sales earned over £745 million for Bentley, and the company reported record revenue and operating profit.

CEO Dr Franz-Josef Paefgen commented: '2007 was a milestone in the history of Bentley as we passed the 10,000 units for the first time. Five years ago we were selling only 1000 units but the development of a strong product line has seen the Company attract new customers in greater numbers. 2007 saw strong growth both in mature markets, such as Germany, the UK and the US, as well as in emerging markets, such as China and Russia.'

More Bentley accessories, this time a branded timepiece and a coffee table made from the cylinder block of a V8 engine.

CHAPTER SEVEN

A GT FOR THE TWENTY-FIRST CENTURY

Designing a new Bentley for the twenty-first century was, quite simply, an awesome task. In the sense that the VW Group could do more or less whatever they wanted, it offered endless opportunities. Yet those opportunities were constrained by eight decades of Bentley history and by the expectations of the marque that had grown up in that period. It says a great deal for the top management at VW Group that they invested the company's resources with almost clinical precision in order to produce a new car, which appeared in 2003 with the name of the Bentley Continental GT.

From quite an early stage, the project to design the new car was known as MSB, those initials standing for Mid-Sized Bentley. That this meant the car would be smaller than existing models was never in doubt, and in fact the plan to create a smaller Bentley had been around for some years before the VW Group took ownership of the marque. It was first revealed in public at the Geneva Motor Show in March 1994, when the Concept Java car (see Chapter 11) was shown on the Bentley stand.

That car never entered production, but there can be little doubt that the VW Group took careful note of the thinking that had gone into it. For Bentley, a smaller and somewhat cheaper range of cars would have increased their sales by making the marque affordable to a wider group of buyers. With careful brand management, and of course the traditional Bentley build quality, no harm would have been done to the Bentley image. It would, instead, have been enhanced.

The VW Group strategy was to build on this set of ideas. Their aim was also to increase Bentley sales by bringing the marque within reach of a wider group of buyers, but they had the advantage of additional resources in the shape of other models. In particular, they wanted to break the dominance of Mercedes-Benz and BMW in the market sector just below that where Bentley operated, and they saw a new and less expensive Bentley as a vital element in a pincer movement against their rivals. The idea was to continue attacking sales of the top-model Benzes and BMWs from below with their own Audi brand, while putting pressure on them from above through the Bentley brand.

So the MSB package came together around new and more compact dimensions; it was around 300mm shorter than the Concept Java car, which itself had been around 300mm shorter than the 'full-size' Bentleys of its day. Yet within those dimensions, VW Group aimed to offer at least as much passenger space as the most spacious coupés then on sale. Equally important was to offer performance and handling dynamics comparable to the best supercars on the market. And on top of that, the car had to look like a Bentley. Even though this would be the first Bentley ever to be designed as a 'virtual' car on computer, before any metal was cut, the design specification represented a very tall order.

The last of those design aims – that the car should look like a Bentley – was in many ways the most critical, and to oversee the new car's appearance VW chief Ferdinand Piech appointed Dirk Van Braeckel as Bentley's new chief designer. Van Braeckel was a Belgian by birth, who had initially joined Ford in Germany but had moved to Audi in 1984 and in 1993 had been appointed to oversee the new models of the Skoda marque that had just been bought by VW. His success at re-defining a brand that had once been considered rather downmarket made him the ideal choice for re-defining the Bentley brand.

It was already clear that the new Bentley would be a two-door coupé like the 1994 Java, and the most recognizable two-door coupé in Bentley's history was the fabulous Continental R of 1952. So Van Braeckel took some styling cues from that car – notably its sleek fastback design. However, he blended that with a much more sporting appearance, achieved by

117

■ A GT FOR THE TWENTY-FIRST CENTURY

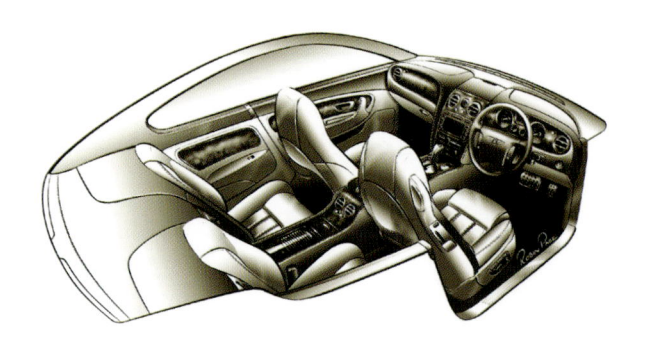

This early sketch of the Continental GT's interior shows the essence of the 2+2 design, featuring traditional Bentley detailing.

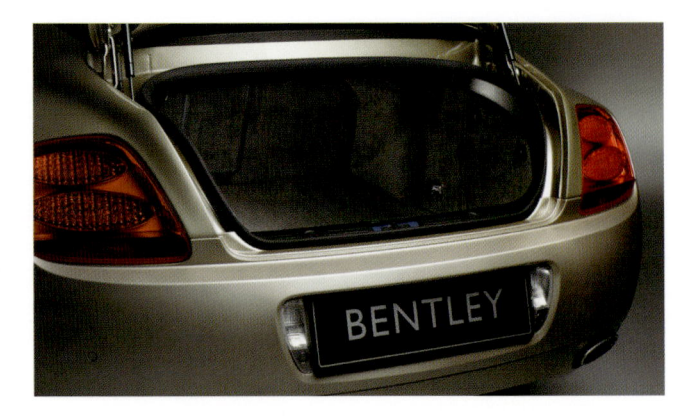

Room had been found for a decent-sized boot, and a movable panel allowed longer loads to be fed through onto the rear seats as well.

The traditional Bentley grille was really the only obvious link with older Bentleys, even though the R-type Continental fastback was said to have been an inspiration. A key feature was the animal-like 'haunches' over the rear wheels.

A GT FOR THE TWENTY-FIRST CENTURY

TOP RIGHT: **Sadly, little of the 6-litre W12 engine was visible under its plastic shroud when the bonnet was opened.**

TOP LEFT: **As originally displayed in press pictures, the cabin lacked some of the contrasting trim that would characterize the car.**

Contrasting trim colours and wood-veneer panels brighten the interior of this later GT coupé considerably.

giving the car 'haunches', which suggested an animal tensed and ready to spring. At the front of the car, he retained the twin headlamps and cross-hatched grille, which had become Bentley trademarks, and with careful use of swooping lines he gave the whole an elegance that fitted perfectly into the Bentley tradition. The design actually came together very quickly: Van Braeckel started work in August 1999 and his design was finished and approved for production by Christmas that year. The only real compromise was a retractable rear spoiler, which the engineers decided was necessary to improve the aerodynamics at high speeds.

Of particular help to Van Braeckel in drawing up the balanced exterior lines of the MSB was the very short engine that VW planned to use in the car. It had been clear from the beginning that a 12-cylinder engine would be necessary to compete with the V12s offered by Mercedes-Benz and BMW, but the VW Group had no V12, and nor did they have any plans to make one. Instead, they had been working for some years on an alternative design to achieve the refinement of a 12-cylinder engine without its length. Their design was a W12, which consisted of four banks of three cylinders each rather than two banks of six cylinders each. It was thus much shorter

■ A GT FOR THE TWENTY-FIRST CENTURY

than a V12, and this factor allowed more of the MSB's length to be given over to passenger space than would otherwise have been possible.

The origins of the W12 can in fact be traced back to the 1980s, when VW needed the refinement of a 6-cylinder engine to fit some of their cars, which had been designed around transverse 4-cylinder engines. A straight-six would have been too long, and a traditional 60-degree V6 too wide. So they designed a V6 with a very narrow angle between its cylinder banks of just 15 degrees. With the cylinders staggered to minimize width, the VR6 achieved its design aims very successfully.

The W12 was created from this design. In effect, what the VW engineers did was to put two VR6 engines on a common crankshaft, mounting them at 72 degrees to one another. With four overhead camshafts, the result was an extremely

SPECIFICATIONS FOR BENTLEY CONTINENTAL GT, GTC, SPEED AND SUPERSPORTS MODELS

Years of manufacture
2003 on (Continental GT)
2006 on (GTC)
2007 on (GT Speed)
2009 on (Supersports and GTC Speed)
2010 on (Supersports Convertible)

Build quantity
Still in production.

Engine
GT and GTC:
5998cc (84mm × 90.2mm) W12 with four overhead camshafts and four valves per cylinder
Bosch Motronic engine-management system and twin Borg Warner turbochargers with air-to-air intercooling
9:1 compression ratio
552bhp at 6,100rpm
479lb ft (650Nm) at 1,600rpm

GT Speed:
5998cc (84mm × 90.2mm) W12 with four overhead camshafts and four valves per cylinder
Bosch Motronic ME7.1.1 engine-management system and twin Borg Warner turbochargers with air-to-air intercooling
8.5:1 compression ratio
600bhp at 6,000rpm
553lb ft (750Nm) from 1,750 to 5,600rpm

Continental Supersports:
5998cc (84mm × 90.2mm) W12 with four overhead camshafts, four valves per cylinder and phased cam timing
Bosch Motronic engine-management system and twin Borg Warner turbochargers with air-to-air intercooling
8.5:1 compression ratio
600bhp at 6,000rpm
590lb ft (800Nm) from 1,700 to 5,600rpm

Transmission
Six-speed ZF 6HP26 automatic gearbox with torque converter.
Supersports with ZF 6HP26A gearbox incorporating 'Quickshift' mode.
Four-wheel drive with 50-50 torque split via torsen centre differential; different splits on some models.

compact 12-cylinder engine that had a swept volume of just under 6 litres – exactly what was needed to compete with the V12s from BMW and Mercedes-Benz.

The VW Group used this engine in the Audi A8, where its compact size allowed room for the extra hardware of four-wheel-drive at the front of the car. Later, it also appeared in the VW Phaeton and the Touareg SUV. At the 2001 Tokyo Motor Show, a 600bhp version of the engine was also displayed in the prototype VW Nardo coupé, a mid-engined supercar with rear-wheel drive, which had broken the 24h world endurance a week before the show, at an average speed of 183.45mph (295.23km/h) over 4,402.8 miles (7,085.6km). Production of this car was certainly under consideration but in the event was not sanctioned.

All this valuable experience with the W12 engine, of course, also fed into the Bentley MSB project – which by the start of

Suspension
Front independent suspension with four-link double wishbones, computer-controlled self-levelling air springs and anti-roll bar.
Rear independent suspension with trapezoidal multi-links, computer-controlled self-levelling air springs and anti-roll bar.
Continuous damping control with four adjustable settings,

Steering
Servotronoic speed-sensitive power-assisted rack-and-pinion type.

Brakes
Ventilated disc brakes on all four wheels, with 15.9in (405mm) diameter at front and 13.2in (335mm) diameter at rear. ABS with Hydraulic Brake Assist and Electronic Brakeforce Distribution. MSR drag torque control, Bosch ESP 5.7 electronic stability programme and ASR electronic traction control.
Carbon/ceramic brakes with cross-drilled discs, 420mm diameter at front and 356mm diameter at rear, standard on Supersports and optional on other models.

Wheels and tyres
19in alloy wheels with 275/40R19 tyres
Split-rim 19in alloy wheels optional
20in split-rim seven-spoke alloy wheels optional, with 275/40R20 tyres
GT Speed: 20in wheels with 9in rims and 275/35x20 tyres
Supersports: 20in wheels with 9.5in rims and 275/35x20 tyres

Vehicle dimensions
Wheelbase	GT, GT Speed and GTC: 108.07in (2,745mm)
Overall length	208.94in (5,307mm)
Overall width	75.5in (1,918mm) (2003–2005 GT, and GTC)
	75.4in (1,915mm) (GT from 2009)
	77.4in (1,966mm) (convertibles from 2009)
	76.6in (1,946mm) (Supersports)
Overall height	54.7in (1,390mm) (standard models)
	54.3in (1,380mm) (Speed models)
Weight	GT: 5,500lb (2,495kg) kerb weight
	GTC: 5,600lb (2,540kg) kerb weight
	Supersports: 4,939lb (2,240kg)

Performance
Max. speed	GTC: 195mph (312km/h)
	GT Speed: 202mph (326km/h)
	Supersports: 204mph (329km/h)
0–60mph	GTC: 4.8sec
	GT Speed: 4.3sec
	Supersports: 3.7sec
Fuel consumption	17mpg (16.6ltr/100km)

A GT FOR THE TWENTY-FIRST CENTURY

the new century was more openly being called the GT coupé. (In fact, four-door derivatives were already being considered, and referring to the new model in this way tended to deflect attention from that aspect of Bentley's plans.) There was no doubt that the W12 had the power, or that it had the refinement, but for the Bentley the VW Group wanted more.

They therefore decided to give the engine twin turbochargers to improve response and torque; the idea was to emulate the legendary 6½-litre Bentley of the 1920s, which was famed for its instant response to the accelerator at virtually any speed. The new Bentley engine, though related to the Audi and VW units, therefore became unique – which was a further important element in the creation of the new car's image. With 552bhp and 479lb ft of torque available all the way from an incredibly low 1,600rpm to the 6,100rpm redline, this engine also delivered astonishing performance.

There was never any question that the new Bentley should have an automatic transmission, and ZF came up with a six-speed type called the 6HP26 to fit the bill, complete with the latest type of manual over-ride and paddle-switch control from the steering wheel. A torque converter lock removed the response delays inherent in traditional automatic transmissions and provided for that instant response to the accelerator.

The decision was also taken early on to give the new car a four-wheel-drive system controlled by a torsen (torque-sensing) centre differential. This provided an even division of torque between front and rear wheels, but could automatically redirect torque away from a wheel that had lost grip towards wheels that still had it. It was a system that would improve the new car's traction and roadholding and, of course, therefore its safety in the hands of an over-exuberant driver. The technology was once again derived from the VW Group's experience with similar systems in its other products – and for those buyers who were going to be more impressed with the specifications when they saw them on paper than with the difference they made, the four-wheel-drive added a feature that rival cars did not have.

Then, of course, it was important not only that the car should accelerate and handle in a way appropriate for the Bentley marque; it should also offer the most comfortable ride possible in a sporting machine. The best solution was to use computer-controlled air suspension combined with computer-controlled electronic dampers. This allowed the suspension to be fine-tuned on the move to cope with surface conditions as the car encountered them, so delivering a soft ride whenever possible but firming up to deal with cornering forces when necessary. In practice, the GT coupé's ride was quite firm, but admirably comfortable.

Finally, of course, the car's interior was designed to live up to Bentley standards of finish. Of course that meant the use of top-quality leather hides and of impeccably matched and finished wood trims, plus an immense choice of optional finishes which would individualize a car. It also meant that the Continental GT became the first car in the world to have a Breitling timepiece (the company did not make mere 'clocks') as standard. This had been carefully designed by Breitling in conjunction with the Bentley team, in order to deliver an item that fitted perfectly into its surroundings on an automotive dashboard while providing the legendary Breitling standards of timekeeping and reliability.

However, living up to Bentley standards also meant that the car really did have to provide room for four occupants: a '2+2' Bentley would never do. In practice, the designers managed to carve out enough room for four people by creating a driving position that was quite straight-backed and high up – in the process, raising the driver up so that he had a commanding view along the bonnet. It was possible to fit four six-footers into the GT coupé – but only just, and the two rear passen-

> ### A COMMON PLATFORM
>
> By the end of the twentieth century, the VW Group had become past masters at 'platform sharing' – creating a basic floorpan and suspension structure that could be adapted to suit a number of its brands and could carry different body superstructures to suit. The group also depended on basic engine designs, which were adaptable to suit different uses. The close, but not always visible, inter-relationship between VW, Skoda, Audi and SEAT cars was one result.
>
> So it was no real surprise to find that the Continental GT's platform was derived from the all-steel understructure of the Volkswagen Phaeton, the group's luxury saloon. The Phaeton was itself something of a failure, mainly because the public found it hard to come to terms with a luxury model from a manufacturer traditionally associated with affordable, everyday cars. Nevertheless, the advanced engineering that lay behind the so-called D1 platform was never in doubt, and was certainly no disgrace to the Bentley marque.

gers might have wanted to stretch their legs more than once on a long journey.

It was in the interior, of course, where the interface occurred between the driver and much of the car's more sophisticated equipment. The very latest trends were in evidence: there was no key to open the doors or start the engine, but simply a remote tag, which the driver had to keep on his person. This automatically unlocked the car and turned on the ignition, when the engine could be fired up with its own 'start' button. In the centre of the dashboard was a large information screen, which provided control of a variety of functions that were not essential to the driving of the car. Its various menus operated the ICE system, the satellite navigation and the climate control system, allowed adjustment of the ride height and manual operation of the rear spoiler, and provided all the various functions of a trip computer.

2004 MODELS – THE CONTINENTAL GT

On its public announcement at the Paris Motor Show in autumn 2003, the Continental GT replaced the long-serving Continental R and short-wheelbase Continental T models in the Bentley range. It was available initially only as a fastback coupé, but it was not hard to see how the design could be turned into a convertible – and indeed a convertible model was already in the design stages.

As far as performance was concerned, the Continental GT did not disappoint. Its makers claimed a maximum speed of 197mph (317km/h) – they had no intention of limiting the car to the 'voluntary' 155mph (250km/h) maximum of BMW and Mercedes – and the GT would simply rocket off the line to hit 62mph (100km/h) from standstill in 4.8sec. True to its design aim, the drivetrain delivered instant response at all engine speeds, and in fact one of the first things a driver new to the GT had to learn was how to drive it at socially and legally acceptable speeds. A mere touch on the accelerator was enough to take the car to motorway speeds before the driver could realize what was happening, and the smooth changes from the ZF gearbox gave no warning of the rapid increase in speed.

It scarcely needs to be said that the Continental GT was a huge success, famously attracting 3,200 deposits at launch from customers who were anxious to be among the first to own one of the new models. In 2004, its first full year on sale, the car sold 5,983 examples, a total that exceeded predictions by a massive 63 per cent. That was a superb result for a company that had barely managed 1,000 cars a year all told in the first years of the twenty-first century. Bentley was forced to take on an extra 1,000 staff to cope with demand, swelling its workforce to 3,500. And the popularity of the Continental GT did not wane as time went by.

Nevertheless, it would have been a miracle if Bentley had got everything right with their new car straight out of the box, and they did not. Customer reactions were generally very positive, but it became clear that the interior design was too unadventurous. So, during 2004, an optional Mulliner Driving Specification was introduced, with a more modern and sporting appearance. It brought diamond-quilted upholstery, an embroidered Bentley marque emblem on the head rests, and indented leather headlining. Dark-stained burr walnut or piano black wood trim was available at no extra cost, and the pedals and footrest were made of drilled alloy, while the gear lever had a knurled finish and a leather covering. For good measure, there were new alloy wheels, too: 20in seven-spoke two-piece wheels with 275/35 R 20 tyres.

2006 MODELS – THE GTC AND THE DIAMOND SERIES

As Chapter 8 explains, the second derivative of the new Bentley platform was not the anticipated convertible, but rather a four-door saloon called the Continental Flying Spur. That made headline news in March 2005, but the convertible GT was not long in coming. Developed under the project code of BY615, it was announced in September 2005 as the Continental GTC, although actual production was delayed until autumn 2006. Would-be buyers of a Bentley convertible were meanwhile offered the new Azure model (see Chapter 9), although they had to pay dearly for the privilege of owning one of these.

Following a precedent established with the original Azure, the convertible element of the GTC had been developed with a specialist, and in this case it was Karmann of Osnabrück in Germany. Karmann also manufactured the complex, hydraulically-operated convertible roof assembly for the car. However, there was much more to creating the GTC than simply removing the roof and fitting a soft top. The sills had been reinforced with steel, there was additional cross-bracing underneath the passenger cabin, and strengthened tubing was used to reinforce the windscreen pillars and windscreen surround. Inside, the space needed for the convertible top had

A GT FOR THE TWENTY-FIRST CENTURY

Once the GT had spawned the four-door Flying Spur, Bentley introduced the GTC for 2006. The two-door model's lines lent themselves very well to the open car, although the rear seats were now rather minimal.

eaten into the already meagre rear-passenger room, and the GTC's front seats had 1.2in (30mm) scooped out of the backs to restore some knee-room.

The body modifications had also altered the weight distribution, which was now 55 per cent at the front (as against 57 per cent on the GT coupé) and 45 per cent at the rear (as against 43 per cent). Partly to cope with this, and partly to accommodate the convertible roof and protect the boot space, the rear suspension had been modified, the dampers mounted lower down the upper lever arms and located by a new trapezoidal link. Other changes reflected the modifications seen earlier in the year on the Flying Spur (see Chapter 8), with a new steering rack, column and ball joints to make the steering response more linear. Strangely, perhaps, Bentley decided not to make this change to the Continental GT coupé as well.

With the same drivetrain and overall dimensions as the fastback GT, the Continental GTC was very nearly as quick, although the extra weight and drag of the convertible top counted against it. Acceleration from standstill to 62mph (100km/h) was claimed to take 5.1sec, while the maximum speed was 189.5mph (304.9km/h) with the top down or 195.1mph (313.9km/h) with the top erected.

When *Autocar* tested a GTC at MIRA for its issue of 13 December 2006, it decided against testing the absolute maximum on the speed bowl, but did achieve 175mph (282km/h) before tyre scrub induced nervousness in the test team. The magazine considered that the ride was the best of any Continental they had yet driven, although 'in "comfort" mode the suspension still allows too much road surface detail into the cabin at times'. Nevertheless, this was 'a fantastic car in which to waft'.

'The wind management is superb' they went on, 'with only a subtly raised volume – chiefly around the mirrors and frameless join between the front and rear side glasses – at motorway speeds betraying the lack of a fixed roof. With the roof lowered, the experience is equally pleasant, and for calmer, two occupants-only cruising there's a standard alloy windbreaker that can be fixed behind the front seats.'

In conclusion, 'with a basic of £130,500, it's not cheap, but it does feel as special as a product featuring such a price tag should'.

A GT FOR THE TWENTY-FIRST CENTURY

'More than two years after sales began, worldwide demand for the Continental GT remains strong,' claimed Bentley CEO Franz-Josef Paefgen in early 2006. 'Eighty per cent of all Continental GT customers are new to the Bentley marque, migrating not only from top-end luxury coupés but also supercars such as Ferrari.'

The occasion of that comment was the launch of a Diamond Series of the Continental GT as a companion to the Diamond Series Arnage (see Chapter 5) that celebrated the diamond jubilee of Bentley production at Crewe. This new special edition of 400 cars had some unique new features, such as the brand-new carbon ceramic brakes (described in Chapter 9) with black-painted eight-piston callipers at the front visible through new fourteen-spoke forged alloy wheels with a 20in diameter and a 9in rim width. Central to the Diamond Series was the Mulliner Driving Specification, to which were added unique tread plates and badges and a Mulliner alloy fuel filler cap. The car could be had in any one of the existing fifteen Continental GT colours, but was also available in three special colours: grey-black Anthracite, Meteor (steel blue-grey) and bright Moroccan Blue.

2007 MODELS – A MILD UPGRADE

Changes to the Continental GT range were relatively minor for the 2007 model-year, although Bentley took no chances and drummed up orders by announcing the specification early, in March 2006.

The model-year changes for the Continental GT brought it into line with the Flying Spur (see Chapter 8) and included the new DVD-based satellite navigation system and Bluetooth telephone connectivity. The Flying Spur's new 19-inch, five-spoke alloy wheels became standard, and customers could now order the 20in seven-spoke type, in bright machined or chromed finish, that had earlier been restricted to the four-door model.

2008 MODELS – THE GT SPEED

During the marque's revival in the 1990s, Bentley had set a pattern of introducing something new every year, and under the VW Group this tradition was continued. So on 1 August 2007, Crewe announced its new high-performance GT Speed model. At £137,500, this cost £17,000 more than the standard Continental GT. Visually, the car was distinguished by larger exhaust tailpipes and a tinted radiator grille, and the more ornate Mulliner Driving Specification interior that was optional on the standard car came as part of the package.

Essentially, as its name suggested, it was a higher performance version of the Continental GT coupé. The W12 engine was uprated to deliver 592bhp, with new pistons and conrods, better crankcase breathing and a new engine-management system. In addition, the standard 0.6 bar (8.7psi) turbocharger

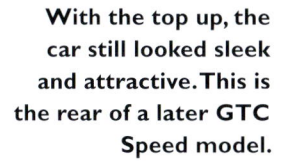

With the top up, the car still looked sleek and attractive. This is the rear of a later GTC Speed model.

125

A GT FOR THE TWENTY-FIRST CENTURY

There were special treadplates for the Speed version of the Continental GT.

boost was slightly increased, to 0.7 bar (10.2psi). The result was more torque right the way through the rev range than was available from the standard engine.

A strengthened gearbox, firmer suspension and further revised steering completed the package, and Bentley had also achieved a weight reduction of 35kg (77lb) over the standard car. The 0–60mph acceleration time dropped to 4.3sec, while maximum speed went up to 202mph (325km/h). However, as *Autocar* found in its road test of 30 August 2007, the car had to be driven hard for its benefits to become apparent.

When the GT Speed was introduced, Bentley had no real idea of how popular it would be. Company estimates suggested it might take anywhere between 15 per cent and 50 per cent of Continental GT sales, but in practice it quickly began to account for 70 per cent. That was a clear pointer to customer preferences, and an indication that the gradual performance development being done on the Continental GT was going in the right direction.

RECORD-BREAKING – ON ICE (1)

Finnish rally ace and four-times World Rally Champion Juha Kankkunen used a Bentley Continental GT Speed model to break the World Speed Record on Ice in early 2007. He broke the previous speed record of 183.9mph (296km/h) held by a Bugatti EB110 Supersport by averaging 199.83mph (321.6km/h) in both directions over the flying kilometre and reaching a maximum of 205.67mph (331km/h).

The record attempt was carried out on the frozen Baltic Sea near Oulu in Finland. The car was largely standard but featured a roll-cage for safety, fuel system modifications to cope with the low temperatures, and some aerodynamic aids.

Juha Kankkunen took the Ice Speed Record in 2007 with a GT Speed model.

126

A GT FOR THE TWENTY-FIRST CENTURY

THE CONTINENTAL AFTERMARKET

The cult for car individualization was so widespread by the time the Continental GT reached the market that aftermarket tuners very quickly began to offer their own modifications. In some cases, the modifications were confined to wheel styles, body addenda and interior re-trims, but some specialists also produced tuned engines to deliver more performance.

In the UK, a noted modifier of the Continental was Project Khan, based in Bradford. In Germany, upgrades were available from MTM (Motoren Technik Mayer, based at Wettstetten, near Audi's home town of Ingolstadt). For 2009, they produced a special version of the Continental GT, which they called the Birkin Edition after the legendary Bentley racing driver of the 1920s whose name had also been used for the Arnage Birkin Edition. This had up to 650bhp and featured a modified four-branch exhaust system and F-Cantronic adjustable suspension, which could lower the car to give greater stability at speed. The wheels were 21in multi-spoke alloys, and the brakes had six-piston callipers and diamond-cut discs. The car could reach 60mph from rest in 4.9sec and had a top speed of 206mph (332km/h).

2009 MODELS – THE GTZ

The Flying Spur enhancements, discussed in Chapter 8, were not the only news for the range in 2008. In fact, three months before the announcement of the 2009 models, another new and even more exclusive Bentley had made its appearance at the Geneva Motor Show. This was the Continental GTZ – a rebodied Continental GT Speed by the Italian coachbuilder Zagato. At the time of the Geneva Show in March 2008, its production future had not been decided, but enough interest was shown for Zagato to go ahead with a limited edition of just nine cars.

In practice, only one or two were built because the economic crash of 2008 affected Zagato's ability to pursue the project. However, production did get under way again in 2010, by which time the faster Supersports derivative of the Continental GT (*see below*) had become available. As a result, at least some of the later GTZ examples were based on Supersports rather than GT Speed models. Most were probably based on LHD cars, which had been Zagato's original intention, but the company did state in 2010 that it would be prepared to build RHD cars at a price.

According to legend, the GTZ came about when Bentley's CEO, Dr Franz-Josef Paefgen, met Dr Andrea Zagato at the 2006 Pebble Beach Concours d'Elegance in the USA. The Zagato company was displaying a selection of its 1950s and 1960s designs alongside more recent work for Aston Martin, Maserati and Ferrari. Paefgen asked Zagato if there had been any Zagato-bodied Bentleys and, on learning that there had not, suggested that the two companies should collaborate on one.

Still recognizable as a Continental GT, the Zagato GTZ was very different from the standard car and the show model featured an attractive grey over green paint scheme.

127

■ A GT FOR THE TWENTY-FIRST CENTURY

Although at first glance the GTZ was immediately recognizable as a derivative of the Continental GT, it was in fact entirely different, and the only common components were the headlights. Zagato removed the original body and built a new one featuring a number of aluminium elements, in the process reducing weight by around 220lb (100kg).

The 'haunch' effect of the rear wings was exaggerated and the roofline was restyled to feature the Italian company's trademark 'double-bubble' style. This flowed back into a lengthened tail that featured new LED tail-lights (which reputedly cost €50,000 on their own). The new roof reduced the rear window to a mere slit, and so rearward vision was supplied by a camera that transmitted images to the dash-mounted screen. Particularly effective was the two-tone paint scheme, which on the show car featured a silver-grey roof and bonnet sides over dark green.

Meanwhile, the interior remained broadly similar to the original, although the seats were re-upholstered to feature a broad band running from top to bottom and containing the Zagato 'Z' motif repeated over and over again.

The GTZ was of course fabulously expensive, costing a minimum of £400,000 on top of the £137,500 cost of the GT Speed on which it was based. Manufacture of each example took four months, and it appears that only one found a UK buyer.

2010 MODELS – THE GTC SPEED AND SUPERSPORTS

The GT coupé and Flying Spur saloons had both already spawned Speed models by the time the 600bhp engine found its way into the GTC convertible in 2009. The development was perhaps predictable, and the name definitely so: the new car was called the GTC Speed model. It took on a discreet rear spoiler, and lowered suspension to improve both steering response and handling; new lower-friction dampers were shared with the standard GTC. Both the new model and the standard GTC also took on a more upright grille, along with other detail changes at the front end, while new trim options were introduced.

Autocar magazine of 23 March 2009 thought it was 'generally lovely, albeit with a clunky sat-nav system' – an item that was coming in for criticism right across the Bentley range at the time. They also found the GTC Speed 'engaging in a way the regular GTC isn't,' but thought that it 'seemingly loses nothing either. Yes, its exhaust note is louder, but is so woofly and rich that it's no unwelcome addition'.

However, there was also another new derivative of the GT coupé. Announced at the Geneva Show in March for delivery to most markets that autumn (North American deliveries would not begin until summer 2010), this new derivative had

The Supersports was recognizable by its special front apron and different grille treatment. This one was pictured at the Geneva Show in March 2010.

A GT FOR THE TWENTY-FIRST CENTURY

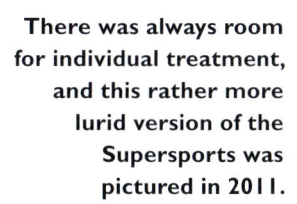

There was always room for individual treatment, and this rather more lurid version of the Supersports was pictured in 2011.

been developed under the project code-name of Victoria. It again mined Bentley's past for an evocative showroom name and, following the high-performance, short-chassis version of the WO Bentley 3-litre made available in 1925, it was called the Supersports.

In fact, the original Supersports was more commonly known as the '100mph' Bentley, a title that would have been completely inappropriate for the new Supersports, which had a claimed maximum of just over 204mph (328km/h). Lead engineer Brian Gush said at the time of the launch that the Supersports had not been in Bentley's original product plan, but was brought about when the engine development team came up with an even higher tune for the W12 engine: in the Supersports it developed 621bhp at 6,000rpm, with 590lb ft of torque between 1,700 and 5,600rpm. So, although the spread of maximum torque was not quite as broad as on the standard Continental GT, the Supersports nevertheless had the distinction of being the fastest and most powerful production Bentley ever made. It was also the quickest off the line, with acceleration from rest to 62mph (99.8km/h) taking just 3.9sec.

Weight had been saved too, and the Supersports was some 110kg (243lb) lighter than the standard GT. Well over half of the weight saving had occurred in the cabin, where carbon-backed racing front seats with manual adjustment replaced the standard electrically-adjusted items, the rear seats were replaced by a carbon-fibre brace bar (intended more to fill the space than to add to the stiffness of the shell) and satin-finish carbon fibre was fitted in place of wood trim.

A Quickshift system on the ZF gearbox reduced shift times by 50 per cent and enabled double downshifts for maximum acceleration, and there had also been changes to the traction and braking systems. A revised torsen centre differential split the torque differently, with 40 per cent now going to the front wheels and 60 per cent to the rears. This was matched by an increased offset for the rear wheels to give a wider track, and the overall effect was better handling balance under power in corners.

The car also sat lower than the GT Speed, by 0.4in (10mm) at the front and 0.6in (15mm) at the rear, and its suspension contained a higher proportion of aluminium components along with stiffer bushes and revised anti-roll-bar geometry. 'The steering proved quick, light, and razor sharp,' enthused *Car and Driver* magazine when they tested one in October 2009. Front and rear, new and lighter 20in alloy wheels carried 275/35 ZR20 Pirelli Ultra High Performance tyres, and were finished in a distinctive gloss black. Behind them were the silicon carbide-carbon fibre brake discs only optional on other Bentleys. The electronic Continuous Damping Control had also been revised to suit the new configuration, and the Bosch ESP system featured a switchable Dynamic mode.

And on top of all this, the Supersports had been designed in line with the new 'greener' policies that Bentley had outlined

A GT FOR THE TWENTY-FIRST CENTURY

in 2008. Its W12 engine was capable of running on either petrol or E85 ethanol – a biofuel available in some countries including the USA, where it is made from corn in the Mid-West. The E85-ready version of the engine did not become available until summer 2010, when deliveries began in the USA, but despite E85's lower energy content than ordinary petrol, Bentley claimed that power and torque were the same with ethanol as with petrol.

The Supersports also had its own distinctive appearance, rather more aggressive than that of the standard car. The front end took on a collection of large air intakes, which were needed to channel extra air to the engine to help it breathe better than the standard type, and the headlamps had dark trim. The rear wheelarches had a subtle framing to accommodate the two extra inches (5cm) of the wider rear track, and the gloss black of the wheel centres was matched by similarly coloured window surrounds and lower-body trim. Then the rear spoiler had an extra lip contour to suit the different aerodynamics of the revised body. Smoked-glass rear lamps and a special lower rear apron around the twin oval-shaped tailpipes completed the picture. The Supersports could be ordered in two new colours, called Ice (white) and Quartzite (grey), and there were also two new matte finishes in dark and light grey.

'As the fastest, quickest, and boldest Bentley ever built,' concluded *Car and Driver* in October 2009, 'we'd say it certainly deserves the Supersports name'.

2010 MODELS – THE SERIES 51

Very clear from sales in recent years was that Bentley customers wanted to personalize their cars as much as possible, and so Crewe's Colour and Trim Department came up with a new set of options that were announced at the Frankfurt Motor Show in September 2009. Orders for the Series 51 derivatives of the GT and GTC could be taken immediately, that name recalling the year (1951) when Crewe's first official styling department had been established by John Blatchley.

The focus of the Series 51 cars was on new interior options. Their cabins were distinguished by the use of three trim colours: a main colour, a contrasting insert colour and an accent colour. Series 51 cars also had non-indented hide for diamond quilting, contrast piping for the seats and doors, and special Series 51 treadplates. The dashboard and centre console finishes – traditionally wood – included dark and bright engine-turned aluminium options and a special limited-edition amboyna veneer unique at this stage to the Series 51. Overmats and boot carpets were also colour-matched and bound in a contrasting colour. The first example of the Series 51 was a Continental GTC displayed on the Bentley stand at Frankfurt and featuring Imperial Blue as a main and secondary leather, Linen seat and door inserts and Newmarket Tan as the accent colour.

There were also some additional exterior features for the Series 51 cars. All had 20in fourteen-spoke polished Diamond wheels with dark centre caps, and all had a special '51' badge on each front wing. Optional was two-tone paint, with one colour running over the bonnet, roof and flowing down to the boot.

The Diamond Series cars were distinguished by a special wing badge and by special tread plates. The Diamond name did not actually appear on the cars.

A GT FOR THE TWENTY-FIRST CENTURY ■

The China series of the Continental GT marked the start of Crewe's special editions for individual overseas markets. There were discreet badges on wings, treadplates and the centre console, and the alternative to this orange paint was an equally striking magenta.

131

■ A GT FOR THE TWENTY-FIRST CENTURY

The Series 51 cars were intended to widen the bespoke offerings even further, although they all carried the same '51' badge on the front wings. The interior options could be extremely attractive; the exterior colours could be eye-catching, like this **GTC** model shown at Geneva in 2010.

132

A GT FOR THE TWENTY-FIRST CENTURY

THE CONTINENTAL SUPERLEGGERA ESTATE

At the March 2010 Geneva Show, Italian coachbuilder Carrozzeria Touring Superleggera had on its stand a remarkably attractive estate car called the Bentley Flying Star. The design of this had supposedly begun in 2008 when the coachbuilder had been commissioned by a private client. However, work actually began in September 2009, and by the time of the Geneva Show, the plan was to build a limited edition of just twenty cars.

The basis of the car was a Continental GTC convertible, chosen because of the additional rigidity of its bodyshell. However, the completed Flying Star ended up weighing some 66lb (30kg) less than the convertible, despite the additional metalwork. The whole body was in fact new from the windscreen pillars rearwards, with lightweight steel sheet used for the roof and aluminium for the doors and tailgate. Steel support bars were concealed inside the roof, and several components of the GTC had to be relocated to create the flat rear floor. Here, 400ltr of load space were available with the rear seats erect, but a huge 1,200ltr opened up when the seats were folded forwards. A five-piece custom luggage set was available as an extra-cost option.

The show car had the standard 552bhp GTC engine which delivered 0–60mph in 4.6sec – the same as the contemporary Continental GT coupé. It originally appeared with multi-spoke Bentley wheels but by the time of the Villa d'Este concours event in May, held at Lake Como, it was on a set of rather leery 20in Borrani wire wheels. It was then expected to return to Bentley to be fitted with a 602bhp Speed engine.

AutoExpress magazine had a brief drive in the car, and reported in May 2010 that, 'What is really surprising is the added stiffness provided by the Touring bodywork. The Flying Star is responsive, and along the very demanding lakeside B-roads of Lake Como, feels as good to drive as the Continental GT. The only difference is the sense of space in the shooting brake set-up, which feels eerily large. The side glasswork now measures 2.4 metres in length! Room in the rear seats is plentiful, too.'

The basic cost of the Flying Star was £510,000 with the standard Continental GT engine, or £575,000 with the 602bhp Speed engine. Such prices – around three times the cost of the Continental GT of the time – guaranteed that not many more than the planned twenty examples would have been able to find buyers.

Proving once again that the art of the specialist coachbuilder was alive and well (at a price), the Flying Star by Touring Superleggera added a new and very attractive option to the Bentley stable.

■ A GT FOR THE TWENTY-FIRST CENTURY

Just another bespoke option… these vented wings could be ordered from late in 2009.

A special front treatment, plus air vents in the bonnet, helped to distinguish the Supersports models. Interiors had the diamond-quilted treatment as standard, with carbon-fibre trim.

2011 MODELS – A SPECIAL FOR CHINA AND A SUPERSPORTS CONVERTIBLE

China had been gradually growing in importance as a market for Bentley since the marque's introduction there in 2002, and by 2010 had grown tenfold. That made China Bentley's third-largest market globally, and so at the Beijing Auto Show in April 2010 the company announced a special edition of the Bentley GT coupé that would be exclusive to China. Called the Continental GT Design Series China, it was accompanied by a special Chinese edition of the Flying Spur, as explained in Chapter 8.

The cars were available only in two unique colours, Orange Flame or Magenta Metallic, specially chosen to suit Chinese tastes. The front wings carried special Design Series China badges. Similar identification was applied to the door sills, while the cabin trim featured an accent colour to match the exterior paint. This accent colour could be applied to the seatbelts, floor mats, seat piping and steering-wheel stitching, and there was further Design Series China badging on the centre console.

OUT WITH THE OLD: THE 80-11 LIMITED EDITIONS

Bentley made sure that the original GTC went out with an appropriate fanfare before the facelifted models arrived for 2012. At the August 2010 Pebble Beach concours event, they announced limited editions for the USA only of the GTC and GTC Speed. These were called the 80-11 Editions; there were eighty of each for the 2011 model-year.

Both had an all-black interior with Piano Black wood-veneer, the leather stitching on the GTC being in white and that on the GTC Speed in red. Both had a Dark Grey Metallic convertible top and the Mulliner fuel filler cap, and both had engine-turned aluminium interior trim. On the GTC, this had a bright finish, and on the GTC Speed the finish was dark. Both also had Union Flag wing badges.

The GTC had 20in fourteen-spoke diamond alloy wheels with a polished finish and black centre caps. The wheels on the GTC Speed were the 20in design otherwise used on the Supersport, but with a dark tinted finish.

Exclusive to the USA for the 2011 model-year were the 80-11 models of the GTC and GTC Speed. The numbers stood for the 80 of each produced as 2011 models.

■ A GT FOR THE TWENTY-FIRST CENTURY

At the same time, in April 2010, but this time for wider global consumption, Bentley introduced the Continental Supersports Convertible as a companion model to the existing Continental Supersports coupé. Its suspension had been softened very slightly as compared to that of the coupé, but it still rode some 0.39in (10mm) lower than a GTC Speed, with tighter dampers and stiffer suspension bushes.

Car magazine drove one in April 2011 and commented that 'the steering is surprisingly light, wonderfully precise and there's no hint of that disconcerting steering column wobble that blights most open cars. The car rides with a firm control, connected but sophisticated enough to filter out unnecessary information, but it's the way it responds to direction changes that is truly surprising. There's little hint that this thing weighs 2.5 tonnes or more two-up.' At £182,000 it was of course among the most expensive full-size convertibles in the world, as well as being unquestionably the fastest.

2012 MODELS – A FACELIFT AND A PROMISE

Ten years into the twenty-first century, Bentley's announcements of future developments seemed to be getting further and further ahead of the actual availability of the cars. So the 2012 specification for the Continental GT coupé, planned for showroom availability in March 2011, was actually announced at the Paris Motor Show in autumn 2010. The similarly upgraded GTC convertible was the focus of attention on the Bentley stand at the Frankfurt Show in September 2011.

The car had been extensively re-worked. At its heart remained the 6-litre W12 engine, but promised for release in the early months of 2012 was a new 4.0-litre V8 featuring direct fuel injection. Meanwhile, the W12-engined car was priced at £135,760, or nearly £10,000 more than the model it replaced.

Although the broad outline and major dimensions of the Continental remained unchanged, there had been many detail revisions. A redesigned front end had new headlights, with the inner pair being larger than the outers and featuring surrounding LEDs, while the bonnet had been reshaped to appear more muscular and was actually longer than before thanks to a more upright and lower-mounted grille. The joint between front wing and bumper had also been eliminated for a cleaner appearance.

Wider tracks (up by 1.6in/41mm at the front and 1.9in/

A GT FOR THE TWENTY-FIRST CENTURY

OPPOSITE, RIGHT AND BELOW:
The facelifted Continental GT announced in 2011 had a number of differences from the earlier models, the relocated outer front light units and new tail lights being perhaps the most obvious.

48mm at the rear) had led to wider wheelarches, while the widened rear had a new diffuser, new tail-lights that showed the twin ellipses of the outgoing model only when lit and, below the spoiler, the bootlid featured the new double-horseshoe shape introduced on the new Mulsanne (see Chapter 10). Overall, the original lines seemed simpler and better defined, largely because the panels were now made by a new process called super-forming, in which aluminium was shaped at high temperature by air pressure to allow more accurate manufacture of large sections.

Also part of the 2011 facelift was a larger infotainment screen.

■ A GT FOR THE TWENTY-FIRST CENTURY

The Mulliner treatment is seen here on a facelifted 2011 Continental GT. Carbon fibre was used for the front bumper splitter and integrated strakes, the rear diffuser around the tailpipes, and for the door mirror bodies.

There were, of course, modifications to the W12 engine. A combination of some new low-friction features and reprogrammed electronics delivered 567bhp as against the 2010 model's 552bhp, and 516lb ft as against the earlier model's 479lb ft. Two features first seen on the Supersports model were now standard, in the shape of the 40–60 split torsen differential and the Quickshift gearchanging enhancement. The claimed performance figures were 198mph (319km/h) and 0–60mph in 4.4sec.

The wider tracks could be complemented by optional new 21in alloy wheels running on ultra-low-profile tyres and re-rated springs, and to make room for these Bentley had redesigned the suspension uprights. These were now made by a new process called cast forging, which allowed the component to be hollow to save weight while remaining extremely strong. They had the further desirable effect of reducing unsprung weight. Meanwhile, a new electronic stability control kept the car more stable in high-speed corners; it came with an 'off' mode, as well as 'normal' and 'sport' settings.

The interior had not been neglected, either, and featured a more curvaceous dashboard with a shape that hinted at the winged B Bentley badge. It incorporated a new touch screen for the control of secondary functions with – at long last – a new and simpler satellite navigation system. The seats, too, had been re-designed to offer more support and yet to be significantly lighter, while thinner backs improved room for the rear passengers to a noticeable degree. Finally, larger door pockets gave more room to stow clutter, and improved sound insulation reduced noise levels in the car.

A GT FOR THE TWENTY-FIRST CENTURY

RECORD-BREAKING – ON ICE (2) … AND THE SUPERSPORTS CONVERTIBLE ISR EDITION

'The last time, I narrowly missed the magical 200mph [322km/h] mark in a Continental GT,' said Juha Kankkunen, Finland's four-time world rally champion. 'When I heard about the Supersports I was determined to go record breaking again with the Bentley Boys. This time, with over 600bhp under the bonnet, a Quickshift transmission and the security of the all-wheel drive system, the Supersports convertible was the perfect car to go for the record.'

So at Oulu, Finland, on 15 February 2011, Kankkunen broke his own ice-speed record of 2007, achieved at the same place in a Continental GT. This time, he achieved an average speed of 205.48mph (330.7km/h) with a Bentley Continental Supersports convertible. The record was broken over a 1,000m long measured distance, and the speed was certified by officials from the Finland Traffic Police and ratified by a representative of *The Guinness Book of Records*.

As before, the car had only minimum modifications from standard. It had a fully welded, heavy-duty safety roll-cage, and a parachute mounted on the rear bumper. Special front and rear spoilers provided optimum high-speed stability. The car also wore special Pirelli SottoZero II winter tyres (size 275/40R20) and, in line with Bentley's carbon dioxide strategy, it ran on biofuel.

Bentley lost no time in capitalizing on Juha Kankkunen's new Ice Speed Record, and at the Geneva Show on 1 March announced a 100-strong limited edition called the Supersports Convertible ISR. The initials obviously stood for the record, and the car had the 631bhp version of the W12 engine.

RIGHT AND BELOW LEFT: **Juha Kankkunen improved on his own Ice Speed Record with a second run, this time using a Continental GTC Supersports.**

BELOW RIGHT: **There were to be just 100 examples of the Supersports GTC ISR car.**

CHAPTER EIGHT

FLYING SPUR

The Volkswagen Group's plans for Bentley took a further interesting new twist at the Geneva Show in March 2005. There, on the Bentley stand, where most observers had expected to see a convertible version of the Continental GT, was instead a sleek four-door saloon.

They called it the Flying Spur. This name came from an earlier Bentley – a four-door derivative of the H. J. Mulliner two-door design on the S-series Continental chassis of the late 1950s and early 1960s. Its origins lay in the 'winged spur' emblem of the Johnstone family, whose Harry Talbot Johnstone was Managing Director of H. J. Mulliner at the time. So the name was an appropriate one, as the new Flying Spur was in its turn a derivative of a Continental, in this case of the new Continental GT.

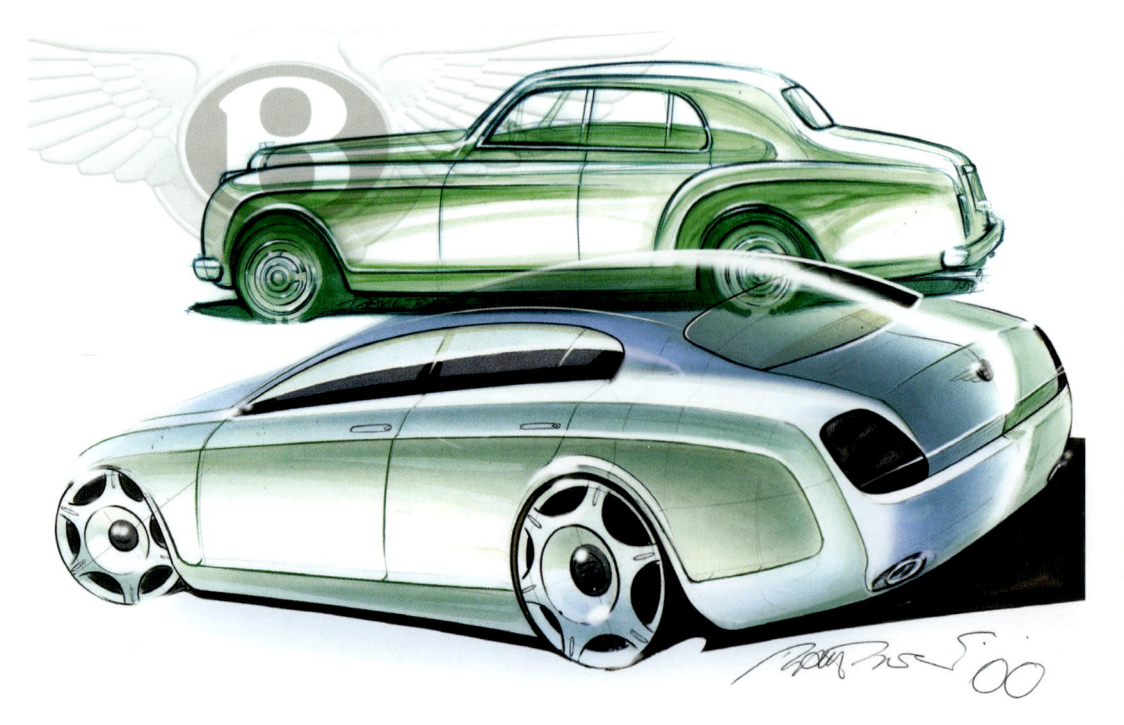

The Continental Flying Spur picked up some of its inspiration from the original Flying Spur four-door model, which is illustrated here for reference. However, the sleek lines were clearly derived from those drawn up for the Continental GT.

FLYING SPUR

In the metal, the car was of course not as sleek as the design sketches had envisaged, but it was well balanced and had the elegance and grandeur that made it instantly recognizable as a Bentley.

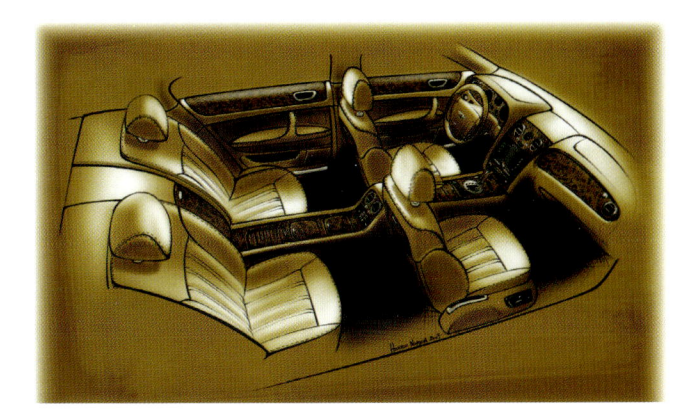

A characteristic of the interior, seen here in a design sketch from 2004, was the full-length centre console that provided stowage and convenience features for the rear seat passengers. The figured wood shown here was very much a Bentley characteristic.

The basic platform of the Flying Spur was the same as that of the Continental GT, but of course the wheelbase had been stretched by 319mm (about 12.6in) to give dimensions more suited to a full four-door saloon. Overall, the car was about 19in (483mm) longer than the GT, and its wheelbase of 120.7in (3,116mm) was very close to the dimension associated with earlier four-door Bentleys. The Flying Spur also had revised steering components to give better response in turns, with reduced friction from a new steering rack, steering column and ball joints.

The dashboard was pretty much identical to that of the Continental GT, and the Flying Spur was mechanically pretty much identical to the GT as well. Particularly impressive, though, was that its performance figures were not far behind, despite the extra weight: the Flying Spur could reach 62mph (100km/h) in 5.2sec from rest and peaked at 194mph (312km/h).

One question on many people's lips after that surprise at Geneva was whether the new Flying Spur was intended as a replacement for the existing Arnage saloon. Only later did it become clear that it was not: the Flying Spur was actually an addition to the range, which now consisted of Continental GT coupé, Continental Flying Spur saloon and Arnage saloon. With no convertible yet in the range, it was again clear what was most likely to happen next. However, the Volkswagen strategy was altogether more ambitious than most observers had imagined. The Continental GT was to sire its own family of less expensive Bentleys and the new Flying Spur, priced at the same £115,000 as the Continental GT coupé, was an aggressive step in the new direction.

In fact, the arrival on the market of the Flying Spur created a problem for Bentley. The car was delivered in accordance with the future products plan that had been drawn up some time earlier, but the success of the Continental GT had taken the company by surprise. Demand was such that the anticipated spare capacity, earmarked for the Flying Spur, had already been eaten up. So the first Flying Spurs for Europe were not assembled at Bentley's factory in Crewe, but rather

■ FLYING SPUR

The actual car ensured that both front and rear seat occupants enjoyed the car's luxury appointments. There was plenty of lounging room in the rear, as customers expected.

at the VW plant in Dresden, Germany, alongside the slow-selling VW Phaeton to which they were of course distantly related. They thus became the first (and only) Bentleys not to be assembled in the UK, although all key components were built at Crewe. Only when pressure eased did production switch completely to Crewe, in October 2006; quite a large number of Flying Spurs had been built by this stage.

Car and Driver magazine tested an early Continental Flying Spur in February 2006, and were impressed by the amount of rear space that had been created in this derivative of the cramped Continental GT. 'Headroom and legroom are immense,' they said, 'with nearly six inches between the headliner and the scalp of an average adult male. However, the seat cushion is surprisingly low and short, so you end up with most of your weight on your behind.'

At the wheel, not everything met with approval. 'The Bentley does suffer from the unfortunate "German disease" of overly complex and non-intuitive controls. You can't even change a radio station, adjust the climate controls, or activate the rear defroster until you pretend to have read the legalese that comes up on the main screen every time you start the car.' In fairness, though, this was hardly an uncommon problem in cars of all types, and the excellence of the Flying Spur's performance provided a massive counterpoint. 'When you drive it in a tidy fashion and make good use of the paddle shifters to manually select your gears, the Flying Spur can charge up or down a mountain at a clip rapid enough to justify its connection with the Bentley racing bloodline. In the process you enjoy a nicely tuned exhaust burble that is subdued but has more character than most turbocharged engines produce.'

The ride, too, was excellent. 'The Yokohama Advan Sports on the Flying Spur… collaborate with the air springs and computer-controlled shock absorbers to deliver a comfortable, quiet ride on good asphalt pavement. Road noise does become more prominent on concrete freeways, and the tires won't absorb every little bump and divot the car encounters.

Sunroof and roof console were exquisitely integrated into the design.

SPECIFICATIONS FOR BENTLEY CONTINENTAL FLYING SPUR MODELS

Years of manufacture   From 2005 on

Build quantity
Still in production.

Engine
Flying Spur:

5998cc (84mm × 90.2mm) W12 with four overhead camshafts and four valves per cylinder
Bosch Motronic engine-management system and twin Borg Warner turbochargers with air-to-air intercooling
8.5:1 compression ratio
552bhp at 6,100rpm
479lb ft (650Nm) at 1,600rpm

Flying Spur Speed:

5998cc (84mm × 90.2mm) W12 with four overhead camshafts and four valves per cylinder
Bosch Motronic ME7.1.1 engine-management system and twin Borg Warner turbochargers with air-to-air intercooling
8.5:1 compression ratio
600bhp at 6,000rpm
553lb ft (750Nm) from 1,750 to 5,600rpm

Transmission
Six-speed ZF 6HP26 automatic gearbox with torque converter and mode control.
Four-wheel drive with 50–50 torque split via torsen centre differential.

Suspension
Front independent suspension with four-link double wishbones, computer-controlled self-levelling air springs and anti-roll bar.
Rear independent suspension with trapezoidal multi-links, computer-controlled self-levelling air springs and anti-roll bar.
Continuous damping control with four adjustable settings; additional 'Comfort' setting on 2010 China edition.

Steering
Power-assisted rack-and-pinion steering.

Brakes
Ventilated disc brakes on all four wheels, with 15.9in (405mm) diameter at front and 13.2in (335mm) diameter at rear. ABS with Hydraulic Brake Assist and Electronic Brakeforce Distribution. MSR drag torque control, Bosch ESP 5.7 electronic stability program (ESP 8.1 from June 2008) and ASR electronic traction control.
Optional carbon/ceramic brakes with cross-drilled discs, 420mm diameter at front and 356mm diameter at rear.

Wheels and tyres
Flying Spur: 19in alloy wheels with 275/40R19 tyres
Flying Spur Speed: 20in wheels with 9.5in rims and 275/35 × 20 tyres

Vehicle dimensions
Wheelbase   Flying Spur: 120.67in (3,116mm)
    Flying Spur Speed: 121in (3,065mm)
Overall length   208.94in (5,307mm)
Overall width   83.39in (2,118mm) across mirrors (Flying Spur)
Overall height   58.1in (1,475mm)
Weight   Flying Spur: 5,546lb (2,475kg) kerb weight
    Flying Spur Speed: 5,379lb (2,440kg) kerb weight

Performance
Max. speed   Flying Spur: 195mph (312km/h)
    Flying Spur Speed: 200mph (322km/h)
0-60 mph   Flying Spur: 4.9sec
    Flying Spur Speed: 4.5sec
Fuel consumption   17mpg (16.5ltr/100km)

■ FLYING SPUR

But the ride will not be a shock to anyone who has spent time in high-performance sedans. And wind noise is exceptionally low. At 100 mph, the driver can converse with rear-seat passengers without anyone raising a voice.'

One way or another, the new Flying Spur proved a big hit with Bentley customers, providing an attractive alternative to the top-model Mercedes saloons, including the high-performance AMG derivatives, which were strictly its direct competitors. The new model added a sporting dimension to the saloon range that even the higher-performance derivatives of the Arnage had been unable to provide. Within a couple of years, the Flying Spur became the most successful 12-cylinder luxury saloon in the world and, according to a 2008 press release, 'played a pivotal role in the revitalization of Bentley'.

2007 MODELS – MINOR ADJUSTMENTS

One of the recurrent criticisms of Bentleys in recent years had been that the satellite navigation system was inadequate, and in particular could not cope with postcodes. So the new DVD-based system introduced for the 2007 model-year Flying Spur (as on other models at the same time) did feature postcode entry programming. Flying Spurs also gained a Bluetooth remote telephone system as standard, and as an option could now be fitted with a rear-seat telephone as well.

The 2007-model Flying Spurs also came with a new style of road wheel, this time a 19in five-spoke design that could be chromed at extra cost. The optional alternative was a 19in five-spoke design with a bright machined finish; this, too, could be chromed and the chroming again cost extra.

Mostly, however, the 2007 Flying Spur specification was all about increasing the possibilities of ordering a bespoke car. New for the model was an exterior paint-matching scheme, which allowed customers to match the colour of a new Flying Spur to that of a favourite object, and this, of course, was additional to the large range of 'standard' colours, which was the same as that for the Arnage. These changes brought the Flying Spur into line with the Continental GT coupé.

The extra bespoke possibilities were not confined to the exterior, but related to the finish of the passenger cabin as well. So contrasting-colour stitching on the leather inside the car was now available, and the boot carpet could also be matched to the carpets inside if the customer so wished. A new Chestnut wood-veneer took the number of wood options up to seven, and a new extra-cost option was veneered picnic tables on the rear of each front seat.

Going even further, the Mulliner Driving Specification was now made available for the Flying Spur as well. This had been available since 2004 on the Continental GT coupé, as Chapter 7 explains. For the Flying Spur, it meant that the 20in two-piece wheels were standard. Inside the car, there was diamond-quilted leather on the seat facings, the doors and the rear quarter panels, and the rear seat facings had an embroidered Bentley emblem. An indented leather headlining and a choice of upgraded veneers (Burr Walnut, Dark Burr Walnut and Piano black) were complemented by drilled-alloy pedals and footrest, and a gear lever finished in knurled chrome and leather.

Further upgrades were promised for late 2006, but were not available at the start of the 2007 model-year. These were vanity mirrors for the rear picnic tables, a refrigerated bottle cooler instead of the ski hatch in the rear seat and a rear entertainment package that consisted of an LCD screen in the back of each front headrest and a DVD multi-changer.

2008 – THE CONTINENTAL FLYING SPUR SPEED

The 2007 model-year upgrades had simply refined the launch specification of the car to meet customer expectations. Few people were surprised when a second version of the Flying Spur became available alongside the original in mid-2008. Both versions benefited from a mild facelift, but only the new Continental Flying Spur Speed model had the 600bhp version of the W12 engine that had been introduced a year earlier for the Continental GT Speed. The price difference between the two Flying Spurs was a massive £16,000, but at that level of the market it made much less difference than those used to lower-priced machinery imagined.

Unfortunately, sales did not get off to the best possible start, because just as the Flying Spur Speed began to reach the showrooms, a major global economic downturn began to affect even Bentley buyers. In October, Bentley announced that it had suffered a global sales drop of 20 per cent in the twelve months to the end of September 2008, and followed this with the announcement of a second cut in production at Crewe in less than two months.

None of that made the Continental Flying Spur Speed model any less exciting. While its name was a bit of a mouthful, Bentley claimed that their new model offered 'the pure

FLYING SPUR

The Speed model of the Flying Spur was introduced at a bad time, just as global recession began to bite in 2008. Nevertheless, its extra performance earned it a permanent place in the range. This picture shows an example at the Geneva Show in March 2010.

driving experience and uncompromising performance synonymous with all Bentleys bearing the Speed legend'. They also claimed a 0–60mph time of 4.5sec and a maximum of 200mph (322km/h) – all from a full-size four-door saloon.

The front end of both Flying Spur models now boasted a new and more upright grille and larger lower air-intakes, while bright tail-lamp bezels were added and there was a new and slimmer rear bumper with wrapround brightware and a black valance. Three new colours and four two-tone paint combinations became available, while the wheel choice was between a new design of 19in five-spoke on the ordinary Flying Spur and a 20in size on the Speed model, which was further distinguished by dark-tinted radiator and air intake grilles and wider, 'rifled' exhaust tail pipes.

Inside, new noise insulation improved refinement at speed, while a wider range of wood marquetry and chrome inlays and seat piping became available for the first time on the Flying Spur, along with two new hide colours. Speed models had a three-spoke Sport steering wheel and 'Speed' treadplates, diamond quilting on the seat facings and door panels, plus drilled alloy foot pedals and a gearlever finished in knurled chrome and hide.

The new Flying Spur Speed was not only faster than the original model; it also had improvements in the suspension. The ride height was lowered, and there were revised spring and damper rates to suit special new 20in multi-spoke alloy wheels with bespoke Pirelli P-Zero UHP high-performance tyres on 9.5in rims. These changes improved agility and body control, while the steering had also been sharpened up. With the steering rack now more rigidly mounted to the chassis, it gave better feedback on lock and felt more positive and solid in the straight-ahead position.

There was extra refinement, too, and perhaps one of the greatest surprises of the Speed model was that it was actually quieter and smoother than the standard Flying Spur. New noise-absorbent measures helped, with acoustic glazing, tri-laminate body undertrays and wheelarch liners now in the specification. Both models could now be fitted with a radar-based Adaptive Cruise Control system, which monitored traffic ahead and managed the accelerator and brakes to maintain a pre-set time gap, up to a maximum set speed selected by the driver. As a further option, the new Naim for Bentley audio system, with its fifteen speakers and 1,100W of power, could be specified for either model. It was, as already noted in this book, the most powerful system offered anywhere in a production car.

As *Automobile* magazine put it in April 2009, after trying out one of the new Flying Spur Speed models, 'The Bentley ranks among the premier freeway cruisers of all time, with more than enough braking and handling to match its deep reservoirs of power. Its rocklike solidity made it easier to negotiate the tight, un-even, and disturbingly blind turns one frequently encounters on the autostrada than is generally the case in many of the more darty Lamborghinis and Ferraris'.

■ FLYING SPUR

2010 – CHINA AND THE SERIES 51

The global recession undoubtedly put the brakes on the Flying Spur new-model programme for a time, not least because Crewe's resources had to be focused on the new Mulsanne (see Chapter 10) if the Arnage was not to outstay its welcome in Bentley showrooms. However, once sales began to recover in 2009, there were more changes for the Flying Spur range to encourage the return of customer interest.

So April 2010 brought a Continental Flying Spur Speed China, as a companion to the Continental GT Design Series China edition. This was specifically targeted at the Chinese market, where Bentley sales were making a strong impact. The car had been revised to suit Chinese tastes and as a result had a new 'Comfort' suspension setting and a quieter exhaust. The rear roof pillars carried a Bentley logo and the winged B was embroidered into the leather upholstery of the rear seats. There was also special identification on the front wings, while the door sills and centre console had special treatment as well. A special vanity touch was a display case for the ignition key.

Then in November, Bentley announced the availability of the Series 51 upgrades, which had been announced in 2009 on the Continental GT coupé. In practice, deliveries were not to start before March 2011. For the Flying Spurs, the Series 51 enhancements meant 19in nine-spoke alloy wheels with a graphite finish, and new blue brake callipers visible through them. Front wing vents were added, and a range of two-tone paint options was made available. The full range of fourteen different interior colour and trim options, recommended by Bentley's designers in Crewe, featured a variety of wood, aluminium and leather combinations. The rear seats now came with matching scatter cushions, and the new Flying Spurs took on the latest touch-screen infotainment system with eight-inch display that was also made available on the contemporary Continental GT coupés.

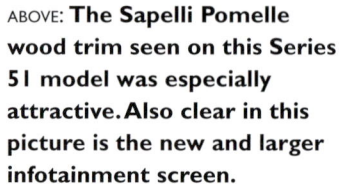

ABOVE: **The Sapelli Pomelle wood trim seen on this Series 51 model was especially attractive. Also clear in this picture is the new and larger infotainment screen.**

LEFT: **The Series 51 models of the Flying Spur once again expanded the range of bespoke options that were fundamental to the Bentley approach. Although they were announced in November 2010, they were in fact available on the 2012 models whose deliveries would not begin until the autumn of the following year.**

146

FLYING SPUR

THE FLYING SPUR ARABIA

Following a new trend towards special editions for individual markets around the world, Bentley Motors announced in autumn 2010 two limited editions of the Flying Spur for the Middle East. Known as the Flying Spur Arabia models, these came in both standard and Speed types. By this stage, the Middle East accounted for 10 per cent of all Bentley sales world-wide.

Both cars had special front wing badges, tread plates and ashtray lids bearing an Arabia motif. The standard model had fourteen-spoke diamond alloy wheels, while the Flying Spur Speed Arabia had bright silver 20in wheels with a ten-spoke design, and could be fitted optionally with carbon-ceramic brakes.

Special editions for individual markets became a feature of Bentley marketing at the start of the century's second decade. This was the Flying Spur Arabia, complete with special tread-plates. It was announced for Middle East markets in autumn 2010.

2011 – CHINA AGAIN

The continuing importance of China to Bentley sales was made apparent in September 2011 when the company announced yet another Chinese limited edition. At the same time, Bentley announced that China had become its second largest and fastest-growing market.

This time, there were to be just ten Continental Flying Spurs with wood-trim elements from the British design company Linley. Although the collaboration was described as unique, there had in fact been an even smaller limited edition of Linley Range Rovers in 1999. The Linley company, which specialized in top-quality furniture, upholstery and accessories, was founded in 1985 by David Linley, nephew of the Queen.

The Linley Flying Spurs were intended to appeal to 'customers who value pedigree and lineage, handcrafted quality and peerless design', according to the Bentley press release. They featured specially selected Linley veneers in Santos rosewood on the facia, centre console, waist-rail and roof console. The waist-rail trims and picnic tables featured the Linley Helix motif as a marquetry inlay, made up of four different types of veneer, which contrasted with the Santos rosewood. In addition, the rear console was modified to incorporate a customer-commissioned Linley humidor.

Further special features were stainless steel Linley tread-plates, a Linley for Bentley rhodium-plated plaque in the glove box, and modified seat fluting with burnt oak contrast stitching and additional burnt oak hide accentuating the storage areas and door pockets. The boot of each car also contained a Linley branded leather bag with a cashmere blanket and other Linley items such as a leather luggage tag.

■ FLYING SPUR

Announced in September 2011 was the Linley for Bentley collaboration, and on ten Flying Spur models destined for China it added the Linley Helix to the wood trim of the waist-rail and picnic tables.

The marquetry work associated with the Linley Helix was complex and demanded great skill. Four different wood veneers were used.

CHAPTER NINE

AZURE AND BROOKLANDS

Developing the mid-size Bentley that became the Continental GT was only one part of the Volkswagen strategy for Bentley Motors. The Continental GT was deliberately positioned to sell at a lower price than other Bentleys, in order to attract new customers to the brand. But Bentley had no intention of forsaking its claim on the very top-end of the market, particularly in view of the obvious plans of its former stable-mate Rolls-Royce to build convertible and coupé models alongside its luxury saloons.

However, one all-new car at a time was quite enough for the early days of Volkswagen's ownership. Developing the Continental GT and investing heavily in the re-engineering of the 6.75-litre V8 engine had consumed enough capital to ensure that Bentley did not break even until 2004 – six years after the Volkswagen take-over. So the decision was taken to build new convertible and coupé models on the basis of an existing platform. That, inevitably, meant using the still relatively young Arnage platform.

This next stage in the development of twenty-first century Bentleys was not begun until after the Continental GT had been signed off for production, but by early 2004 some serious work was under way. The new coupé and convertible appear to have carried project codes BY825 and BY835 and the coupé was also known as the Havana project. Although they were closely related, priority was given to the convertible because it was going to be far easier to develop a closed coupé from a bodyshell that had been designed with the torsional stiffness needed for an open car than to start with the closed car and try to stiffen the shell after removing the roof. As a result, the first prototype, running by spring 2004, was of the convertible.

It was nevertheless a huge job to create a satisfactory two-door convertible from the four-door Arnage. The basic 122.6in wheelbase dimension remained unchanged, and the body forward of the windscreen also remained true to the original. However, almost everything else was new, or at least

The lines of the new Azure had links to both the Corniche of the 1970s and to the more recent Continental R-based Azure. This European-market example shows the chromed highlights characteristic of the early cars – wheel trims, grille surround and mirror bodies.

149

■ AZURE AND BROOKLANDS

The convertible top was a superb piece of work, and when erected was as sleek and as soundproof as the metal roof of a coupé.

Careful arrangement of the folding top and its mechanism ensured that there was only minimal intrusion into the rear seat area.

redesigned. As is usual with open cars, there were reinforcements to the sills, the A-pillars and the underbody. A reinforced rear sub-frame was found necessary, and to ensure that the roofless bodyshell was as stiff as its customers had every right to expect, the engineers working under Ulrich Eichhorn designed a pair of immensely strong but light cross-braces made of carbon fibre. These were incorporated under the floor, one linking the deepened sills to the front sub-frame and the other linking them to the rear sub-frame. When the car entered production, Bentley claimed that the resulting bodyshell was 300 per cent stiffer than that of the last Bentley convertible – the Azure that had last been built in mid-2003.

The car was given a shallower and more steeply raked windscreen than its Arnage parent, and the convertible top was designed with the expected power operation. Rather than impinging on the boot space, the body designers gave the hood its own special compartment under the rear deck and in front of the boot. The convertible top stowed away completely out of sight and, when the appropriate button was pressed, a hinged metal lid opened automatically to allow it to rise smoothly into place. Everything was achieved automatically – again, as customers expected by this stage – and the hood could be raised or lowered in 25sec. The operation could even be done on the move, although a speed of 20mph (32km/h) had been set as a maximum, and safety cut-outs prevented the hood from being moved at higher speeds. In line with current practice in the motor industry, rollover hoops popped up automatically from behind the rear headrests if sensors detected that the car was about to turn over. In tandem with the reinforced windscreen pillars, these were capable of supporting 2.5 times the car's considerable weight and so protecting the occupants from serious injury.

The convertible top itself was a minor masterpiece, combining sleek lines when erect with sound-proofing, which

AZURE AND BROOKLANDS

Operation of the hood was fully automated, and impressive to watch. These three pictures show the sequence of events: the cover panel behind the seats lifted automatically to allow the hood to emerge, and then closed again afterwards. This car has the seven-spoke alloy wheels rather than the six-spoke type pictured earlier.

The driving compartment of the first new Azures had the usual attractive combination of figured wood-veneers, parchment-coloured instrument faces, and finely stitched leather. Just visible here, in the closed position, is the pop-up satellite navigation system that was less of a success.

151

■ AZURE AND BROOKLANDS

SPECIFICATIONS FOR BENTLEY AZURE AND BROOKLANDS MODELS

Years of manufacture 2006 on (Azure)
2008 on (Brooklands)

Build quantity
Azure still in production.
Brooklands limited to 550; still in production at the time of writing in 2011.

Engine
6750cc (104.14mm × 99.06mm) ohv V8
Bosch ME 7.1.1 engine-management system; two Garrett T3 turbochargers with air-to-water intercoolers
7.8:1 compression ratio
Azure: 450PS (444bhp) at 4,100rpm and 875Nm (645lb ft) at 3,250rpm
Azure T: 500PS (494bhp) at 4,200rpm and 738lb ft (1,000Nm) at 3,250rpm
Brooklands: 530PS (523bhp) at 4,000rpm and 774lb ft (1,050Nm) at 3,250rpm

Transmission
2006 models only: Four-speed GM 4L80-E automatic gearbox with torque converter; switchable Sports mode and converter lock-up on top gear.
2007 and later models: Six-speed ZF 6HP26 automatic gearbox with mode control.

Suspension
Independent front suspension with coil springs, twin wishbones, anti-roll bar and electro-hydraulic dampers.
Independent rear suspension with coil springs, twin wishbones, anti-roll bar and electro-hydraulic dampers.

Steering
Power-assisted rack-and-pinion steering.

Brakes
Four-channel ABS standard.
Azure: Ventilated disc brakes on all four wheels, with 13.7in (348mm) diameter at the front and 13.5in (345mm) at the rear.
Brooklands and Azure T (optional): Lightweight carbon and silicon carbide discs with 16.6in (420mm) diameter at the front and 14in (356mm) diameter at the rear; eight-piston callipers.

Vehicle dimensions
Wheelbase   122.6in (3,116mm)
Overall length   212.2in (5,389mm)
                      Brooklands: 213.03in (5,411mm)
Overall width   76in (1,930mm)
                      Brooklands: 81.81in (2,078mm) over mirrors
Overall height   59.6in (1,514mm)
                      Brooklands: 58in (1,473mm)
Weight   6,107lb (2,770kg) kerb weight
                      Brooklands: 5,853lb (2,655kg)

Performance
Max. speed   171mph (275km/h) (Azure); 166mph/267km/h with top down
                      179mph (288km/h) (Azure T)
0–60 mph   5.9sec (Azure)
                      5.2sec (Azure T)
                      5.0sec (Brooklands coupé)

Fuel consumption   14.5mpg (19.5ltr/100km)

made the car as quiet as an Arnage saloon when the top was up. It was of triple-layer construction, and none of the seven hood bows could be seen from inside. All were concealed under the smooth headlining, which – a 'first' in a convertible – contained a reading light for rear-seat passengers. The dashboard was essentially the same as in the Arnage, and worked very well in the open car. There was also plenty of rear legroom thanks to the retention of the saloon's wheelbase, and rear-seat passengers actually enjoyed some 20 per cent more width than in the saloon.

Nevertheless, the overall lines of the body, penned under the direction of Bentley design chief Dirk van Braeckel, were readily identifiable as coming from the same stable as the Corniche, and the 1995 Azure. In fact, at the launch Bentley designers cited the Azure and the 1955 Park Ward drophead coupé on the S1 chassis as the primary influences in shaping the new convertible. The Park Ward car's influence was most obvious in the deep body with its single feature line that ran along both flanks and rose to create powerful rear haunches that had some family resemblance to the haunches at the rear of the Continental GT (*see* Chapter 7). It was an enduring style that was elegant and timeless, and it was clearly what the customers wanted. However, to be absolutely sure that they were on target with their thinking, Bentley presented the new car as a concept at the Los Angeles Motor Show in January 2005 in order to gauge reactions. They called it the Arnage Drophead Coupé.

They need hardly have worried. The car went down a treat and so production went ahead as planned, and the car was introduced to the buying public at the Frankfurt Motor Show in September 2005. By this time, it had been given the name of Azure, as many commentators had expected it would. Unimaginative it may have been in view of the earlier car of the same name, but a lot of the Bentley appeal rested on tradition of one sort or another, and there was no doubt that the Azure name was ideally suited to a big, expensive and luxurious convertible like this. Expensive it most certainly was, too: at £222,500 without extras when the first cars were delivered to their owners in spring 2006, it cost twice as much as a Continental GT. In fairness to Bentley, though, it was still £8,390 cheaper than the last of the old Azures had been, three years earlier!

These first Azures had the same twin-turbo V8 engine as the contemporary Arnage saloon. Though very much heavier than that car, they nevertheless delivered astonishingly rapid performance. A heavy right foot could achieve 0–60mph acceleration in 5.9sec, and the car would power on to 171mph (275km/h) – or a mere 166mph (267km/h) if the top was not erected. Even fuel consumption was surprisingly reasonable in view of the car's size and weight, although figures of between 13mpg and 17mpg (17–22ltr/100km) were in the frightening category for the average motorist of the mid-2000s. Using all of the car's performance a lot of the time quickly brought single-figure mileage returns, as some contemporary road-testers discovered, too.

Relatively few cars were delivered with the original engine and four-speed gearbox combination, however. For 2007, the Azure took on the latest version of the 6.75-litre V8 with low-inertia turbochargers, and with that came the new six-speed gearbox from ZF. Its changes were slicker than those available with the General Motors four-speed, and there were three separate drive modes, as well as a torque converter lock-up feature. Among the road-testers who were lucky enough to test-drive examples of the 2007 models for the media, there was an unfortunate tendency to look back on the old four-speed gearbox as somewhat clunky and inadequate. In reality, it was nothing of the kind; the new gearbox was simply qualitatively better.

2008 – THE BROOKLANDS

The coupé version of the two-door models based on the Arnage platform was not introduced to the public until March 2008 at the Geneva Show. However, by that time there were only fifty left to order, with deliveries due to begin before the middle of 2008 and to continue over the next few years until the promised total had been sold.

That promised total, designed to ensure the exclusivity of the Brooklands coupé, was strictly limited to 550 cars. Word that the new model was on its way had reached likely customers some time in advance of the car's actual introduction and so, by mid-February, when *The Times* newspaper previewed the new model, Bentley Motors had already taken deposits on 500 examples. For a car that cost £230,000 in basic form – before the Mulliner individualization that large numbers of clients were expected to specify – that was a formidable statement about the surplus wealth available in the world just before the economic meltdown that affected the West later in the year.

The cost, exclusivity and specification of the Brooklands coupé immediately elevated it to the position of flagship in the Bentley range, and to date it remains the only model to have a very special handbuilt version of the 6.75-litre V8.

AZURE AND BROOKLANDS

This had been further developed from the 450PS/1000Nm (444bhp/738lb ft) derivative used in the Arnage T by means of a new air induction system, a less restrictive sports exhaust (tuned to give an awe-inspiring roar under hard acceleration), altered valve timing and a recalibrated management system. The turbochargers were also new, being made by Mitsubishi. The results were 530PS and 1050Nm (523bhp and 773lb ft) of torque, figures thrown into sharp relief when compared with the 198bhp of the V8 engine in its original 6.23-litre naturally-aspirated form in 1959. This was the most powerful production V8 engine ever seen, and when its full performance was used, the Brooklands coupé could reach 60mph from rest in just 5sec and would power on to a maximum of 184mph (296km/h). The six-speed ZF gearbox, in its latest Arnage form with stiffened casing, delivered the usual seamless and responsive changes.

Not surprisingly, the very special nature of the latest V8 engine was immediately apparent when the bonnet was opened. Although the engine was shrouded as usual in plastic fairings and sound-deadening, a brushed aluminium plate at the front of the engine bay proclaimed not only that it was a 6¾-litre V8, but also that it was fitted in a Brooklands coupé. The turbochargers lying on top of each cylinder bank were embossed with the Bentley logo, and as usual there was a smaller plate carrying the number of the engine and the signature of the technician who had hand-assembled it.

The addition of a fixed roof to what was in effect the lower body of the Azure convertible had considerably stiffened the structure. That allowed Bentley to provide the car with even more performance than was already available in its other models, and it also allowed the car to ride on lower-rate springs, so improving ride comfort to levels that the company equated with that of an Arnage R, while giving handling and roadholding equivalent to that of an Arnage T.

The standard brakes were the same ventilated steel discs as used for the Azure, but it was also possible to order the Brooklands coupé with the special upgraded lightweight braking system that had been introduced on the Continental GT

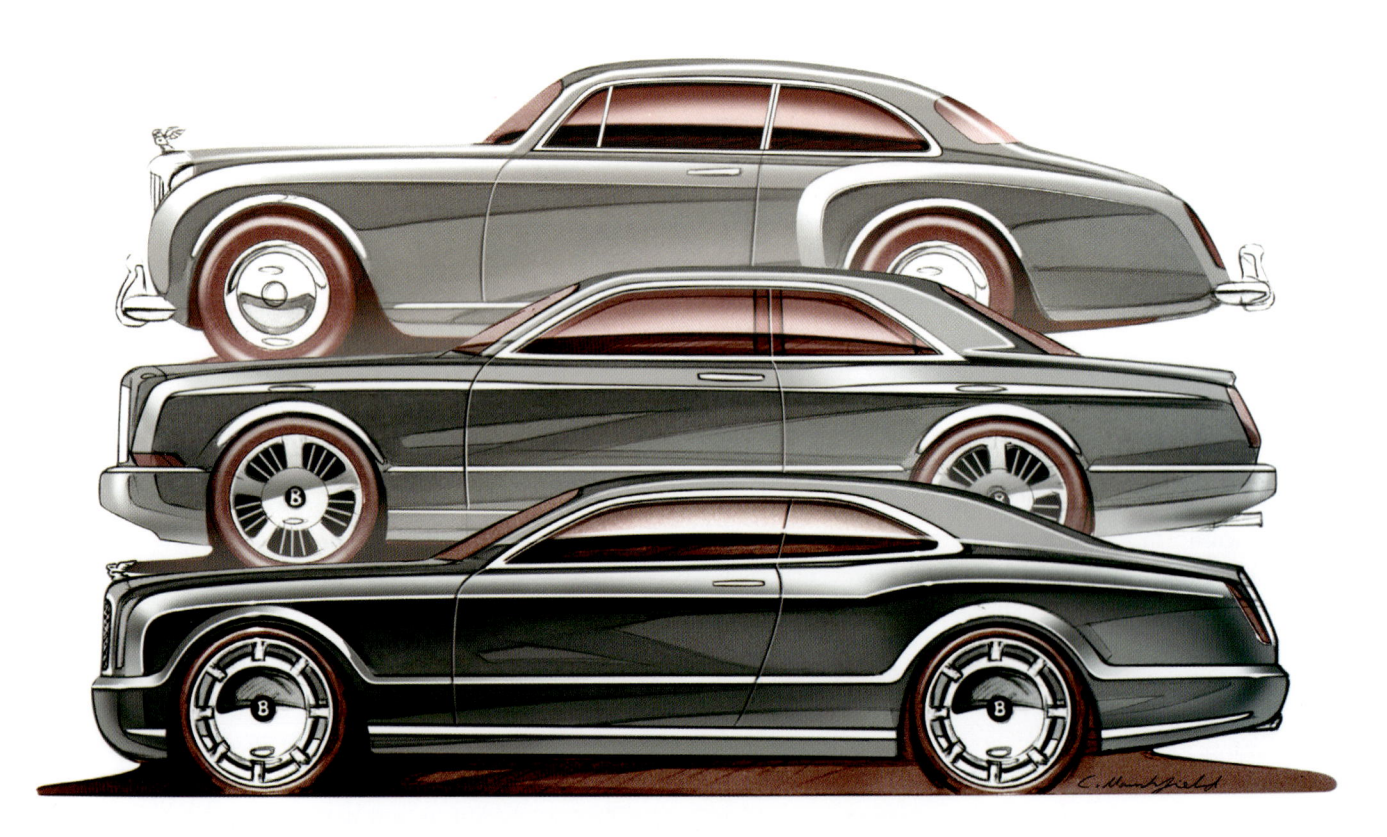

Bentley marketing was coming to rely increasingly – some might argue, too much – on the marque's history in this period. This design sketch shows the relationship of the Brooklands coupé to its predecessors, the S3 Continental (top) and Continental R (centre).

Another design sketch for the Brooklands makes clear that the intention was always to have a shallow window line to give a streamlined effect.

Diamond Series in 2006. This was formidably expensive, adding some £14,000 to the cost of the car. It featured cross-drilled and ventilated discs made from a combination of carbon and silicon carbide. With a 420mm (16.5in) diameter at the front and a 356mm (14in) diameter at the rear, these discs were claimed to be the largest fitted to any production car then on sale, and were expected to last the lifetime of the car without needing replacement. Pad life was also expected to be double that of the standard system. The unsprung weight saving with this system was 17.6lb (8kg), with benefits to steering response, acceleration and ride.

As was now to be expected on Bentley models, the new Brooklands had an array of sophisticated electronic systems to assist the driver to keep control in all manner of unfavourable circumstances. The standard ABS came with EBD (Electronic Brakeforce Distribution) and HBA (Hydraulic Brake Assist) – the latter able to detect an emergency brake application and to apply maximum braking even more quickly than the driver. There was ASR (Anti-Slip Regulation) to enhance traction, an aquaplaning detection system and an MSR or engine-drag torque control system, which, in the Volkswagen Group's own words, 'prevents the driven wheels from locking due to the braking effect of the engine on slippery surfaces when the driver suddenly takes his foot off the accelerator or rapidly shifts down a gear'. The Bosch 5.7 ESP traction control system was also set up to monitor the car's overall stability rather than simply loss of grip to the wheels, and to restore power earlier and more progressively if an intervention did become necessary. Then, of course, there was also a tyre-pressure monitoring system.

Adding that pillarless fixed roof to the two-door bodyshell, developed originally for the Azure convertible, had not been done the easy way. On the car's announcement, Bentley

The plan for the Brooklands was to create a full-size four-seat coupé, without the rear-seat legroom compromises so obvious in the Continental GT.

Motors drew attention to the 'floating' rear screen, which they described as a 'contemporary take on traditional coach-built Bentleys'. The lower edge of the screen sat well above the upper edge of the bootlid to provide a line that flowed through to the rear, and this (according to press material of the time) could not be achieved in mass production. It could only be achieved by hand-welding the rear wings to the rear body pillars. In fact, the whole bodyshell demanded no fewer than 130 hours of hand-welding – and that was before final preparation and painting.

There were other special exterior features of the Brooklands that differentiated it further from the Azure. Most noticeably, it had a body-colour grille surround instead of the chromed type used on the open car. It came as standard with 'Le Mans' air vents low down on the front wings, with a dark-

■ AZURE AND BROOKLANDS

Despite the elegance of its lines, the Brooklands coupé had a somewhat brutal appearance. Wing vents and the body-coloured grille surround and mirror bodies were touches that differentiated the car from the Azure to which it was closely related.

tinted grille matrix, and with what Bentley called a 'jewelled' fuel filler cap, which was made from aluminium billet. There were two large-diameter oval tailpipe finishers, themselves exquisitely detailed with rifling on their inner surfaces. And, of course, there were special wheels; this time, the standard wear were 20in alloys with a sixteen-spoke design and 8.5in rims that rode on Pirelli P-Zero 255/40ZR20 tyres. However, five-spoke, two-piece sports wheels were available as an alternative.

Opening the doors to the Brooklands coupé revealed sill tread plates carrying the 'Bentley Brooklands' name. The seats and door trims featured the latest diamond quilting, and the headlining was a single piece of leather. Bentley designers had managed to make the cabin wider than that of the old Conti-

nental R, the additional 10 per cent width at the rear reflecting similar gains in the Azure's interior. However, the Brooklands had two separate rear seats rather than the full-width bench of the Azure, and between them was a new centre console with both stowage room and the inevitable cupholders. The cushions of the rear seats were set some four inches (101.6mm) further back than their Azure equivalents, and just over an inch (25mm) lower, so justifying Bentley's claim that this coupé offered its occupants more leg, knee and headroom than any other currently in production. Those rear seat cushions could also be powered forwards electrically to give the ideal combination of under-thigh and back support.

The Brooklands could be had with the full Bentley range of twenty-five interior hides and the full range of eight top-qual-

156

Chromed five-spoke alloy wheels, special door tread-plates and a retractable winged B mascot were all available for the Brooklands coupé.

ity unbleached veneers. Seats featured new 'sandwich' piping, where the piping sat flush with the stitching rather than standing proud of it. For the driver, there were special features on the dash and for some of the controls, too. The footrest was made of aluminium, and the pedals were of drilled aluminium; the gear knob was of knurled chrome, and several handles and switches had a matching knurled finish. Also different from the Azure was a separate 'Sport' switch on the dash to control the damper settings. On the convertible, the dampers' Sport mode had automatically been engaged when the Sport mode was selected on the gear lever, but customer feedback had indicated a preference for separation of the two.

The underlying theme throughout was, of course, exclusivity. No other car on the market offered the combination of space, performance and sheer cachet associated with the Brooklands coupé, and Bentley Motors offered so many different 'standard' options to enable customers to personalize their cars that the chances of any two ever being exactly alike were therefore very remote indeed. The company calculated that there were 3.5 billion possible permutations of colour, trim and equipment – and that was before the possibilities available through the Mulliner personalization scheme were

■ AZURE AND BROOKLANDS

LEFT AND BELOW: **The interior was as opulent as ever, with diamond-quilted upholstery contrasting with highly polished wood-veneer and chrome detailing. This is a European-specification car, with kilometres-per-hour speedometer.**

MIDDLE LEFT: **The rich, warm tones of this dark maroon leather are complemented by wood-veneer waist-rail trim with inlaid Bentley logos.**

BOTTOM LEFT: **The Brooklands boot was spacious, too – and contained a pair of umbrellas as standard.**

158

AZURE AND BROOKLANDS

New for the Brooklands was a 530PS version of the V8 engine. Bentley were traditionally cautious about releasing pictures of their engines to the press, but they made an exception this time.

For most people, however, this was all they would get to see of the Brooklands coupé's engine. It was beautifully presented, as ever, and the special plaque with the Brooklands name was a nice touch.

added into the equation. Here, customers could more or less order whatever they wanted, as long as they were prepared to pay for it. And, for starters, Bentley offered as Mulliner options a NavTrak automatic driver recognition system (which would prevent the car being started by any driver not programmed into the system) and a retractable flying-B bonnet mascot in place of the standard flat type.

2009 – THE AZURE T

Inevitably, some of the features pioneered on the Brooklands coupé also found their way onto the Azure, in particular through the new Azure T derivative that was announced in November 2008 at the Los Angeles Auto Show as a 2009 model. This was the third Bentley to bear the T designation, the first being the 1996 Continental T coupé and the second the 2002 Arnage T. The word from Bentley Motors was that most of these cars were expected to go to the Middle East.

Like other Bentley models bearing the letter T in their designations, the focus of the Azure T was performance. Its engine and three-mode transmission were the same as those already available in the Arnage T and Arnage Final Series saloons. So the twin-turbocharged 6.75-litre V8 delivered 500PS (494bhp) at 4,200rpm and 1,000Nm (738lb ft) at 3,250rpm, and drove through a six-speed ZF automatic gearbox.

These figures represented increases of 11 per cent in power and 14 per cent in torque over the standard Azure engine of the time, and more than 90 per cent of that huge torque figure was available between 1,800 and 3,800rpm to deliver the characteristic Bentley 'wave of torque'. The 0–60mph dash was despatched in just 5.2sec and maximum speed was quoted as 179mph (288km/h). So it was again unsurprising to find the Azure T equipped as standard with the full panoply of electronic driver aids already standard on the Brooklands, while the lightweight carbon-silicon carbide braking system could also be specified, albeit at the usual considerable cost.

There were of course subtle visual distinctions between Azure and Azure T, too. At the front, the distinguishing features of the Azure T were its 'Le Mans' air vents low down on the front wings and the body-colour grille surround with dark-tinted upper and lower grilles – just as on the Brooklands coupé. Most cars also came with the new retractable Flying B mascot on the grille, but it was possible to order the flat grille badge if the customer so wished. Body-colour door-mirror mountings and a 'jewelled' filler-cap made from aluminium billet were smaller touches, but the car also had 20in two-piece alloy wheels with a five-spoke design, running on 255/40ZR20 Pirelli P Zero tyres. All forty-two standard exterior colours could be ordered, and all the Mulliner options and the associated bespoke colour-matching service were available to create an individual car if the customer wanted.

■ AZURE AND BROOKLANDS

Many of the innovations introduced with the Brooklands spilled over onto the Azure T. This picture shows the wing vents, body-colour grille surround and mirror bodies, and the two-piece 20in wheels.

Special features of the Azure T included the aluminium billet filler cap and turned-aluminium instrument surround.

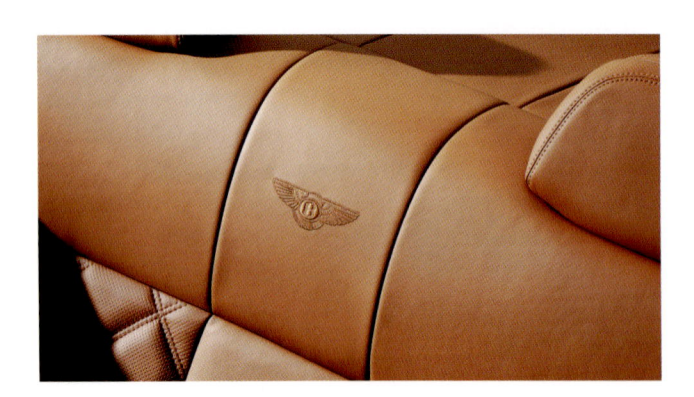

The Bentley logo between the rear seats was another Azure T feature.

The interior of the Azure T was also made special, and came as standard with many interior features previously unavailable or available only as cost options on the standard Azure. So the seats and door panels had diamond quilting, the dashboard had an engine-turned aluminium finish, and the instrument faces were black rather than the standard dark grey Parchment. The front seat backs and centre of the rear seat also carried embroidered Bentley emblems, while the leather trim extended past the rear seats and onto the parcels shelf to emphasize the dimensions of the rear compartment. Thorax airbags were fitted to cover the rear seats, and the full range of twenty-five interior colours was available alongside the eight standard unbleached wood-veneers.

Just as on the Brooklands coupé, there were special features on the dash and for some of the controls, too. The pedals were drilled, and the gear knob and various handles and switches had a matching knurled finish. There was a new ICE head unit with a larger display screen, an SD memory card slot instead of the single CD slot and an iPod USB interface. For even better audio, the Naim for Bentley audio system could be ordered at extra cost, with ten speakers, a dual-channel sub-woofer and an 1,100W amplifier, plus eight individual DSP modes to reproduce a 'live' concert-like sound. With this system, the sub-woofers were located in the rear passenger footwells and contained within a special enclosure to ensure that the sound of the music remained as far as possible within the cabin, even with the roof open.

160

CHAPTER TEN

A NEW GRAND BENTLEY

Once the Continental GT had been signed off for production to begin in 2003, the next major challenge facing Bentley was the renewal of the existing Arnage saloon platform. There was plenty of life in it yet, of course, as it had only been introduced in 1998 and was already earmarked as the base of the new two-door Azure and Brooklands models. However, within four or five years it would definitely need to be replaced, and in the meantime the Bentley designers knew they would have to take into account the competition from some formidable new rivals. These were the Maybach limousine from Mercedes-Benz and the Phantom (and, later, the smaller Ghost) from Rolls-Royce.

Size was obviously going to be a key issue. The Maybach could be bought with a variety of wheelbases, but all of them offered a great deal of interior room. The Rolls-Royce Phantom was simply enormous, even in standard form. So Bentley's first response was the limited-production Arnage limousine in 2004 (*see* Chapter 5), which matched the interior room available in these rivals by a massive increase in its wheelbase.

Back at Crewe, several options seem to have been under consideration. One, reported by *Autocar* magazine in May 2004, was an Arnage stretched by about 9.8in (250mm) – giving a wheelbase of about 132.5in (3,365.5mm) – and a 600bhp engine. The idea was to use a naturally-aspirated derivative of the 8-litre Volkswagen W16 engine planned for the Bugatti Veyron supercar, with around 600bhp. This proposal, according to *Autocar*, was known at Crewe as the BQA, which stood for Bloody Quick Arnage. However, Bentley foresaw a production run of no more than about 250 cars. Like the Arnage Limousine, this could never be a long-term solution, and in the end it did not see production.

Work on the new car started under the project code-name of Kimberly. While Bentley Motors debated the ideal size for the new model, and reviewed a number of naming options, which eventually settled (rather unadventurously) on Mulsanne, their engine teams examined the powertrain options. Their conclusion was that a further-developed version of the long-serving V8 would be the best option. The engine was far less complicated than the W12 and W16 types from Volkswagen and, despite the age of the basic design, could be successfully re-engineered to deliver both the performance and the low emissions that would be necessary. Although six-speed gearboxes were only just making their appearance at Bentley, ZF were working on an eight-speed type that would deliver the responsiveness, smooth shifts and fuel economy that the new big Bentley saloon would need. So this was incorporated into the programme as well.

In re-engineering the V8, Bentley's intention was to incorporate all the latest engine technologies and so to keep the engine in production for several more years. Exactly how long they had in mind has not yet been revealed, but it was probably a minimum of five years and a maximum of ten from the planned 2010 introduction date. So the engine had to meet planned and anticipated emissions and power requirements up to at least 2015 and possibly 2020. For a basic design that would already be fifty years old when the re-engineered derivative was introduced, that was a massively tall order.

Two key innovations were at the heart of the new V8. The first was cam phasing, in which electronics altered the valve timing to give optimum performance at different engine speeds, and the second was almost euphemistically known as variable displacement. The principle behind this was to deactivate some of the cylinders at cruising speeds so that they were not consuming fuel when they were not needed. Variable displacement was not a new idea, and had been tried by General Motors in the early 1980s on some of their large V8 engines. The GM engines had not been a great success, partly because of the crude nature of their cylinder deactivation systems, but the Bentley engineers were sure that modern electronics could enable them to produce a wholly reliable and seam-free system for their engine.

As these new systems were designed into the engine, all the V8's major building blocks were modified to a greater or lesser extent. The original cast-iron cylinder block gave way

■ A NEW GRAND BENTLEY

to an aluminium alloy version, saving some 50lb (22.7kg) in weight. The forged crankshaft, the pistons and the con-rods were all lightened to reduce reciprocating mass and internal friction, so giving faster response to the accelerator. By the time the engine was ready for production, more than 300 of its components were either new or had been significantly re-engineered. Nevertheless, some features of the original design were retained because they happened to help in the quest for low emissions: examples were the short exhaust ports and the wedge-shaped combustion chambers.

The new engine's headline power figure of 512PS (505bhp) was still some way below the 530PS (523bhp) delivered by the ultimate derivative of the 'old' V8 in the Brooklands coupé, but the biggest achievement of the re-engineering process had been the torque delivery, which was now 1,020Nm (751lb ft) from as low as 1,750rpm. What this meant was that the trade-mark Bentley 'wave of torque' was available from just above idling speed and carried on almost right the way through the engine's rev range.

There were other important benefits, too. Deactivation of four cylinders at light-throttle cruising speeds up to 74mph (119km/h) reduced fuel consumption (which was probably of little concern to most Mulsanne buyers), and the combined effect of this and the other engine changes was an overall improvement in fuel economy of 15 per cent. Carbon dioxide emissions were reduced by the same amount, these results being entirely in line with the commitment that Bentley had made to an environmental strategy in March 2008.

The engine and transmission were only elements of the new Mulsanne, of course. Crewe decided to design it around a completely new platform, which would rely on an air-suspension system. All recent Bentleys had relied on steel springs,

The new Bentley Mulsanne was unveiled at the Pebble Beach concours d'élégance event in California, in August 2009. Its appearance was very much in the mould of the new Bentleys designed under Volkswagen, and its role was to replace the older Arnage as the company's flagship saloon.

162

A NEW GRAND BENTLEY

'Floating' rear lamps were a design element of which Bentley were very proud. The car is seen here at the Geneva Show in March 2010, with Bentley's chief engineer, Dr Ulrich Eichhorn.

The car's side view made clearer how big it actually was, not least because the rear quarters were rather heavy in appearance.

163

■ A NEW GRAND BENTLEY

These five-spoke alloy wheels looked much more sporting than the rather formal multi-spoke design seen on the Pebble Beach car. Somehow, they also made it look lighter.

The Mulsanne's front end had a new version of the twin headlamp design that had characterized all the Dirk van Braeckel Bentleys. This time, the outer light units were dropped slightly below and behind the headlamps.

controlled to a degree by high-pressure hydraulics, but air suspension was now becoming the norm on top-end luxury models and Bentley could not risk stepping out of line. The new platform was designed to be lighter and stiffer than the one it replaced, and to give the best possible combination of ride and handling, an electronic-suspension control system was incorporated. This became known as Continuous Damping Control or CDC, and among other features it automatically reduced the ride height at speed to reduce lift and improve cornering stability.

The steering system chosen was a Servotronic speed-sensitive type, which also incorporated a degree of electronic control. This was arranged so that the driver could choose the degree of steering sharpness and feel, and there were two different settings. Crewe's engineers also linked the steering and suspension systems electronically through what they called the Drive Dynamics Control system. This was operated by a switch next to the gear selector, and calibrated the suspension and steering into one of four modes. Three were pre-set, and the fourth was a Custom mode, which could be adjusted to suit the driver's preference. The pre-set modes were called Bentley, Sport and Comfort – the Bentley name sounding rather better than 'standard', which was what it really meant!

A particular challenge in designing the suspension system was the need to use large wheels with very low-profile tyres. By the start of the 2000s, wheel size had become an important factor in appearance, and customers for cars in all classes tended to like stylish wheel centres that filled the arches and showed only minimal depth of rubber around them. Bentley had to follow suit, and the new Mulsanne was designed around huge 20in alloy wheels with rims 9in wide. The tyre size chosen for production was 265/45ZR20, but as always there had to be options. So a 21in wheel size was also prepared, and even lower-profile 265/40ZR21 tyres were chosen for this. In fact, there would be two 21in options: one would be a 'classic' alloy wheel, while the other would be a two-piece type. The narrow sidewalls on the associated tyres offered relatively little flexibility, with the result that the suspension had to be tuned to soak up the bumps that on taller tyres might have been absorbed by the sidewalls.

All these features demanded that Bentley should embrace the very latest technology, but for many customers they were items that would simply be taken for granted. The eighty ECUs located around the car to cover dozens of functions were, in any case, designed to be neither seen nor heard. For the typical new-Mulsanne customer, the car's overall appearance was likely to be the most important factor in the decision to buy or not to buy, followed closely in importance by the interior ambience. So here, Crewe once again took very great care.

Once the overall dimensions of the car had been decided, the design teams under Dirk van Braeckel were able to get to work shaping the body. The wheelbase of 128.6in (3,266mm) that was chosen made the new Mulsanne longer and more spacious than the long-wheelbase derivatives of earlier modern Bentleys – although, of course, the limited-production Arnage Limousine of 2004 had been larger and the massive limousines on the 8-litre chassis of 1930 had wheelbases as long as 156 inches. Getting the proportions right, while retaining a recognizable Bentley family look, was thus a very special challenge.

The style chosen for production featured a long bonnet, very short front overhang and a long rear overhang. This gave the required impression of power, which was reinforced by a kick-up in the body crease towards the rear, giving the car the muscular 'haunches' that had worked so well on the Continental GT and other models. The nose was a variation on the modern-Bentley style established under Volkswagen, with twin circular light units flanking the classic Bentley mesh grille with its body-colour surround. However, for the Mulsanne, the outer light units were dropped some way below the inner headlamps, perhaps to help distinguish this car more easily from such models as the less expensive Continental Flying Spur. Polished stainless steel was used for the window frames, as indeed it would be for all the brightwork on the car, and the front wings carried air vents low down behind the wheels. These, though, were not the overtly sporting Le Mans-type vents seen on other models. For the Mulsanne, something far more discreet was considered appropriate.

At the rear, there were 'floating' elliptical light clusters and the rear screen was enveloped in the body sheet metal to give the same sort of flowing line of which Bentley had been so proud on the Brooklands coupé. The centre high-mounted stoplight had been something of an eyesore on cars like the Arnage Limousine, and for the Mulsanne it was discreetly incorporated into the rear parcels shelf moulding. Then, of course, there were large oval exhaust outlets that deliberately hinted at the power and performance available.

Drawing up the shape was one problem; getting it into production was quite another. This was clearly going to be a very large car and was therefore likely to be heavy; weight compromises fuel economy and exhaust emissions, and therefore has to be reduced as far as possible. This was a problem that was affecting the motor industry as a whole, but more especially the makers of large cars, and the solution adopted by Jaguar and others was to lighten the structures by making extensive use of aluminium alloys.

Using aluminium alloys played into Bentley's hands in one way. The complex shape of the front wings for the new Mulsanne was going to be very hard to create by traditional stamping methods in steel. Using lighter aluminium alloy would allow it to be made using the latest superforming process, which involved heating the metal sheet to around 450°C and then using air pressure to mould it against a single-sided press tool. This process enabled the panel to be made thinner and therefore lighter than by conventional pressing; it also enabled more complex shapes to be made accurately; and it delivered a surface finish not obtainable from conventional methods. So the new Mulsanne's wings were made of superformed aluminium.

Superformed aluminium was also used to create the structure of the doors, while their side impact beams were made from extruded aluminium. The bonnet was also an aluminium pressing, but for the boot lid something special was reserved. A problem on many recent car designs had been incorporating the aerials for satellite navigation, radio, mobile phone and tracking systems, and all too often these had ended up under an ugly plastic-covered moulding at the back of the roof. Bentley's solution was elegant, if expensive. The aerials were incorporated in the boot lid, which was constructed of composite polymer in order not to interfere with signal transmission and reception.

A keyless entry system gave access to the cabin, and this was programmable so that a given key would set the car up to its owner's favoured settings. So the 'personalized' keyless 'key' would adjust the seats, the steering wheel, the phone

■ A NEW GRAND BENTLEY

A stylish modern version of the winged B mascot adorned the bonnet, but it would not have met pedestrian safety regulations if it had not retracted into the metalwork on impact. The same design had already been seen on the Brooklands coupé (see Chapter 9).

book stored in the multimedia system (about which more in a moment), the rear window blinds and even the radio. The multimedia system depended on a 60Gb hard disc and was accessible through an 8in touch-screen that was normally discreetly concealed behind an electrically-operated veneered door in the upper dash. It controlled the satellite navigation system, the audio and video systems, personal data storage, the telephone functions and included Bluetooth wireless connectivity. All the connectors needed for various plug-in systems could be found in a leather-lined drawer below the touch-screen, and this drawer also served as stowage for an iPod or MP3 player. The standard audio system came with fourteen speakers, but of course the twenty-speaker Naim for Bentley system with its 2,200W output could also be fitted to order.

The cabin was, of course, trimmed exquisitely in leather and wood. The waistrail was designed as what Bentley called a 'ring of wood', and the shape of the dash and console was said

As was expected in a Bentley, the cabin was exquisitely trimmed in leather and wood-veneer. This early right-hand-drive car shows the new 8in touch-screen that controlled a number of secondary functions.

A NEW GRAND BENTLEY

ABOVE: **Piano black wood-veneer was an alternative to the figured walnut seen in the previous picture.** The driver lacked for nothing, and there was even a digital date readout on the main instrument panel, just below the digital speed readout. Here, it reads '19.4.2010'. The aviation-style dials, with needles operating anti-clockwise, were new for the car.

RIGHT: **Three seat-belts were provided in the back, together with a retractable centre headrest.** However, the Mulsanne was really designed to carry just four passengers. The centre armrest opened to give access to a variety of controls, and those cup-holders were both practical and attractive.

167

■ A NEW GRAND BENTLEY

There was plenty of leg-room in the rear, cold-air outlets in the centre console and, of course, picnic tables. The basics were familiar, but their execution for the Mulsanne was undeniably modern and stylish.

to have a subtle resemblance to the winged B mascot of the Bentley marque. There was the usual selection of nine standard wood-veneers. As for the seats, those at the front had twelve-way power adjustment, and the rear seat was divided into three sections. The centre section was fixed and, when not in use, folded down to provide a large armrest with stowage and convenience features. The outer pair of rear seats had eight-way electric adjustment.

The dashboard still featured the traditional bright-finish eyeball vents so much liked by Bentley customers and unique to the Mulsanne were stylish 'black glass' switches. Aviation-style speedometer and rev counter dials had needles that worked their way round anti-clockwise from the top. This was more styling caprice than functional, but for drivers who had difficulty, the car's speed was also displayed on a digital readout between the two main dials. There was a large Stop/Start button for the engine that worked in conjunction with the keyless 'key', and the steering wheel incorporated paddle shifts for rapid gear selection – the first time these had been seen on a production Bentley.

Most interesting, perhaps, was that Crewe had gone to a great deal of trouble to create the interior ambience that its customers wanted. Modern leather tanning methods were efficient but did not produce leather with the same smell as that produced by traditional tanning methods. Bentley customers had shown a preference for that traditional smell, and so in the Mulsanne that was what they got. All the leather used – there were twenty-four different colours to choose from – was tanned in the traditional manner. It may have been more expensive than modern methods, but Crewe knew that its customers were happy to pay.

The Mulsanne's interior had also been planned carefully to provide maximum comfort. So there was acoustic glazing in the side and rear windows to reduce noise transmission from the outside, and the glass had an infra-red layer to reduce heat transmission as well. Only the windscreen did not have this infra-red layer, which would have hindered the operation of automatic toll readers and other devices that depended on a transceiver located inside the windscreen.

A NEW GRAND BENTLEY

Then, of course, there were the Mulliner personalization options. As more or less anything could be had if a price could be agreed and a way could be found, there was obviously no formal list of these. However, at the launch of the new Mulsanne, some samples were listed. Notably, it was possible to have the seats embroidered with a personalization feature (such as a name or coat of arms), and such a feature could also be included on the kick-plates that adorned the sill of each door.

With such a complex specification, it was no surprise, as Bentley said at the car's launch, that each example took nine weeks to build. More than 170 hours went into hand-building the interior, of which up to 15 hours might be spent on hand-stitching the steering wheel. Nearly 30 hours were spent hand-building each engine, which of course carried a plate with its builder's signature. And of course the vast combination of choices ensured that the build process could not be automated further than it already was. No ordinary car assembly line could cope with 114 different paint options, twenty-four upholstery colours, twenty-one carpet options and those nine different veneers – to say nothing of all the variations introduced by the Mulliner personalization process.

Bentley Motors chose an unusual venue for the introduction of the new Mulsanne. Rather than show it to the public in the traditional way at a motor show, they took it to the Pebble Beach Concours d'Elegance at Monterey in California, which opened on 16 August 2009. This car show has focused on classic cars since it was first held in 1950, and always attracts the sort of wealthy car enthusiasts to whom Bentley hoped their new model would appeal. They displayed it there along with the 1930 8-litre model that had once been owned by the marque's founder, W.O. Bentley, and is now preserved by the company's heritage department. The allusion was deliberate: the new Mulsanne was another

The latest version of the 6.75-litre twin-turbo engine was beautifully presented when the bonnet was opened, but was largely hidden under plastic cowlings.

A NEW GRAND BENTLEY

LEFT AND OPPOSITE: **As was now standard Bentley practice, each engine carried a plaque with the signature of the man who had built it by hand. The assembly process was quite unlike that used by mass-market manufacturers to build engines.**

'grand' Bentley that represented the pinnacle of the luxury car in its time.

However, very little information about the new car was released at Pebble Beach. Not until the Frankfurt Motor Show that opened on 15 September did a more detailed specification become available, and the car was then introduced to the US market at the Detroit Auto Show in January 2010. Its basic price in the USA was $285,000; in the UK it cost £222,000. However, Bentley hoped that almost every car ordered would eventually cost considerably more as buyers plundered the options lists and personalized their purchases.

So what was it like to drive? Possibly the first in-depth test was published by Britain's *Autocar* magazine, in its issue dated 28 April 2010. The car was obviously a pre-production model, but had presumably been prepared to be representative of the production standard. The evaluation was written by Andrew Frankel, whose main criticism was that the car was somehow slightly bland, without the endearing flaws of the Arnage that it replaced. However, there was no criticism of the driving dynamics:

'It's as effortless as a flagship Bentley should be, as luxuriously appointed and as capable and rewarding as any car flying the wings should be. It may be slightly less lovable than an Arnage, but much of that car's charm lay in its flaws. Those failings have been exorcised and what remains is a breathtakingly able, utterly admirable and endlessly enjoyable new Bentley.'

That effortlessness was clearly a dominant characteristic:

'It's so effortless that you almost wonder if the Mulsanne even needs a gearbox, let alone one with eight choices of ratio.' But this was no bloated limousine: 'It handles and rides like a Bentley too. The Mulsanne may look like a limo but it doesn't drive like one. There is an underlying firmness to the suspension even in its softest setting that brings outstanding levels of body control at the inevitable cost of some compromise to bump isolation.

'If you want a magic carpet ride, it is to Rolls-Royce and not Bentley that you must turn. But if you want to drive a car that copes with difficult roads with more grace and precision than any 2.6-tonne, four-seat saloon has a right to, look no further. The Mulsanne is not agile – nothing this heavy, sitting on that wheelbase, ever could be – but it is responsive, accurate and communicative. To call it fun would be no exaggeration.'

There was similar praise from John Simister, writing for *The Independent* newspaper of 9 May that year. He found the new Mulsanne to be 'all a flagship luxury car should be' and 'amazingly agile for what it is'. He also liked the fact that 'you feel much more at one with it than you would ever feel in the old Arnage. It helps that you sit a little lower.'

The first examples of the new Mulsanne were delivered to customers in September 2010, but some months before that every car planned for production during 2010 and 2011 had already been sold. The car had reached the market at a time when its most obvious rival, the Rolls-Royce Phantom, was already beginning to look a little old. The battle was now on.

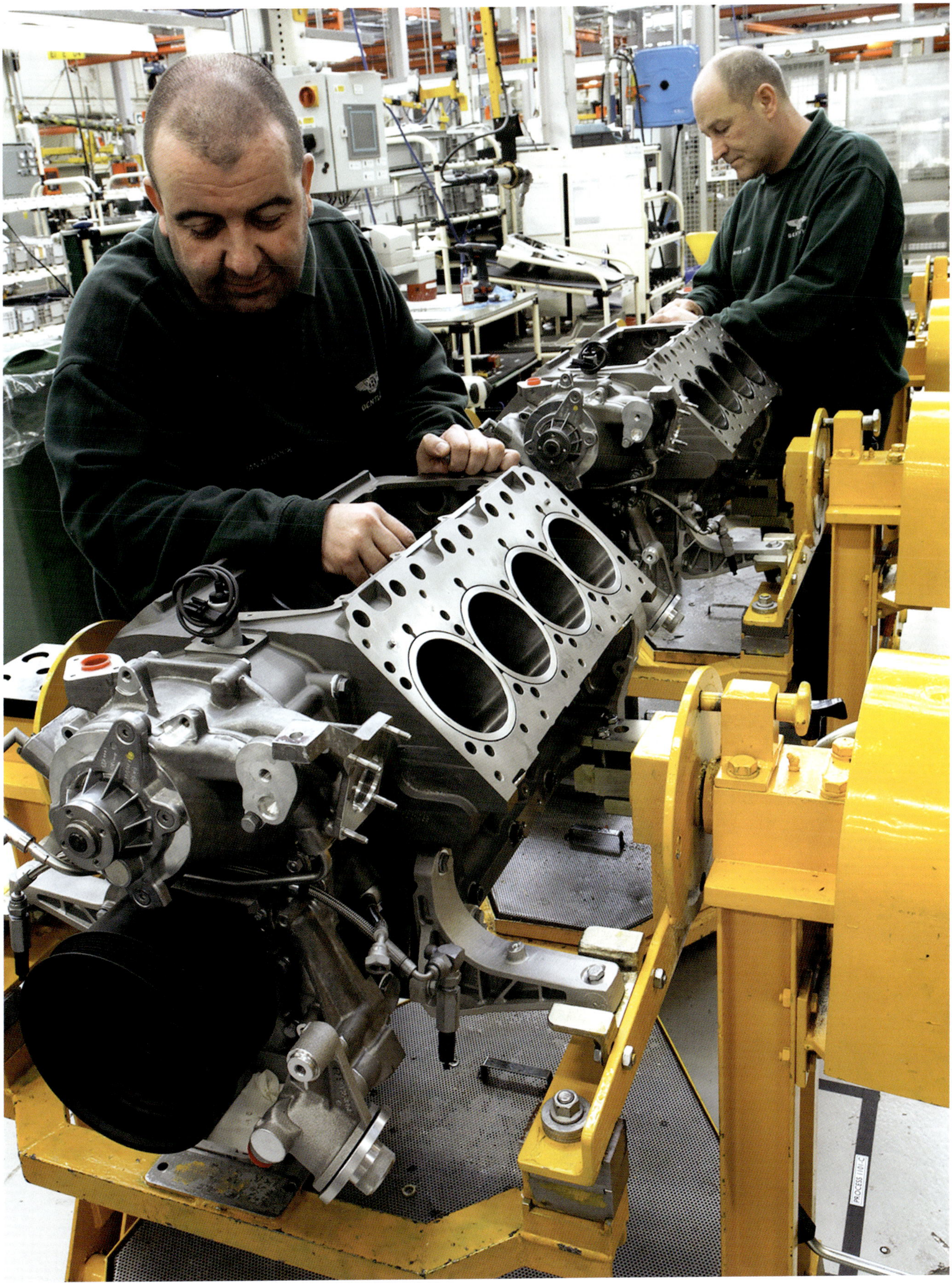

■ A NEW GRAND BENTLEY

Bentley is justifiably proud of its continuing use of traditional skills in car manufacture. To demonstrate the point, these images of the Mulsanne build process were issued when the car was announced.

SPECIFICATIONS FOR BENTLEY MULSANNE MODELS

Years of manufacture From 2010 onwards

Build quantity
Still in production.

Engine
6750cc (104.14mm × 99.1mm) ohv V8
Bosch engine-management system; twin turbochargers with intercoolers
8.5:1 compression ratio
505bhp (512PS) at 4,200rpm
752lb ft (1,020Nm) at 1,750rpm

Transmission
Eight-speed ZF automatic gearbox.

Suspension
Independent front suspension with double wishbones, electronically controlled air springs and automatic ride height control.

Independent multi-link rear suspension with electronically controlled air springs and automatic ride height control.

Steering
Servotronic speed-sensitive power-assisted type with two selectable settings

Brakes
Two-piece disc brakes on all four wheels, with iron discs and aluminium hubs; 15.7in (400mm) at front and 14.6in (370mm) diameter at rear. Twin servos; ABS and EBD, linked to Electronic Stability Control system with traction control, hydraulic brake assist, electronic brake prefill and automatic hill-hold control.

Electronic Parking Brake with drive-away assist and hill hold feature.

Vehicle dimensions
Wheelbase	128.6in (3,266mm)
Overall length	219.49in (5,575mm)
Overall width	75.8in (1,926mm) with mirrors folded
Overall height	59.88in (1,521mm)
Weight	5,700lb (2,585kg) kerb weight

Performance
Max. speed	186mph (299km/h)
0-60 mph	5.1sec
Fuel consumption	14mpg (20ltr/100km)

CHAPTER ELEVEN

VERY SPECIAL BENTLEYS

Most modern Bentleys have been built to a largely standard production pattern, even though bespoke finishing has become part of the Bentley DNA. However, for some customers, Bentley's volume-production offerings have not quite hit the mark, and so specialist coachbuilders have been tasked with creating a number of one-off or small-volume conversions.

It is impossible to list every example here, but there have been two-door conversions of the four-door saloons, convertible versions of both the two-door and the four-door models (in some cases anticipating the two-door convertibles that Bentley eventually did make), stretched-wheelbase cars and estate-car conversions. Some aftermarket companies have specialized in creating faster Bentleys, and in making both major and minor alterations to the coachwork in order to individualize the cars.

On top of that, Bentley itself has created some remarkable concept cars, notably the Java in 1994 and the Hunaudières in 1999, and has built two very special State Limousines for the Queen. And perhaps most interesting of all to Bentley enthusiasts are the bespoke creations of the mid-1990s for the Royal Family of Brunei.

THE JANKEL CONVERSIONS

Among the leading builders of modified Bentleys in the 1980s and 1990s was Robert Jankel Design in Weybridge. The company had a contract with Rolls-Royce to build long-wheelbase derivatives of the Silver Spur between 1983 and 1989, and under its own name also built a number of bespoke conversions, such as two-door saloon versions of the Bentley Turbo

The Jankel Val d'Isère conversion not only made a viable estate car out of the SZ models, but also added a four-wheel drive system, as the '4WD' script on the tailgate badge reveals. These cars had a shortened rear overhang to give better proportions; the car was also available as the Jankel Provence with standard rear overhang.

VERY SPECIAL BENTLEYS

R. Jankel were proud of the fact that they never disclosed the identities of those who had ordered these highly individual vehicles.

A notable Jankel conversion was the Val d'Isère estate car conversion of the Turbo R. Available on either standard or long-wheelbase variants of the SZ range, it had a shortened rear overhang and one-piece tailgate hinged from the roof. An alternative model called the Provence was also available, with a longer estate compartment.

The Val d'Isère came as standard with a four-wheel-drive transmission system that could also be fitted to other SZ models and was optional on the Provence. Engaging Low or Reverse in the transmission automatically engaged a hydraulic drive system, which drove the front wheels through motors built into modified hub assemblies. The hydraulic pump that powered these motors was driven from the transmission by a toothed belt. At speeds above 30mph (48km/h), the system disengaged automatically to return the car to normal rear-wheel drive mode. A number of these cars were built for the Brunei Royal Family.

THE 1994 BENTLEY JAVA

A second and less expensive model-line had been under consideration at Rolls-Royce on and off for many years, as Chapter 1 shows. By the mid-1980s, the purpose of this second model-line had been defined as broadening the appeal of the two marques into the market that the most expensive Mercedes-Benz and BMW models had made their own. Project SX, drawn up as a Rolls-Royce, was a four-door saloon that had reached the full-size mock-up stage before it was cancelled.

However, the idea of that second model-line did not go away, and by the early 1990s it had been linked to the revival of the Bentley brand. Again, the idea was to broaden the brand's appeal by creating a less expensive model, but this would be very different from the formal four-door saloon that had been SX. Project Java (the name had also been used for an earlier project, as Chapter 1 shows) was drawn up as a two-door model with convertible and coupé derivatives.

The car was drawn up by Design Rights Associates, the company set up by former Rover design chief Roy Axe, under the watchful eye of Rolls-Royce chief designer Graham Hull. Light weight was an important issue, and the convertible prototype supposedly weighed no more than 1,725lb (782kg) – extraordinarily light for a Bentley. That prototype was also drawn up around a new engine that was designed in conjunction with Cosworth Engineering, the Vickers subsidiary that had taken over production of the V8 engines for Rolls-Royce and Bentley when space at Crewe became too tight.

The Cosworth engine was a twin-turbocharged V8 with a swept volume of 3.5 litres and four valves per cylinder and, on the prototype, it drove through a four-speed automatic transmission. Exactly how far development had proceeded by the time that prototype was shown at Geneva in March 1994 is unclear, but the car was displayed strictly as a concept to show how a future, smaller Bentley might look. Pictures released at the time also showed the hardtop coupé version.

However, these were difficult times for Rolls-Royce and Bentley, and parent company Vickers decided against funding production of this new model-line. More important was to

175

■ VERY SPECIAL BENTLEYS

The Java was a concept for a smaller and less expensive Bentley. The design was extremely attractive, and was drawn up with both convertible and coupé variants. Sadly, it never entered volume production – although a number of copies and derivatives of the show car were built for the Brunei Royal Family.

put money into the new manufacturing facilities that the company needed so badly. So it is probable that the decision not to go ahead with Java had been taken before the car appeared at Geneva. Nevertheless, it made a fine advertisement for Bentley, and of course whetted customer appetites for the new Azure convertible that would be announced a year later (see Chapter 4).

The concept car was bought straight off the show stand by the Sultan of Brunei when he learned that it would not go into production. As explained later in this chapter, it was modified before delivery to him, and he commissioned Bentley to build a whole series of copies, including coupé and estate derivatives.

Although Project Java itself did not become a series-production reality, the idea of a smaller and less expensive Bentley did not go away, and in fact was incorporated into the strategy that the Volkswagen Group adopted for Bentley when they bought the company in 1998. The long-term result was the Continental GT of 2003.

CARS FOR THE ROYAL FAMILY OF BRUNEI

Bentley's best customers, during the 1990s, were the Brunei Royal Family. Both the Sultan and his brother, Prince Jefri,

176

were well-known car enthusiasts, and the Royal collection amounted to thousands of cars. Of these, well over 400 were Bentleys (the *Daily Mirror* newspaper reported on 21 February 2011 that the total was 441). It has been said that the patronage of the Brunei Royal Family was a major factor in keeping Rolls-Royce and Bentley afloat during a particularly difficult time in the mid-1990s. Prince Jefri alone is said to have spent $475 million on the two brands.

The first Bentleys delivered to the Brunei Royal Family seem to have arrived in 1989, but the main period of deliveries was the mid-1990s, from around 1994. However, the Brunei commissions dried up after 1997, when Prince Jefri's investment company collapsed as a result of the Asian financial crisis. Jefri himself was obliged to pay a huge sum of money back to the Brunei Government. Many of the vehicles in the royal car collection were sold, although most of the Bentleys remained in Brunei and a few are still kept in the UK for use when the sultan or members of his family make a visit.

Many of the Brunei Bentleys were simply standard production models, albeit with personal touches. The collection included some historically important examples, such as the red car which introduced the Continental R to the public at motor shows in 1990, and the 1994 Bentley Java prototype. There were also many coachbuilt conversions of standard cars, such as drophead conversions of the Turbo R and original Mulsanne, and around ten examples of the Jankel Val d'Isère estate conversion.

However, the collection also contained a number of very special vehicles that were built to the Sultan's requirements in small batches. These cars were based on proven Bentley components but were coachbuilt to give them an individual style and their own kind of exclusivity. They also carried Bentley insignia, and were given type names of their own. Most were built in batches of six, which was probably the minimum number that was viable for Crewe to produce.

Bentley Motors refuses to discuss or even to confirm the existence of these cars, on the grounds that it has a duty of confidentiality to its customers. However, the cars are often seen in public on state occasions in Brunei, and some are even kept and used in the UK. Over the years a band of dedicated researchers has identified large numbers of them, but many details are still not known.

At the time of writing, pictures of some of these cars were available on the web (www.supercars.net/gallery/129612/976/2.html and at www.bentleyspotting.com).

Coachbuilt Cars

These cars were coachbuilt conversions of production models, and therefore retained their standard VIN codes.

Bentley B2 (1994–96)

The Bentley B2 was a two-door convertible with a body designed, and almost certainly also built by, Pininfarina in Italy. The front featured elongated faired-in light units next to the Bentley grille.

These cars appear to have been built on Continental R platforms and had right-hand drive with twin airbags. There were three in the 1994 model-year, ten in the 1995 model-year and four in the 1996 model-year. Sample VINs are SCBZ-B04C5RCH52042 (a 1994 model registered in the UK as M1 STY) and SCBZB04C5SCH52435 (a 1995 car registered as M347 MYF in the UK).

Bentley B3 (1994–95)

The B3 was a two-door coupé based on the Continental R and with a body designed by Pininfarina. Although similar to the B2 models, which were built in the same period, the B3 had a different front-end treatment. It appears that Pininfarina subcontracted the construction of the bodies of at least some of these cars to Coggiola SpA, a specialist prototype builder in Beinasco near Turin. Two examples were built in the 1994 model-year and ten more in the 1995 model-year.

Specially Commissioned Cars

The Brunei Royal Family ordered a number of highly individual cars, which were built exclusively for them. Almost all of these were based on the running-gear of the Turbo R or Continental R, although a special 'Sultan-spec' version of the engine was drawn up for them. This had twin turbochargers and developed 500bhp (at a time when production engines had no more than 450bhp). The special engines were developed with Cosworth under the code-name of Blackpool and had a special alloy crankcase.

The special Bentleys built for Brunei have a distinctive H code identifier in the fifth position of the VIN code, which normally indicates the model type; this probably stands for 'hand-built', although some observers have suggested that it stands for Hassanal, the Sultan's given name. They also have special serial numbers from the sequence below 01001 at which standard production numbers begin. In the lists below, the cars are arranged as far as possible in serial number order.

Bentley Spectre (1994–96)

The Bentley Spectre appears to have been the earliest of the special-commission models built for Brunei. Nine examples have been identified, six dating from the 1995 model-year and the remaining three from 1996. Their body configuration is unclear.

A sample VIN is SCBZH04A9SCH00125, which was one of the 1995 model-year cars. These had serial numbers running from 00121 to 00126; the 1996 cars had serial numbers 00470 to 00472.

Bentley Phoenix (1994–96)

Eight examples of the Bentley Phoenix have so far been identified, of which five were built in the 1995 model-year and three more in the 1996 model-year. The sequential serial numbers suggest that there were at least six 1995 models. It is not clear what body configuration these cars had. One of the 1995 cars (SCBZHO4A7SCH00141) was registered as M1 NTS in the UK.

The 1995 cars had serial numbers 00141 to 00146, and the 1996 cars ran from 00473 to 00475.

Bentley Sports Estate (1992–95)

Although only fourteen Sports Estates have been positively identified, the sequential serial numbers suggest that at least seventeen were built. Of the identified cars, six were built in the 1993 model-year and the remaining eight were 1995 model-year cars. They appear to have been based on Continental R bodyshells.

The 1993 cars had serial numbers from 00201 to 00209 (although 00203, 00207 and 00208 have not been confirmed). The 1995 cars had serial numbers from 00210 to 00217. A sample VIN is SCBZH04D5PCH00205, which was registered as BN 1968 in Brunei.

Bentley Silverstone (1994–96)

Seven Bentley Silverstone models have been identified, built in two batches. Five were 1994 model-year cars and the remaining two were from 1995. The sequential serial numbers suggest that there may have been at least one additional 1994 example. They were built on the Continental R platform, but their body configuration is unclear.

The 1994 cars had serial numbers 00301 to 00306, and the 1996 cars ran from 00476 to 00477. So far unconfirmed is 00305. A sample VIN is SCBZH04A0RCH00301, the first of the 1994 batch, that was registered as KF 8877 in Brunei.

Bentley Monte Carlo (1994–95)

There were six examples of the Bentley Monte Carlo, another two-door coupé. These were built in the 1995 model-year and had consecutive serial numbers. The platform was that of the Continental R.

The serial numbers of these cars ran from 00322 to 00326. A sample VIN is SCBZH04C9SCH00322, which was registered as BN 9000 in Brunei.

Bentley Imperial (1994–95 and possibly later)

The Imperial may have been a two-door drophead coupé. There were six examples in all, with consecutive serial numbers in a special sequence. At least four were built in the 1995 model-year, with serial numbers from 00341 to 00344. The other two, 00345 and 00346, may have been built later. A sample VIN is SCBZH04C4SCH00342, registered as BQ 11 in Brunei.

Bentley Grand Prix (1994)

The six Bentley Grand Prix models were built as a batch in the 1994 model-year and had consecutive serial numbers. They were again sleek two-door coupés, possibly with a 2+2 seating configuration and on a shortened Continental R platform.

Serial numbers ran from 00361 to 00366. A sample VIN is SCBZH04C9RCH00363, which was registered as BP 9996 in Brunei.

Bentley Camelot (1994–95)

Just two Bentley Camelot models have been identified, but the spread of serial numbers suggests there may have been at least six in all. One of the known cars was built in the 1994 model-year and the other in 1995. It is not clear what bodies they carried.

The known serial numbers are 00403 and 00408. SCBZH-04C5RCH00408 was registered in Brunei as BP 818.

Bentley Dominator (1998)

There were six Bentley Dominator models, all built in the 1998 model-year with consecutive serial numbers. These cars appear to have used the bodyshells, and possibly also the chassis, of the contemporary Range Rover. The engine code of 98 in the VINs does not correspond to any other associated with Bentley, and may have been a BMW V8; Land Rover were experimenting with such engines in Range Rovers at the time, but they were not adopted for production. Also interesting is the letter T in fourth position in the VINs, which indicates they were not built on a standard Bentley platform.

The cars were definitely built in the UK, supposedly at Crewe, although one story suggests that there was also input from the Mulliner Park Ward division in Willesden. Land Rover has declined to comment on any involvement in the project.

These cars had serial numbers 00422 to 00427. A sample VIN is SCBTH98C2TCH00426, which was registered as BQ7570 in Brunei.

Bentley Rapier (1995–96)

There were six examples of the Bentley Rapier, all based on the Continental R and with sequential serial numbers. The VIN codes indicate that they were built in the 1996 model-year. Their configuration is not clear.

These cars had serial numbers 00428 to 00433. A sample VIN is SCBZH16C6TCH00430, which was registered as KF 9991 in Brunei.

Bentley Buccaneer (1996)

Six Bentley Buccaneer cars were built in 1996 as a batch with consecutive VINs. They were based on Continental R running gear, possibly on a shortened wheelbase. These cars were sleek two-door coupés with some similarities in overall shape to the special R-type Continental built by Pininfarina on chassis BC49C in 1954. Some commentators have detected hints of modern Zagato styling in their bodywork, but Dr Andrea Zagato's comment in 2006 to Franz-Josef Paefgen that there had never been a Zagato Bentley (see Chapter 7) seems to contradict this.

The Buccaneers had serial numbers 00434 to 00439. A sample VIN is SCBZH16C9TCH00437, which was registered in Brunei as KF 9997.

Bentley Pegasus (1995–96)

There may have been as many as fourteen examples of the Bentley Pegasus, although only nine have so far been confirmed. It is not clear what their configuration was. Their VIN codes suggest that all were based on the Continental R and that all were built in the 1996 model-year.

The known serial numbers are 00440 to 00443, 00446 to 00449 and 00452 to 00453. A sample VIN is SCBZH-16CXTCH00446, which was registered as BQ 9919 in Brunei.

Bentley Java

The original Bentley Java was a two-door convertible shown at Geneva in 1994 as a concept. It was not put into production, but the show car was bought by the Sultan, who ordered a further batch of cars based on it. The exact number of Javas built was probably eighteen, although details of only twelve are known. There were certainly coupés and estates, as well as convertibles – six of each if the total was indeed eighteen.

The original show car had a prototype Cosworth engine and is known to have been modified before delivery to the Sultan. It seems very likely that the prototype Cosworth engine was removed. As Bentley did not at the time have another engine small enough to fit into the Java, the subsequent models were given BMW 4-litre V8s, modified by Alpina in Germany to run twin turbochargers, and intercooled. It seems probable that the original show car was also given one of these engines.

The first six cars had serial numbers 00480 to 00485, were known as P700 types and were built in the 1994 model-year. These presumably included the original concept car and were convertibles. Five (and probably all six) of the last six cars were P710 types and were built in the 1996 model-year. These had serial numbers 00492 to 00497 and may have been the estates. Serial numbers 00486 to 00491 have not been confirmed but may have been coupés built in the 1995 model-year.

A sample VIN is SCBVH99D2RCH00483, which is one of the 1994-model convertibles and was registered in Brunei as BP 9997. The V in the fourth position presumably stands for Java; the engine code 99 in the sixth and seventh digits presumably stood for the twin-turbo 4-litre BMW V8. The build location is shown conventionally as C for Crewe, although the cars were engineered and built on behalf of Bentley by MGA in Oxford, a specialist prototype engineering company.

■ VERY SPECIAL BENTLEYS

Project Hunaudières was built on the basis of a Lamborghini Diablo to save time, but was intended to explore public reactions to a Bentley 'supercar' in the modern idiom. Though it was a head-turner, no production Bentley has yet gone down the same route, so presumably Bentley customers gave this concept the thumbs-down.

THE 1999 PROJECT HUNAUDIÈRES CONCEPT

One of Bentley's first public moves after the Volkswagen take-over was to prepare a concept car to explore perceptions of the marque. The Hunaudières concept (named after a straight section of the Le Mans circuit) appeared at the 1999 Geneva Show and was a deliberately provocative exercise to help Bentley determine how far they could safely stray into traditional supercar territory. Tony Gott, acting Chief Executive of Bentley, told observers that he thought there would be enough buyers for around 300 such cars a year... but what he did not say was that such figures were too small to be viable for the Volkswagen Group's vision of Bentley's future.

In order to put the car together quickly, its designers had started with an existing mid-engined supercar – the Lamborghini Diablo VT. A new body was created, made from aluminium and carbon fibre, with a roofline some 3.3in (85mm) higher than the Diablo's to give better headroom, accessibility and visibility out of the cabin. The car was painted in metallic British Racing Green – an early indication that Volkswagen was prepared to mine the Bentley tradition for all it was worth – with chromed lower body panels and chromed 20in wheels. These touches were largely theatrical, to make sure the car looked good under the lights on the exhibition stand.

The cabin of the Hunaudières was trimmed in typical Bentley fashion, with a combination of green and tan leather and

BENTLEY HUNAUDIÈRES DETAILS

Wheelbase:	104in (2,650mm)
Length:	174in (4,430mm)
Width:	78in (1,980mm)
Height:	47in (1,190mm)
Track:	68in (1,738mm) front, 65in (1,645mm) rear
Tyres	265/30ZR 20 (front), 335/30ZR 20 (rear)

An indication of what might follow in production was the engine, an 8004cc W16 related to Volkswagen's modular VR engine, and in effect two V8s joined together side-by-side. This had a claimed 623bhp at 6,000rpm and 560lb ft at 4,000rpm. It drove all four wheels through a five-speed gearbox, and the car was said to be capable of 220mph (350km/h), with 60mph coming up from rest in an estimated 4sec.

THE 2002 STATE LIMOUSINES

In 2002, Crewe presented Queen Elizabeth II with two very special State Limousines on the occasion of her Golden Jubilee. These were the first Bentleys ever to be accepted as State Limousines, and they took over front-line duties from some special Rolls-Royce Phantom VI models. Although Bentley actually designed and built the cars, they were funded by a consortium of British Motor Industry manufacturers and suppliers.

Work began on the project in February 2000. Although

nubuck for the seats and dashboard, and with aluminium on the dashboard and centre console. A panel on this console concealed the ICE and air-conditioning controls, and monitor screens to the left and right of the speedometer and rev counter relayed the views from a pair of rear-facing cameras fitted behind the front wheels.

Getting Royal agreement to build a pair of State Limousines was a feather in Bentley's cap, and a poke in the eye for former stable-mates Rolls-Royce. Here, one of the two very special cars is seen under construction at Crewe.

■ VERY SPECIAL BENTLEYS

ABOVE: **Bentley's Franz-Josef Paefgen is seen with other company representatives on the occasion of the new State Limousine's presentation to the Queen and Prince Philip. The sheer size of the car is apparent in this photograph.**

LEFT: **One of the State Limousines is seen here with the rear panels removed to give the public the best possible view of the interior and its occupants. The black roof panel and window pillars have a trompe-l'oeil effect, making the car look less bulky than it really is.**

VERY SPECIAL BENTLEYS

Before construction of the two State Limousines began, a full-size model was built. The coats of arms were left off the doors on the real cars, and Bentley were permitted to add discreet red Bentley logos on the rear pillars. The mock-up is seen here with the rear window shrouds in place.

VERY SPECIAL BENTLEYS

their running-gear was based on existing production Bentley hardware and the front ends had a Bentley grille and other recognizably Bentley elements, the cars were completely custom-built. The Queen herself had requested certain design elements, in particular the large rear window, which enabled her to be seen easily by the crowds on State occasions when she was riding in the car.

These cars were the largest Bentleys built in modern times, with a wheelbase of 155.3in (3,946mm) or 33in (830mm) longer than the standard Arnage of the time. The bodies had no real resemblance to any other Bentley design, but were custom-designed by Dirk van Braeckel, with Crispin Marshfield taking the major responsibility for the exterior design. The high roofline made the cars 10in (255mm) taller than the contemporary Arnage, while the overall width was 2.7in (68mm) greater.

Both cars were finished in the traditional Royal Claret, and carried a Royal crest on the roof above the windscreen. They had winged-B Bentley bonnet mascots, but when the Queen was aboard, these were removed and replaced with her personal mascot of St George slaying the dragon. The rear doors had their hinges at the rear so that they could open to 90 degrees for ease of entry and exit, and there were removable cover panels for the large rear window. These were stowed in the boot when not in use.

The front compartment was upholstered in dark grey leather, with seats for the chauffeur and for a police protection officer. However, the rear compartment, which was used by the Queen and other designated occupants, was upholstered in special light grey lambswool sateen cloth made by British textile manufacturer Hield Brothers.

These cars had modified versions of the Arnage R's twin-turbocharged 6.75-litre V8 engine, with 400bhp and 616lb ft. Their theoretical maximum speed was 130mph (210km/h), although they spent most of their time being driven at very slow processional speeds. In accordance with Bentley's Flex-Fuel strategy, an announcement in January 2009 revealed the plan to convert both State Limousines to run on biofuels.

Each State Limousine carried a plaque engraved with the names of those who had worked on it.

APPENDIX

BENTLEY IDENTIFICATION NUMBERS SINCE 1965

1966–80 Seasons

The car-numbering system introduced for the first monocoque Bentley models was quite different from the one used earlier. Each car had an eight-digit identification number, which consisted of a three-digit prefix code and a five-digit serial number. A typical (fictitious) example might be DBX01234.

The prefix codes break down as follows:

(First letter)
- C Used for all two-door cars up to serial number 6646 in mid-1969; thereafter used only for two-door saloons (it initially stood for 'coachbuilt', and later probably for 'coupé')
- D Drophead coupé (from mid-1969)
- L Long-wheelbase saloon
- S Standard saloon

(Second letter)
- B Bentley (Rolls-Royce equivalents were identified by R)

(Third letter)
- H RHD (the H stood for Home market type)
- X LHD for export markets

From 1972, North American cars had their own sequence of letters in place of the X. These letters indicated the model-year of the car, as follows:

A	1972
B	1973
C	1974
D	1975
E	1976
F	1977
G	1978
K	1979
L	1980

1981 Season Onwards

From the start of the 1981 season, Bentley cars carried Vehicle Identification Numbers (VINs), which followed a pattern agreed by the International Organization for Standardization. These numbers had seventeen digits, of which the first twelve were type identifiers and the remaining five a serial number. A typical (fictitious) number might be SCBYB00000AH12345.

Cars destined for California in the USA, and built during the 1980 model-year, had an eighteenth identification digit. This was a letter C at the end of the otherwise standard seventeen-digit VIN string.

The prefix letters decode as follows:

APPENDIX

Digit(s)	Letter(s)	Interpretation
1 & 2	SC	(Manufacturer code: Rolls-Royce/Bentley)
3	B	Bentley brand
4 & 5	LB	Arnage, Arnage Green Label, Arnage Birkin
	LC	Arnage Red Label, Arnage Le Mans, Arnage R
	LE	Arnage Limousine
	LF	Arnage T
	YD	Corniche, to 1982
	YJ	Camargue (only one car)
	ZB	Continental R, Continental S
	ZC	Corniche S
	ZD	Corniche and Continental, 1982–96
	ZE	Eight from 1987, Brooklands
	ZF	Brooklands LWB
	ZK	Azure
	ZN	Mulsanne LWB, Mulsanne Turbo LWB, Turbo R LWB, to 1989
	ZP	Turbo R LWB, to 1989
	ZR	Turbo R, from 1989
	ZS	Mulsanne, Mulsanne Turbo, Eight to 1987, Turbo R to 1989
	ZT	Turbo S
	ZU	Continental T
	ZZ	Continental SC
6 & 7	00	6.75-litre V8, naturally aspirated, non-catalyst exhaust system
	02	6.75-litre V8, naturally aspirated, catalytic converter, from 1988
	03	6.75-litre V8, single Garrett turbocharger, catalytic converter, cross-bolted crankshaft, from 1988
	04	6.75-litre V8, single Garrett turbocharger, cross-bolted crankshaft, non-catalyst, from 1988
	05	6.75-litre V8, single Garrett turbocharger, catalytic converter (Turbo S)
	06	6.75-litre V8, turbocharged, non-catalyst (Turbo S)
	11	6.75-litre V8, naturally aspirated, catalytic converter, OBDII
	12	6.75-litre V8, naturally aspirated, catalytic converter, OBDI
	13	6.75-litre V8, naturally aspirated, non-catalyst
	14	6.75-litre V8, single Garrett turbocharger, catalytic converter, OBDII
	15	6.75-litre V8, single Garrett turbocharger, catalytic converter, OBDI
	16	6.75-litre V8, single Garrett turbocharger, non-catalyst
	17	6.75-litre V8, naturally aspirated, catalytic converter, OBDI, with Traction Assistance
	18	6.75-litre V8, naturally aspirated, non-catalyst, OBDI, with Traction Assistance
	19	6.75-litre V8, low-pressure single Garrett turbocharger, catalytic converter, OBDII, non-intercooled
	20	6.75-litre V8, low-pressure single Garrett turbocharger, catalytic converter, OBDI, non-intercooled
	21	6.75-litre V8, low-pressure single Garrett turbocharger, non-catalyst, non-intercooled

APPENDIX

Digit(s)	Letter(s)	Interpretation
	22	6.75-litre V8, single Garrett turbocharger, catalytic converter, OBDII, intercooled, 400bhp
	23	6.75-litre V8, single Garrett turbocharger, catalytic converter, OBDI, intercooled, 400bhp
	24	6.75-litre V8, single Garrett turbocharger, non-catalyst, intercooled, 420bhp
	25	6.75-litre V8, single Garrett turbocharger, catalytic converter OBDII, intercooled, 420bhp
	26	6.75-litre V8, single Garrett turbocharger, catalytic converter, OBDI, intercooled, 420bhp
	27	6.75-litre V8, single Garrett turbocharger, non-catalyst, intercooled, 420bhp
	28	6.75-litre V8, single Garrett turbocharger, catalytic converter, OBDI, intercooled, 325bhp
	29	6.75-litre V8, single Garrett turbocharger, catalytic converter, OBDII, intercooled, 325bhp
	30	6.75-litre V8, low-pressure single Garrett turbocharger, non-catalyst, intercooled, 325bhp
	31	6.75-litre V8, twin turbochargers, catalytic converter, OBDII, intercooled, 400bhp
	32	6.75-litre V8, twin turbochargers, catalytic converter, OBDI, intercooled, 400bhp
	33	6.75-litre V8, twin turbochargers, non-catalyst, intercooled, 400bhp
	34	6.75-litre V8, twin turbochargers, catalytic converter, intercooled, 450bhp
	36	6.75-litre V8, twin turbochargers, non-catalyst, intercooled, 450bhp
	37	6.75-litre V8, twin turbochargers, catalytic converter, intercooled, 400bhp
	38	6.75-litre V8, twin turbochargers, non-catalyst, intercooled, 400bhp
	50	4.4-litre BMW V8, non-catalyst
	51	4.4-litre BMW V8, catalytic converter
8	0	'Blank' digit used for all markets except USA before 1987
	A	Active seat belts (fastened by seat occupant)
	B	Passive front seat belts (attached to door)
	C	Twin airbags
	D	Driver's airbag only
	E	Twin airbags and belt pre-tensioners
	F	Twin airbags plus side 'curtain' airbags
9	0	'Blank' digit used for all markets except USA before 1987
	0–9 or X	Check digit to prevent VIN forgeries
10	A	1980 model-year
	B	1981 model-year
	C	1982 model-year
	D	1983 model-year
	E	1984 model-year
	F	1985 model-year
	G	1986 model-year
	H	1987 model-year
	J	1988 model-year
	K	1989 model-year
	L	1990 model-year

APPENDIX

Digit(s)	Letter(s)	Interpretation
	M	1991 model-year
	N	1992 model-year
	P	1993 model-year
	R	1994 model-year
	S	1995 model-year
	T	1996 model-year
	V	1997 model-year
	W	1998 model-year
	X	1999 model-year
	Y	2000 model-year
	1	2001 model-year
	2	2002 model-year
	3	2003 model-year
	4	2004 model-year
	5	2005 model-year
	6	2006 model-year
	7	2007 model-year
	8	2008 model-year
	9	2009 model-year
	0	2010 model-year
11	C	Crewe factory
12	H	Right-hand drive
	X	Left-hand drive
13–17	12345	Serial number

INDEX

1987 changes, SZ range 53
1998 changes, Continental range 71
2007 changes, Flying Spur range 144

ABS 53
accessories, branded 115
acoustic glazing 168
Adaptive Shift Control 58
air suspension 162
airbags, arrival of twin 55
Alpina 85
Apex Motorsport 110
Aquaplaning detection system 155
armour-plating 93
Arnage convertible concept car 98, 153
Arnage Diamond Series 99
Arnage Final Series 102
Arnage Green Label 90
Arnage Limousine 96, 165
Arnage long-wheelbase 92
Arnage R 96
Arnage Red Label 88, 96
Arnage Series 2 93
Arnage T 94
Arnage T-24 96
ASR (Anti-Slip Regulation) 155
Audi 109
Automatic Ride Control 54
Automatic Stability Control 87
Automatic, 4L80-E type 55
Axe, Roy 175
Azure (1995) 80
Azure Final Series 84
Azure Mulliner 84
Azure T 159

B2 (Brunei special) 177

B3 (Brunei special) 177
bankruptcy of Rolls-Royce, 1971 16
Bengal project 9
Bentley Continental (1952) 7
Bentley marque ownership 6
Bentley marque positioning, 1960s & 1970s 11
Bentley MkVI 7
Bentley R-type 7
Bentley S-type 7
Bentley T-series 10
biofuels 108, 184
Birkin Arnage 92
'black glass' switches 168
Blackpool project 177
Blatchley, John 11, 24, 45
Blundell, Mark 113
BMW 850 seats 83
BMW, and purchase of Bentley 104
Borneo project 9
BQA (Bloody Quick Arnage) project 161
Brabham, David 113, 116
British Motor Corporation (BMC) 9
Broadspeed 50
Brooklands (1992) 56
Brooklands coupé 153
Brooklands R (1998) 61
Brundle, Martin 110
Brunei Royal Family, special cars 176
Buccaneer (Brunei special) 179
Bugatti Veyron 161
Burma project 8
BY615 project 123
BY825 project 149
BY835 project 149

Camargue (one-off Bentley) 31
Camelot (Brunei special) 178

INDEX

Capello, Rinaldo   113
carbon ceramic brakes   125, 154
centre stop lamp   165
Clare, Simon   93
Coggiola SpA   177
Continental bodies, 1960s   8
Continental drophead from 1992   36
Continental drophead, 1984   33
Continental Flying Spur   see Flying Spur
Continental GT   123
Continental GT Birkin Edition   127
Continental GT Design Series China   135
Continental GT Diamond Series   125
Continental GT Series 51   130
Continental GT Speed   125
Continental GT, 2012 models   136
Continental GTC   123
Continental GTC 80-11 Edition   135
Continental GTC Series 51   130
Continental GTC Speed   128
Continental GTC Speed 80-11 Edition   135
Continental GTC, 2012 models   136
Continental GTZ   127
Continental R Le Mans   80
Continental R Millennium Edition   80
Continental R Mulliner   73
Continental R, development   66
Continental S   68
Continental SC   72
Continental Superleggera Estate   133
Continental Supersports   128
Continental Supersports Convertible ISR   139
Continental T   70
Continental T Le Mans   80
Continental T Mulliner   73
Continuous Damping Control   129, 164
Corniche   28
Corniche development   30
Cosworth Engineering   85, 175, 177

D1 platform   122
dealer special editions, Azure   84
dealer special editions, Continental   84
dealer special editions, SZ range   63
Delaney Gallay   13
Design Rights Associates   175
Dominator (Brunei special)   179

Dresden assembly plant   142
Drive Dynamics Control system   164
Dürheimer, Wolfgang   106

EBD (Electronic Brakeforce Distribution)   155
Eichhorn, Dr Ulrich   106, 150
Eight, 1984   51
Elleray, Peter   109
environmental strategy   107
ESP (Electronic Stability Program)   94, 129
ETAS (Electronic Traction Assistance System)   60
ethanol fuel   130
EXP Speed 8   110

F6 engine   94
F-60 4-litre engine   8, 9
F-Cantronic suspension   127
Feller, Fritz   45
first-series T-series cars   16
Flying Spur   140
Flying Spur (by HJ Mulliner)   7
Flying Spur Arabia   147
Flying Spur Linley   147
Flying Spur Speed   144
Flying Spur Speed China   146
Flying Spur Speed Series 51   146
Flying Spur, assembled in Dresden   142
Flying Star   133
four-wheel drive   122, 175
fuel injection first introduced   19

GM Northstar 8   85
Gott, Tony   85, 180
Grand Prix (Brunei special)   178
grille surround unpainted; origins   45
Grylls, Harry   11

Harvey Bailey Engineering   17
Harvey-Bailey, Alec   7
Havana project   149
Hawal Whiting   85
HBA (Hydraulic Brake Assist)   155
Heffernan and Greenley   65
Herbert, Johnny   113, 116
Hield Brothers   184
Hollings, John   17
Hull, Graham   85, 175

INDEX

Hunaudières concept   174, 180
Hydramatic gearbox   16

Imperial (Brunei special)   178
infra-red heat-resistant glass   168
intercooler   54

James Young bodies   23
Jankel (Robert Jankel Design)   174
Java concept, 1994   117, 174, 175, 179
Java project, 1962   9
Joest Racing   115
Johnstone, Harry Talbot   140

Kankkunen, Juha   126, 139
Karmann   123
Kevlar   60
Keyless entry   165
Korea project   8
Kristensen, Tom   113

L380 engine   45
L410E engine   45
L725 engine   45
'Labels'   73
Lamborghini Diablo VT   180
Le Mans, the return   109
Leitzinger, Butch   110
Light Pressure Turbo engine   60
Lotus   85

Maybach   161
Mayflower   85
Mercedes-Benz 600   13
Mercedes-Benz V8   85
MGA, Oxford   179
Mitsubishi turbochargers   102
monocoque construction   23
Monte Carlo (Brunei special)   178
MSB (Mid-Sized Bentley) project   117
MSR (engine drag torque control system)   155
MSX   85
MTM (Motoren Technik Mayer)   127
Mulliner Driving Specification   123
Mulliner personalisation service   73, 105, 107, 159, 169
Mulliner special series, SZ range 1998   61
Mulliner-Park Ward   10, 23, 24, 25, 179

Mulsanne S   54
Mulsanne Turbo   48
Mulsanne, 1980   39, 45

Naim for Bentley audio system   103
new model plans, 1950s   8

Ortelli, Stéphane   110
Oulu   126, 139

P3000 project   85, 90
P700 project   179
P710 project   179
paddle shifts   168
Paefgen, Dr Franz-Josef   106
Park Distance Control   90
Park Sheet Metal   83
Pebble Beach event   169
Pegasus (Brunei special)   179
Phoenix (Brunei special)   178
Piech, Ferdinand   117
Pininfarina   31, 72, 83, 177
Pininfarina T-series coupé   38
Plastow, David   39, 64
platform sharing   122
polymer, for Mulsanne boot lid   165
power figures for Mulsanne Turbo, revealed in Germany   50
Pressed Steel   16, 83
problems in early 1990s   41
production figures, SY two-door models   38
production figures, SZ models   49
production figures, Turbo RT   48
Project 90, 1985   64
Project Khan   127
Provence estate conversion   175

Quickshift system   129

Randle Engineering Solutions   85
Range Rover   179
Rapier (Brunei special)   179
rationalised range   7
record-breaking on ice, 2007   126
record-breaking on ice, 2011   139
retractable mascot   159
Ricardo   53
Rolls-Royce Camargue   30, 50

191

INDEX

Rolls-Royce Silver Cloud 7
Rolls-Royce Silver Dawn 7
Rolls-Royce Silver Seraph 84, 86
Rolls-Royce Silver Shadow 10
Rolls-Royce Silver Spirit II 55
Rolls-Royce Silver Spur II 55
Rolls-Royce Silver Wraith 7
RTN (Racing Technology Norfolk) 109, 115

sales success, 2007 on 116
Sapelli Pomelle wood option 146
Sebring race 113
second-series T-series cars 17
Silverstone (Brunei special) 178
Smith, Guy 110, 113, 116
specifications, 2003 Le Mans cars 115
specifications, Arnage 88
specifications, Azure (1995-2003) 66
specifications, Azure (2006 on) 152
specifications, Brooklands coupé 152
specifications, Continental drophead 27
specifications, Continental Flying Spur 143
specifications, Continental GT 120
specifications, Continental R 66
specifications, Corniche 27
specifications, Hunaudières concept 181
specifications, Mulsanne 173
specifications, SY (T2) models 18
specifications, SY (T-series) models 15
specifications, SZ (Mulsanne) models 46
specifications, two-door SY (T-series) cars 27
Spectre (Brunei special) 178
Sports Estate (Brunei special) 178
state limousines 181
superformed aluminium panels 165
SX project 175
SY model 10

SZ range, design and development 45

Tibet project 8
Tonga project 9
Touring Superleggera 133
traditional tanning of leather 168
Transient Boost Control 57
Turbo R Sport 58
Turbo R, 'new', 1996 58
Turbo R, 1985 52
Turbo RT 61
Turbo S 56
turbocharged engine, initial development 50
Turbo-Hydramatic gearbox 16
twin headlights, 1988 54

V8 engine, 1959 7
V8 engine, re-engineered 90, 93, 107, 161
Val d'Isère estate conversion 175
Van Braeckel, Dirk 106, 117, 153
Van der Poele, Eric 110
variable displacement 161
Vibrashock mountings 13
Vickers plc 104, 175
Volkswagen Group, guiding lights 106
Volkswagen investment in Bentley 105
Volkswagen Nardo coupé 121
Volkswagen Phaeton 122, 142
Volkswagen strategy for Bentley 107, 117, 149

W12 engine 119
W16 engine 161, 181
Wallace, Andy 110

Zagato 127
ZF six-speed gearbox 102, 122, 154
Zytek engine management 58, 69